0034

THE COMPLETE

SPECIAL EVENTS
Handbook

PAULINE CARTER

DIRECTORY OF SOCIAL CHANGE

Published by
Directory of Social Change
24 Stephenson Way
London NW1 2DP
Tel. 08450 77 77 07; Fax 020 7391 4804
email publications@dsc.org.uk
www.dsc.org.uk
from whom further copies and a full books catalogue are available.

Directory of Social Change Northern Office
Federation House, Hope Street, Liverpool L1 9BW
Policy & Research 0151 708 0136

Directory of Social Change is a Registered Charity no. 800517

First published 2009

ISBN 978 1 903991 95 4

British Library Cataloguing in Publication Data
A catalogue record for this book is available from the British Library

Cover and text designed by Kate Bass
Typeset by Marlinzo Services, Somerset
Printed and bound by Page Bros, Norwich

CONTENTS

Foreword   ix
About the author   x
Acknowledgements   xi
Aims of this book   xii

1   Introduction   1
1.1   Who should read this book?   1
1.2   How to use this book   2
1.3   What are special events?   3
1.4   Special events: pros and cons   4

2   Strategy and planning   5
2.1   Establishing a strategy   5
2.1.1   The basis for a strategy   5
2.1.2   Reviewing an existing strategy   5
2.1.3   Key questions to consider   6
2.1.4   Some tools for strategic analysis   7
2.2   Identifying aims and objectives   12
2.2.1   Identifying the primary goal or aspiration   13
2.2.2   Setting specific objectives and targets   13
2.2.3   Identifying secondary aims   14
2.3   Ideas: what sort of event is appropriate?   17
2.3.1   Ways of finding ideas   17
2.3.2   Be critical   18
2.4   Supporter and market research   19
2.4.1   Deciding who your supporters are   19
2.4.2   Finding out more about your supporters   19
2.4.3   Surveys: asking the professionals   20
2.4.4   Using national statistics   21
2.4.5   Analysing the results   21
2.5   Risk management   22
2.5.1   Identifying risks: consider the worst   22
2.5.2   Likelihood and impact   23
2.5.3   Managing risks   24
2.5.4   Unmanageable risks   26

2.6	**Timescale and timing**	**27**
2.6.1	Allowing enough lead-time	27
2.6.2	Timing is key	27
2.7	**Budget**	**29**
2.7.1	Establishing a realistic budget	29
2.7.2	Forecasting costs	31
2.7.3	Estimating income	32
2.7.4	Using and controlling your budget	33
2.7.5	Return on investment ratios	34
2.7.6	Budget templates	35
2.8	**Review**	**38**
2.8.1	What to review	38
2.8.2	Collecting information	38
2.8.3	Reviewing against aims and objectives	39
2.8.4	Ongoing review	40
3	**Making it happen**	**44**
3.1	**Putting a team together**	**44**
3.1.1	The special events organiser	45
3.1.2	Trustees and senior staff	50
3.1.3	Events committee	50
3.1.4	Event staff team	53
3.1.5	Other staff	53
3.1.6	Volunteers	54
3.1.7	Professional event organisers	57
3.1.8	Checking and vetting	57
3.2	**Project management**	**60**
3.2.1	What is a project?	60
3.2.2	The life-cycle of a project	61
3.2.3	Identifying what needs to be done	61
3.3	**Finding the funds**	**70**
3.3.1	Reserves or fundraising budget	71
3.3.2	Corporate sponsorship and partnership	71
3.4	**Finding a venue**	**88**
3.4.1	How to find a suitable venue	88
3.5	**How to book entertainment and catering**	**90**
3.5.1	When to book	90
3.5.2	What type of entertainment?	90
3.5.3	What type of catering?	91

3.6	**Negotiating prices**	**91**
3.6.1	How to negotiate prices	92
3.7	**Establishing contracts**	**92**
3.7.1	How to establish contracts	92
3.7.2	Managing contracts	96
3.8	**Before the event**	**97**
3.8.1	What you need to do before the event	97
3.9	**At the event**	**101**
3.9.1	What you need to do at the event	101
3.10	**After the event**	**103**
3.10.1	What you need to do after the event	103
4	**Making the most of it**	**107**
4.1	**Publicity and marketing**	**107**
4.1.1	What is marketing?	107
4.1.2	Planning your marketing	108
4.1.3	Methods for promoting and publicising your event	110
4.1.4	Designing materials	114
4.2	**Working with the media**	**116**
4.2.1	Writing a press release	116
4.2.2	When to send your press release	119
4.2.3	Where to send a press release	119
4.2.4	What happens next?	120
4.2.5	At the event	120
4.2.6	After the event	120
4.3	**Interviews**	**120**
4.3.1	Print media	121
4.3.2	Radio and TV	122
4.4	**Photographs**	**127**
4.4.1	Hiring a photographer	127
4.4.2	Getting a press photographer to your event	128
4.4.3	Doing it yourself	128
4.4.4	Sending pictures to the newspaper	130
4.5	**Gaining the edge: attention to detail**	**130**
4.6	**Treating supporters well**	**131**
4.7	**Internal promotion**	**131**
4.8	**Celebrities**	**132**
4.8.1	How to find an appropriate celebrity	132

4.9	Added value: auctions	134
4.9.1	How to hold an auction	135
4.10	**Gift Aid**	**138**
4.10.1	Gift Aid and donations	138
4.10.2	Gift Aid and ticket sales	139
4.10.3	Gift Aid and sponsorship	140
4.10.4	Gift Aid and auctions	141
4.10.5	Keeping records and claiming Gift Aid	142
4.10.6	Template/checklist	142
5	**Types of event**	**144**
5.1	Balls and dinners	144
5.1.1	How to organise a ball or dinner	144
5.1.2	Additional entertainment	151
5.1.3	Fundraising	152
5.1.4	Master of ceremonies	152
5.1.5	The 'wow' factor	153
5.2	Royal events	159
5.2.1	How to organise a royal event	159
5.3	Sporting and challenge events	165
5.3.1	How to organise sporting and challenge events	166
5.4	Musical and cultural events	181
5.4.1	How to organise musical and cultural events	182
5.5	Conferences	192
5.5.1	How to organise conferences	192
5.6	Receptions	198
5.6.1	How to organise receptions	198
5.7	Family events	200
5.7.1	How to organise family events	201
5.8	Festivals	209
5.8.1	How to organise a festival	209
6	**Essentials: Legal requirements and risk management**	**212**
6.1	Charity law and regulations	212
6.1.1	Charity name and registration number	213
6.1.2	Restricted purposes	213
6.1.3	Professional fundraisers and commercial participators	214

6.1.4	Public collections	215
6.1.5	Duty of care	215
6.2	**Data protection**	**216**
6.2.1	Data protection principles	216
6.2.2	Data controller	217
6.2.3	Registering with the Information Commissioner's Office	217
6.2.4	Responding to requests for information	218
6.3	**Health and safety**	**219**
6.3.1	Risk assessment	219
6.3.2	Fire regulations	220
6.3.3	Emergency plan	222
6.3.4	Crowd control	222
6.3.5	First aid	223
6.3.6	Food	223
6.3.7	Overseas events	223
6.3.8	Be prepared	223
6.4	**Insurance**	**224**
6.4.1	Public liability insurance	224
6.4.2	Third-party insurance	225
6.4.3	Equipment insurance	225
6.4.4	Contractors' insurance	225
6.4.5	Venue's responsibility for insurance	225
6.4.6	Bad weather insurance	226
6.4.7	Cash	226
6.5	**VAT**	**226**
6.5.1	Exemptions	227
6.5.2	VAT and sponsorship	227
6.5.3	Tax and Gift Aid	228
6.6	**Licences**	**228**
6.6.1	Premises licences	228
6.6.2	Music licences	229
6.7	**Best practice**	**229**
6.7.1	Fundraising Standards Board	229
6.7.2	Institute of Fundraising Codes of Best Practice	231

7	**If things go wrong**	**232**
7.1	Crisis? What crisis?	232
7.2	Project planning schedule takes longer	233
7.3	Inaccurate estimates	233
7.4	Technical difficulties	234
7.5	Unforeseen absence of resources	234
7.6	Venue lets you down	235
7.7	Entertainer or celebrity lets you down	236
7.8	Not enough tickets sold or people attending	236
7.9	Too many people attending	237
7.10	Adverse weather	238
7.11	Transport breakdown	238
7.12	Illness or injury at the event	239
7.13	Failure or breakdown in communication	240
7.14	Cancelling an event	241
Postscript		243
Appendix 1: Bibliography		244
Appendix 2: List of websites		247
Index		251

FOREWORD

Special events have a particular role to play in the fundraising mix and no fundraising strategy is complete without them.

Events can be part of an annual programme or they can be one-off. Whichever it is, they are special for many reasons. They bring supporters to the charity who otherwise may not get involved; they often take place in extraordinary places; they appeal to supporters from all walks of life; they involve extraordinary people, who are sometimes famous; their success is often dependent on the whims of our climate, and if they come off well, they generate not just money but pages of good, free publicity.

So often though, events are misunderstood. Just because they are special, they are not a licence to print money, and many events make financial losses however high profile they are. It takes hard work, dedication and, above all, imagination to turn an idea on a page or in someone's head into an income-generating reality.

This book is a practical guide. Its author knows this subject inside out. She has written it to help you with every aspect of events organisation, from development through to delivery, so that you and your charity have the best chance of making your event a rip-roaring success.

Judy Beard
Director of Development and Alumni
Imperial College

ABOUT THE AUTHOR

Pauline Carter has been involved in fundraising at a senior level since the early 1980s, first with Save the Children, then with ActionAid. In 1995 she became an independent consultant and has worked with a significant number of charities and organisations. Her work has included offering strategic development and advice on a wide range of fundraising and management issues, including managing special events and capital appeals. Pauline has supported a number of charities with advice on recruitment, selection, coaching and mentoring fundraising individuals and teams. In addition, she has planned and organised a number of conferences.

Pauline is a longstanding member of the Institute of Fundraising and was a member of its executive committee for six years. During this time Pauline was responsible for writing and delivering the special events management courses run by the Institute of Fundraising, and then the Directory of Social Change; additionally, she has also delivered in-house training programmes for charities on a wide variety of fundraising subjects.

Prior to joining the charity sector Pauline was a senior fencing coach working with individuals and teams at the international level. She coached individual women's silver and men's Olympic bronze medal winners in modern pentathlon. She has organised national modern pentathlon and fencing competitions, and lectured on coaching and team development.

ACKNOWLEDGEMENTS

The author and publishers are grateful to the following individuals and organisations that have given freely of their time and experiences in order to provide case studies and examples of good fundraising practice.

Al Bell (trainer), Judy Beard (Director of Development and Alumni, Imperial College), Bernard Ross (The Management Centre), Ken Burnett (White Lion Press), Caroline Chilton (PR consultant), Celia Davies, MBE (Heritage Music and Peckleton Arts), David Davies (The Brainwave Centre), Jeremy Gane (Charity Challenge), Teresa Greener (The Royal British Legion), Adam Stewart-Koenig (Queens' College, Cambridge), Bob Lamoon (photographer), Alan Machin (WaterAid), Geraldine Mannion and John Overton (Acorns Children's Hospice), Karen and Sean Ross (Rosie's Helping Hands), and Guy Woodcock (Montpellier Marketing Communications Group).

Particular thanks go to Zoe Willems, who was instrumental in shaping the book and whose ideas, feedback and additional writing were invaluable in bringing the project to fruition. We are grateful that she found the time to work on the book among her other consultancy work (www.zoeconsulting.org.uk), being a trustee of Charity Trustee Networks and a director of the Fundraising Standards Board.

Also, special thanks to John Martin (Head of Publishing at Directory of Social Change) for his support and enthusiasm. To my husband, William Carter, I owe my thanks for his encouragement. Finally, I would like to thank all those who have attended my training courses, and all the fundraisers I have worked with over the years for their inspiration and commitment.

Aims of this book

This book is aimed at all who are managing special and major events and it is written especially for you. It is founded on more than 20 years' experience of managing special events, and more than ten years of writing and delivering training courses for the profit and non-profit sectors. It is a practical guide designed for today's market: a realistic guide to special events management which will benefit both large and small charities and other organisations. It is a new approach to the subject, developed from hands-on experience.

This book is a working guide structured to take the special events organiser through the stages required to plan and implement a major or special event, using proven project planning methods in order to ensure a successful outcome. It is developed with basic 'nuts and bolts' techniques through the conception, planning and management of events.

The book is user-friendly and places particular emphasis on the 'how to do it' and how to avoid unnecessary pitfalls. It includes a selection of case studies from organisations which offer sound and practical advice on the reality of special events management. There are tips from experienced special events managers which include how to be effective and save money. However, staging special events is not just about making money; by creating a well-run, professionally managed event, your organisation will attract new supporters, major donors and companies who want to be a part of your success.

1 INTRODUCTION

1.1 Who should read this book?

This book has been designed to be used either as a practical start-to-finish guide for beginners to special events fundraising, or as a useful reference book into which the more experienced can dip. It is relevant to anyone involved in or considering special events fundraising, and has examples from both large and small charities' experience.

- *Board members and directors* – this book will be a useful guide when you come to decide whether and how special events fit into your overall strategy, and will give you insight into what is involved in organising them. Some board members may be involved in special events fundraising themselves.
- *Chief executives and senior management* – this book will describe the importance of looking at special events within a fundraising strategy framework, and will give you an understanding of the level of resources needed and the need to focus on correct measures of success.
- *Special events fundraisers* – this book will guide you through the techniques required for planning and delivering special events, from project management, budgeting and risk planning through to marketing and delivering a successful event and following up from it. It can be used as a start-to-finish guide, or can be dipped into for inspiration and information at any stage in the event planning process.
- *General fundraisers* – this book will give you an insight into how special events can be used as part of a wider fundraising strategy, and how they link into other areas of fundraising such as corporate and major donors. It may help those who do not have responsibility for special event management but wish to develop their skill base.
- *People in other departments* – special events may impact on your work, either requiring your support or contributing to your own goals and targets.
- *Volunteers on special events committees* – this book will help you to understand your role, and provides tools and ideas for implementing a successful event.

- *Trainers and independent consultants* – this book will provide you with a useful reference resource and the basis of a toolkit for the times when your brief includes special event management.

1.2 How to use this book

You can use this book either as a learning guide if you are new to special events fundraising, or as a reference handbook when you want to be reminded of how to do things or gain some inspiration for your next event.

Therefore, the contents are arranged in roughly chronological order. They start by dealing with developing an overall fundraising strategy for events, before going on to individual event project planning and then greater detail about planning and implementing events, including risk assessment and management, the legal requirements and what to do when things go wrong. There is also a list of resources and further reading.

Each chapter is laid out in a similar format to make it easier to find what you need when using it for quick reference. The chapter format includes the following.

- *An introductory paragraph* – this paragraph briefly sets out the purpose of the relevant entry.
- *'How to'* – this is a more detailed section getting to the nuts and bolts of the issues, with practical suggestions for how to use the information provided.
- *Tools* – specific tools and methodologies are highlighted in boxes.
- *Case example* – wherever possible, real-life case examples from a variety of sizes of charity have been included to help illustrate the practical value of the key points covered.
- *Template/checklist* – these are included as hands-on aids for you to copy and use whenever appropriate.
- *Top tips* – a range of professionals in the sector have provided their advice throughout the book.
- *Dos and don'ts* – these summarise the key points in each chapter.

There is an index that includes the tools, case examples and templates to help you find the ones you want more easily.

1.3 What are special events?

There are different views in the sector about what makes a special event, and whether or not to include local community fundraising under the same general umbrella. The definition this book uses is:

A high-profile event, which stands out from normal fundraising events by offering exclusive activities and involving intensive planning and organising, often using the support of a dedicated voluntary steering committee.

Examples of special events include:

- sporting events
- balls and dinners
- musical and cultural events
- receptions
- exhibitions, fairs and festivals
- conferences and challenge events.

There are more details about these types of event in Chapter 5.

For the purposes of this book, local 'bread and butter' events such as coffee mornings and jumble sales are not included within the definition of 'special events'. Local community fundraising plays an important part in income generation for a charity – local events can spread the word and reach parts of local communities that central fundraising cannot, but the main difference is that usually they are run by small, dedicated volunteer committees, with minimum central support from the charity. While this can give them scope to be more adventurous and to be run more frequently, usually they do not require or attract major sponsorship, or have value added tax (VAT) implications. Therefore, on the whole they are simpler to organise and run, but this is by no means to denigrate the importance of volunteer and local fundraising. However, inevitably elements covering planning and organisation as covered in this book may be of some help, or local groups may be encouraged to plan something larger scale with the support of the charity for which they raise funds.

Increasingly, special events are playing a major part in charities' fundraising programmes. Because they involve special skills and a good deal of time and dedication to organise, many charities have a designated person or team to plan and manage special events.

Trustees and senior management have to give serious commitment to any special event project or programme. They need to recognise both the possibilities and limitations of a special event programme, the resources needed to ensure that an event is successful, and a realistic awareness of the risks involved. Often they will be needed to give ongoing support to the special events team by providing useful contacts and attending as and when required.

When planned well, special events can help to support wider organisational strategy, raise the profile of a charity and, of course, raise funds. They can go hand-in-hand with a corporate fundraising programme as a way of encouraging companies to get involved and demonstrate their corporate social responsibility, and as a good way to develop a long-term partnership with a company.

1.4 Special events: pros and cons

Pros	Cons
• Directly rewarding in terms of income generation	• Results unpredictable, particularly when insufficient planning has taken place prior to the event
• Can support further income generation as part of a fundraising strategy – links to corporate partnerships, major donors	• Needs to be planned well in advance
• Raises profile for the charity	• Requires a great deal of time and effort
• Generates publicity and promotion for the charity	• High-risk element
• Manageable as part of a three to five-year strategy	• Potentially high cost to income ratio
• Reaches a wide audience – not only those already interested in the cause, but those interested in the event itself	• Can appear attractive to amateurs, but requires a professional approach to be successful
• Attracts new audiences that may be strategically important to the organisation	

2 STRATEGY AND PLANNING

Sir David Green, a mentor of mine at Save the Children and currently chair of The Dartington Trust, always said that 'failing to plan means planning to fail'. It is a mantra that I always keep in mind when planning a special event. Before you plan and organise an individual event, it is important to take the time to look at how it fits into the overall fundraising strategy for your organisation, and to understand how this is linked with the strategy for the organisation as a whole. If you work in a relatively small charity you may have responsibility for all fundraising activity, or just for delivering the events targets set out for you. However, it is important to know what the organisational, fundraising and events strategies are, since they set the overall direction and context which your individual event should fit into and help to deliver. This chapter will explain the key features of an events strategy, and give you some tips on how to develop your own.

2.1 Establishing a strategy

2.1.1 The basis for a strategy

An events strategy sets the framework and direction within which any individual event will be planned. It is not set in stone, and may need to be revised as circumstances change, but it is important to have considered some basic and strategic points, and if necessary to have obtained trustee or senior staff agreement, otherwise you may be undertaking individual events piecemeal and with no clear sense of purpose.

2.1.2 Reviewing an existing strategy

Even if you are working within an established framework, it will be worth your while to take a step back to review your strategy. Look at what your charity has been organising in the way of events in the past. Do you want to continue in the same way? Have previous events achieved their objectives? Is the same format still appropriate, or are there good reasons to change, for example: fewer resources in your events team; change of key staff; change in the focus of the charity; change in giving patterns; change in profitability?

2.1.3 Key questions to consider

At this stage of thinking, you need to decide on the following.

- *Should we be doing events at all?* Do you have sufficient resources to invest in an events programme? Are other sources of fundraising more reliable or profitable? Do not carry on doing events just because you have in the past, or start doing them because others are – they are not for everyone, and you need to be clear what your positive reasons are for doing them at all.

- *How do events fit within the organisation's strategy?* What does your organisation exist to do, and is there a natural tie-in with particular types of event? Are there things coming up in the organisational plan which could be supported by events, such as a name change, new campaign or project, or a plan to grow the organisation? Remember that events can help to raise your organisation's profile or launch an appeal, as well as raise money for ongoing activity. Creating synergy between your events plan and your organisational plan can maximise the potential of both.

- *How often will we put on events?* Are you just looking at a one-off to support a particular need, or do you want to develop events as a regular source of income for your charity? Do you want one major event on an annual basis or a regular number of smaller events, or both? It takes a lot of effort and expertise to run a successful event, and however many you do, and whatever their profile, you need to make sure that you are realistic about the level of resources that you will need to do it.

- *How far ahead will we plan and budget for?* Many organisations have a three to five-year rolling plan, but smaller organisations may plan for one or two years ahead. A three to five-year plan will set a clear direction of travel, but you may need to be flexible and keep it under review as the organisational plan changes and depending on your own progress and external circumstances. However, you do need to allow a realistic lead-in time for organising major events (see section 2.6 for more detail).

- *Who needs to sign off or agree the strategy?* Because events can be resource-intensive and high-risk, you need to make sure that the overall strategy is known, approved of and supported at the highest level in your organisation. You may need to prepare a paper outlining the overall strategy for events, highlighting the benefits and risks, the assumptions (such as the level of resource provided) and contingency plans, and have it agreed by the trustees, chief executive and/or head of fundraising.

- *What is your long-term aim or objective for events?* We will look later at how to set specific aims and objectives for each event, but here we are thinking about what you hope to achieve with an events programme: what is your total financial target, and over how long a period? How many new supporters do you hope to enlist, and is there an overall message about your organisation that you want to get across over several events?

- *What is your past experience with events?* How long did they take to organise, how much did they cost, what was the net income? Look at both successes and problem areas, and consider whether they can be replicated or overcome in your current circumstances, especially with regard to staffing and resources.

2.1.4 Some tools for strategic analysis

There are many tried and tested tools used in the wider strategic planning environment which can be applied equally to help you to focus and assess your strategy with regard to special events. These tools provide a framework to help you look at internal factors, such as organisational strengths and weaknesses, as well as prompting you to look at the wider world and how it is likely to impact on what you plan to do.

Remember, these are just tools. In order to be helpful, you need to make sure that good information goes into them, and intelligent analysis is made of the results. Other publications specialising in strategic analysis (see Appendix 1) go into more detail about how to use these and other tools, should you want to pursue this area further.

SWOT analysis

A SWOT analysis (Strengths–Weaknesses–Opportunities–Threats) is a useful general technique that is extremely helpful at the early stages of a planning process. Using a SWOT analysis will help you to discover how your special event strategy is performing currently, and the key issues that need to be addressed in a new or revised strategy (that is, where you are now, where you could be and what you might need to do to get there). You need to look at what resources you have at your disposal (strengths), where there are gaps in knowledge, experience or resources (weaknesses), what possibilities are out there that you could convert to your advantage (opportunities), and what could go wrong and work against you (threats).

SWOT is just a list of things: it is up to you what you do with them. Do not be put off if you have listed lots of weaknesses and obstacles; do be creative about how you can overcome them. Your SWOT analysis will be a good indicator of what you are capable of: if you have a fantastic team, lots of experience and a well-known charity name behind you, then it is likely that you will be able to plan an extensive programme of large national events; if you are not so lucky, you may want to consider starting small and building up to something larger when you have gained in experience and confidence.

Example of SWOT analysis

Strengths:
- we have a good fundraising team
- we have enthusiastic supporters and volunteers throughout the country
- we have a high national profile

Weaknesses:
- we have not run events before
- we are worried about reputational risk
- we have a lot of new faces on the trustee board
- we do not have a big budget for events
- lack of focus
- too few resources
- poor record of risk management
- inadequate communications within the organisation and with the outside world

Opportunities:
- we are launching a new appeal in six months
- we have a lot of new faces on the trustee board
- we have supportive trustees and senior managers

Threats:
- short timeframe for the new appeal
- may clash with another major charity event
- complacency – we have always done things this way
- other charities have cornered the market with these sorts of events.

Analysis

You need to win trustee and organisational support for an events programme. You probably do not need or want to do a single major event, given the lack of experience on your team, the short timeframe, lack of budget and concern for reputational risk. However, you have a good team and an enthusiastic supporter and volunteer base throughout the country, so you could pilot a smaller scale local event in one region, with the aim of rolling it out across the country to coincide with your new appeal launch. You can make sure that you time it to avoid clashing with another major charity event. With the experience and confidence you build up, you might go on to make this an annual nationwide event, and develop other events for major donors in a year or two. Alternatively, if you win sufficient trustee support for a major event, you might consider contracting out to professionals, or to keep your costs and risks low by 'piggybacking' on someone else's existing event – such as asking a leading art fair to hold a special preview night for your charity.

PEST analysis

PEST (Political–Economic–Social–Technological) is another well-used method for looking at the overall external environment in which you are operating. It works in the same way as SWOT, by listing any key factors under each heading which may have either a negative or positive impact on your plans. The crucial part is to analyse what the overall impact might be, and what your best strategy would be, given the constraints and opportunities that the environment provides for you.

Political:
- Consider the possible impact of a new prime minister or new political party in government.
- Is public service delivery going to continue to be a political priority?
- Are there any changes in legislation which affect you?
- What is the public benefit and what health and safety legislation, discrimination laws and licensing regulations do you need to consider?

Economic:

- What is the likely trend in inflation and interest rates, and how might this affect your charity's activities and your fundraising?
- How will any reduction in public spending affect you?
- What might the 'Olympic effect' be?
- Are you affected by announcements in the Budget (e.g. the impact of income tax cuts on available Gift Aid from donations)?
- Think about impacts on the amounts you aim to raise, at what level you can price and sell tickets, etc.

Social:

- How does the ageing population affect you and your strategy?
- Does immigration have an impact on your activities or fundraising?
- What are the trends in social cohesion versus social fragmentation?
- What is the employment situation?

Technological:

- Are there developments in the internet and communications sectors of which you need to be aware?
- How are people using the internet, phones, etc. differently from when you last set your strategy?
- How do virtual worlds, YouTube and online community forums such as Facebook impact on you?
- Consider whether you are making the best use of your website to advertise your special events programme, inform supporters and enable them to get involved and give more easily.

Unlike the SWOT exercise, there is little you can do to change the external environment (unless that is what your charity does), but you need to be aware of it in order to plan your activities in order to take account of it, create opportunities where you can, and be realistic about constraints.

Boston Matrix

This is another tool you can use to assess the success of previous events in order to decide your future strategy: which ones to invest more in, which ones to drop and which ones form part of a reliable core activity and income stream. In using this tool, it is important to be aware of the product life-cycle (see section 3.2.2 for more details), and where your events are on this curve – just because an event has been a runaway success in previous years does not mean that it will continue to be so forever – you may need to find ways of refreshing it or leaving on a high.

To use this tool, first list your current events. Without thinking too deeply about it, write next to each one the reasons why you do it. Be honest: if you do it because it is a fixture, say that it is a fixture. If you do it because it is the chair's favourite, write that down. If you do it for the income, write it down.

When you have finished looking at the actual reasons why you do these events, find out how much each one costs to put on (remember to include staff costs), and how much income each generates. Then try to fit your current events to their place in the following matrix:

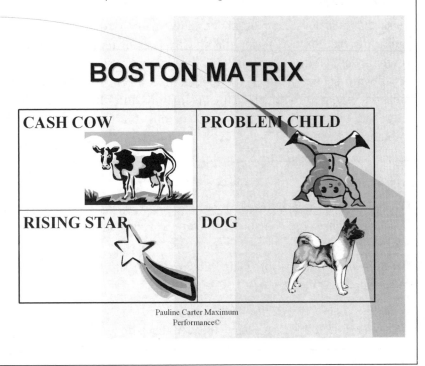

BOSTON MATRIX

| CASH COW | PROBLEM CHILD |
| RISING STAR | DOG |

Pauline Carter Maximum
Performance©

2.1.4.1 Cash cows

These are special events that have a high market share and are easily reproduced. They have a reputation of being excellent events: tickets sell well, the committees are already set up and although they still require a good amount of time and effort, they will not be not too much of a problem to organise. There is still a need to look at the product life-cycle and to avoid being complacent.

2.1.4.2 Rising stars

These are new events requiring time and effort to reproduce, which have winning prospects of becoming a cash cow, and are worth investing in and developing.

2.1.4.3   Problem children

These events can consume cash and resources at an alarming rate. They are problems, but can they be turned into a cash cow? They cannot be allowed to continue as they are – one option is to get rid of them, but it may be worth spending some time and effort researching how they can be resurrected. You may be able to change around poorly performing events by being clearer about your goals, better at marketing and making the most of opportunities.

2.1.4.4   Dogs

These have a low market share, low growth and do not generate significant cashflow: time for the charity to shut its ears to cries of 'But we really enjoy these events!' from supporters and bite the bullet. If they do not sell or achieve their objectives and are a pain to produce, then kick them into touch. Time is money and the charity would be better off spending that time and money on rising stars and even problem children.

Dos and don'ts

Do use these tried and tested tools as something you can use to your advantage, to help provide some structure to your thinking and planning of events.

Do review your reasons for doing certain events, and make sure that they are still appropriate.

Don't get bogged down with process.

Don't keep doing things because you always have done.

2.2 Identifying aims and objectives

It is easy to get carried away with the excitement and challenge of putting on an event, but you need to be clear about why you are doing it. You also need to know whether it has been successful, and you can do that only if you have some idea beforehand about what success would look like.

Your events strategy should set out the overall aims and objectives for all the events you plan to hold, often over a longer period, which allows for some individual events to do less well as long as others can pick up the slack. If you do organise just one event a year, there is more pressure on that event to do well, and all the more need for focus and clarity about what you want to achieve. However, you also need to be clear about the aims of each individual event and how they will contribute to the overall strategy.

This section sets out to take you through the process of identifying clear and realistic aims and objectives for individual events.

Mind maps

For many, mind maps have proved to be an invaluable tool to help their thinking in the strategy and planning processes. Mind mapping was invented by Tony Buzan and is a simple technique that enables you to plot a considerable amount of information and relate and link activities and ideas together in a simple visual way. It is a creative aid that can really help you to work through your thoughts and get them down on paper in a helpful way (see Appendix 1 for Buzan's books on how this tool might help you).

2.2.1 Identifying the primary goal or aspiration

Events can have multiple purposes, but you need to know what the primary goal for your event is, so that you can focus on taking the necessary steps to achieve it. Is your goal:

- fundraising?
- raising the organisation's profile?
- thanking supporters?
- gaining new supporters?

Look at your event in the context of the wider event strategy and decide what the primary goal or aspiration for the event is.

2.2.2 Setting specific objectives and targets

At this point, you can go on to set more specific targets that you want the event to meet.

- *How much do you plan to raise?* £1,000? £10,000? £100,000? Give yourself a specific target, but choose a realistic, even cautious, figure rather than wishful thinking. You have to feel that you can achieve or even exceed it, in order to stay motivated. Make sure that your target figure is the amount you raise after costs, so it represents the real return to your charity. If you plan to increase the level of long-term support arising from this event, put a figure on this as well, and a timeframe in which you are going to measure this.

- *How many people do you want to attend or participate?* What messages do you want to get across through the event? How much wider coverage do you hope to achieve, and do you want this in the local, regional or national press? Remember that profile will be about quality as well as quantity, so add a measure that counts how much *positive* coverage or feedback you get.
- *How many supporters do you want to attend?* The aim here should be for them to enjoy the event, but also to feel even more engaged with the cause, and you may need to find a way to measure this (for example, through feedback forms). If your primary aim is to thank supporters rather than to fundraise at the event, you need to be very clear about how much you can spend, but do remember it is an investment in ongoing support.
- *How many new supporters do you aim to gain?* You may want to measure not only those attending the event, but also those who continue to support the charity.

2.2.3   Identifying secondary aims

Most events will have secondary aims. For example: you want to raise £25,000, but you hope to gain new supporters as well; or you want to raise the profile of the cause, and hope that in doing so you will move people to give more to support it. You should identify these aims and set yourself targets, in order to make sure that you do not miss opportunities when organising the detail of the event. However, do be clear about the main purpose of the event, and do not allow yourself to be distracted.

Acorns Children's Hospice Marquee Week

Geraldine Mannion, corporate functions manager

The main focus of this week-long series of events is to fundraise and to gather together volunteers, staff supporters and families to thank them and celebrate the work of the charity. The annual general meeting has been incorporated also as a central feature of the week:

> By law, we have to hold an annual general meeting, but we have found that holding it on the site of one of our hospices, and incorporating it into a full programme of events, makes it far more appealing. This year, we enjoyed the company of almost 100 members of the Association [Friends of Acorns] at our annual general meeting, compared with a mere 30 members in the past when we took the event outside of Marquee Week.

2.2.3.1 Tools for identifying aims and objectives

The following box describes how to use the SMART system (Specific–Measurable–Achievable–Realistic and Relevant–Time-based) in order to help you define useful targets. This will help you to:

- target the events most in keeping with your organisation's ethos and strategy;
- put a logical case together to 'sell' to your internal market – management, trustees, staff and supporters;
- focus your research;
- assess how much time you have to spend on each event;
- form a realistic budget;
- identify your market when it comes to marketing and ticket selling.

SMART

- Specific – you have defined clearly what you want to achieve.
- Measurable – clear parameters of quality, cost, quantity and time have been established, so you know when you have achieved your targets.
- Achievable – you have set your goal within the resources you have available (both financial and human), drawing on strengths and yet challenging, but it must be realistic.
- Realistic and Relevant – specific targets and goals should fit in with the overall strategy (the business need), and be within the time, experience and resources available.
- Time-based – you should make clear when results are required, and make sure that there is enough time to achieve the goal.

Examples of SMART and non-SMART objective-setting

'Hold the biggest ball by the end of next month' is not specific, realistic, achievable or possible within the time given – this fails the SMART test of an objective.

'Arrange a ball to a high standard, to be held next summer with several A, B or C celebrities in attendance, within a budget of £20,000, and with the aim of raising a minimum of £100,000 for the appeal' is more specific. You know the type of event expected, and at whom it is targeted. It sets out measurable parameters of cost, quantity (income), time and quality (although you may want to go into more detail about what is expected of 'high standard'), and has a more realistic and achievable timeframe and budget attached.

2.2.3.2 Event aims and objectives template

This is a document to keep on the top of the file or posted on the wall as a constant reminder to keep you focused on what you are trying to achieve.

Name and type of event	Response
It fits into the overall fundraising strategy by:	
Primary aim of event:	
Secondary aims:	
Primary objectives: What do you need to put on? How much can you spend? How much do you need to raise? What level of quality should you achieve? By when?	
Secondary objectives: How many additional supporters? How much positive press coverage?	

Top tips

You cannot use the argument, 'This did not make money, but it was a ***great*** *PR opportunity'. You can use the argument, 'This* ***won't*** *make money, but* ***is*** *a great PR opportunity'. If it is an awareness-raising opportunity, do it wholeheartedly. If it is meant to make money, it has to.*

— Teresa Greener, special events manager, The Royal British Legion

Dos and don'ts

Do be clear what your primary aim is.

Do set yourself realistic and measurable targets.

Don't change the aim at the end of the event to fit the results.

2.3 Ideas: what sort of event is appropriate?

This section aims to help you avoid the pitfall of following something through simply because 'it seemed like a good idea at the time'. By now you should have a strategy for events within your organisation, and be clear about the aims and objectives for an individual event. Now you need to find an event to match. Of course, often someone will have had an idea for an event, and it is easy to get carried away with it, trying to squeeze it to make it fit the strategy and aims (particularly if the idea has come from someone senior). However, it is likely to take a lot of work to try and make it fit where it does not, and the end result may not be successful, however good an idea it seemed to be at the time. Remember that what works for one organisation may not work for you. Consider what your organisation does, what your aims and objectives are, who your supporters and likely audience are and, crucially, what resources you have to plan and implement the event.

Also, do try to do something a bit different, or take an existing event and change the format to make it more uniquely your charity's own. In the increasing competition for attention, it is worth giving some thought to what will make your event stand out from the crowd.

2.3.1 Ways of finding ideas

If you are not lucky enough to have an enthusiastic trustee bringing a new idea to your desk every week, then you will need to start by looking at a list of possibilities. Try not to go with the most obvious and first thing that comes to mind – it is worth looking more widely and bringing in other people's ideas to try and find something innovative that will set your charity apart from the many others.

Here are some possible sources of ideas to consider.

- *Brainstorm with your team or committee.* This is the perfect way to bring in wider experiences, and allow your ideas to bounce off each other.
- *Look at what other charities are doing.* Rather than following blindly, consider what it is that attracts people to join in or buy tickets, and whether there are ways to tweak what has gone before and make it fit your charity.
- *Look at adverts for other events* (for example, in newspapers, magazines and on websites). This does not have to be a charity event, as long as it looks interesting and catches your imagination.

17

- *Ask supporters or beneficiaries for ideas.* This might take a bit more time and resources, and you will need to manage expectations (not every idea will be a good one, and you will not be able to do everything suggested), but this will help supporters to feel involved and perhaps more committed to making the event a success.
- *Network.* To a fundraiser, networking is one of the most valuable skills to develop. Meeting people inside and outside of the sector can provide surprising and beneficial leads, whether it be for new volunteers, sources of sponsorship or very specific and particular help. Before attending a social or business event, set yourself goals of what you want to achieve, and if there is a list of attendees available in advance, note down your priorities of whom you want to speak to and why. After the event, keep good notes of your findings and research. (I have a vast collection of business cards, usually with notes on the back, as *aide memoirs*. I also keep my own cards on me at all times: you never know when they might be useful.) If you make good contacts through networking, make sure that you follow up straightaway by email or phone while the lead is still warm.

2.3.2 Be critical

Once you have a list of ideas, look at each one critically. Consider whether:

- it fits with your aims and objectives;
- it fits with your charity – what it does and its ethics;
- it is likely to be popular with your audience;
- you have the resources to organise the event.

Type of event	Does it fulfil the charity's objectives?
Dinner	
Inspirational talk (lunch or dinner)	
Ball	
Auction	
Concert	
Reception and speakers	
Challenge event	
Picnic in the park	
Art or photographic exhibition	
Other	
Other	

Dos and don'ts

Do try and think of something new, or add your own twist to an old idea.

Do speak to other special events organisers – make the most of networking opportunities at conferences and training events.

Don't mistake popular with successful. Supporters may be reluctant to change a time-honoured format, however it may prevent you from doing something even better.

2.4 Supporter and market research

It is likely that you will start with a good idea of the profile of your existing supporters, and therefore your most likely core audience or participants in any event. However, it is worth looking at this in a little more depth, to make sure that you are informed about who your audience is, and how to make your event appeal to your target audience, thereby maximising its potential to be successful. This is important not only when you come to market the event (see Chapter 4), but in checking whether you have chosen the right event for your audience in the first place.

2.4.1 Deciding who your supporters are

First, you need to decide who you want to aim your event towards primarily. If you have established your aims and objectives, you should have a clear idea of whether your main audience is your existing supporters, the general public or any particular social, geographic or interest group. It is likely that your existing supporters will form a core group to make your event successful, even if tickets are sold or participation is invited more widely.

2.4.2 Finding out more about your supporters

You need to gain an understanding about your supporters or target audience in order to decide what kind of event might appeal, what level of income you can realistically expect and how to recruit people to participate. If you hold information on regular supporters, then you should see what you can establish about them from your existing database. However, you may need to build up that information, in which case you may consider undertaking a survey of your supporters. Think carefully about what information you actually need to know and are likely to use, since there is no point asking for and holding random information that you do not use.

What you might want to know about your audience

- Age group
- Social demographic:
  - education level
  - income
  - working status or job
  - newspapers they read
- Interests:
  - dancing
  - gardening
  - sport
  - reading
  - painting
  - history
  - galleries
  - concerts (and what sort)
- Gender
- Children
- Marital status
- Geographic location
- Giving record
- Other charities or causes supported

2.4.3 Surveys: asking the professionals

If that seems too daunting, or you want to do something on a larger scale, there are professional firms which offer to undertake statistical surveys on your behalf. You should make sure that the questions are the ones you want to know the answers to, that you are clear about the sample size, and what the results mean for you. You may want to take the opportunity to find out even more detail about your supporters, what they currently think of you, and what sort of event would make them respond positively, by doing a qualitative survey (i.e. one which involves a discussion or interview, usually over the phone, allowing for follow-up questions and responses which go beyond ticking boxes). However, this is usually more expensive than quantitative surveys, so do be clear about your purpose if you follow this route. Overall, it should be recognised that surveys by external professional organisations may not be within the budget of, or be appropriate for, smaller organisations.

If you want to go beyond your existing supporters, you may need to commission a public opinion survey. Again, there are specialist firms that will help you to design and carry this out according to your needs: make sure that you identify the right sort of sample size, regional mix, gender, age and demographic spread.

Instead of commissioning a survey that is tailored fully to your specific needs, which can be costly, you can commission a 'piggyback' survey, which involves purchasing a certain number of additional questions to be added to an existing survey. This is a less expensive way of obtaining useful statistical information, but be aware that you do have less control over the overall sample parameters (that is, who and how many are being surveyed).

2.4.4   Using national statistics

A less expensive and detailed option would be to look at national statistics and published public opinion surveys to give you information on the general attitudes of certain social, geographic or age groups, as well as background economic trends and income and expenditure patterns.

2.4.5   Analysing the results

The results of surveys need to be treated with care. A small sample size and even smaller return rate may mean that the information collected is not really representative of the wider group. Care has to be taken in the phrasing and presentation of the questions themselves to avoid unintended consequences, such as only time-rich people (probably retired) bothering to respond to a particularly lengthy questionnaire. Also, inevitably those that do respond are likely to be the keener and more committed ones, so be prepared to assume that not everyone else has the same level of enthusiasm or support for your cause.

Dos and don'ts

Do use the information you have to target your event at an audience likely to be interested.

Do find out more about your supporters and what they like.

Don't treat survey responses as gospel truth – they are only indications.

Don't collect information just for the sake of it – make sure that it is relevant and will be used.

2.5 Risk management

Event fundraising is inherently risky. It often involves a lot of upfront investment of financial and time resources, and relies on many elements which are not entirely in your control – the weather being a classic example, but also the number of people who show up, the amount of sponsorship raised by participants, or whether the headline act has a sore throat on the day.

There are three reactions to this level of risk.

1. *Run away* – avoid risk by not doing events at all. However, since all areas of life contain some element of risk, this is not usually a sensible reaction.
2. *'Ostrich head in sand'* – ignore the fact that there are risks and go forward blithely and blindly. This is not sensible at all – be very afraid, because things are more likely to go wrong and you will not have planned for them.
3. *Look risk in the eye* – by clearly identifying risks, you can plan to minimise them, and run a successful and happy event. This is the most sensible way to deal with risk, and the rest of this section looks at how you can go about doing it.

2.5.1 Identifying risks: consider the worst

Your first challenge is to identify the main risks to be faced in organising your particular event. Referring back to the aims and objectives of your event, you need to consider anything that could happen to stop you from achieving those aims and objectives and from holding a successful event. This involves putting on negative, devil's advocate glasses in order to think of the worst case scenario at every stage in the process of organising the event: what if the printer goes bankrupt? What if there is a snowstorm on your sunshine picnic day? What if everyone goes down with food poisoning following the 'Homes for Ponies' dinner?

This is just an exercise in thinking about what could possibly go wrong. In some cases, such as your responsibility for the health and safety of an event, it is essential that you do a detailed risk assessment that covers this aspect in particular (see section 6.3.1). It makes sense to do an overall risk assessment at the start, covering everything you can think of, so that you can build into your planning ways of addressing and minimising these risks.

Worked example: possible risks for a dinner event

- Do not sell enough tickets or tables (financial)
- The venue double-books (financial, reputation)
- Caterers go bust (financial, reputation)
- Guests get food poisoning (health and safety)
- Speaker or celebrity fails to turn up (reputation)
- Guests get bad service (reputation)
- Sued by guest for damage (to clothes, if they trip or fall, etc.) (health and safety)
- Power cut during cooking or event (reputation)
- Guest taken ill (health and safety)
- Guest is disruptive (reputation, health and safety)
- Gatecrashers (financial, health and safety)
- Fire (health and safety).

2.5.2   Likelihood and impact

Once you have a list of what could go wrong, you need to give each a score for likelihood (for example, a snowstorm in July or August would be highly unlikely, but heavy rain is quite probable) and impact (for example, if the balloon supplier goes bankrupt, you may not have the decorations you want, but it will not stop the event). However, while salmonella may not stop the event at the time, it would be disastrous for your reputation and could be very costly in claims against you, more than wiping out any funds you may have raised. You can either choose a numerical scoring system, or use the simpler 'High, Medium and Low' (HML) system, which can be combined easily with the traffic light colours red, amber and green to identify the key areas of risk to be managed.

Worked example: possible risks, their impact and likelihood

Risk identified	Impact (HML)	Likelihood (HML)
Don't sell enough tables	H	M
Venue double-books	H	L
Caterers go bust	H	L
Guests get food poisoning	H	L
Speaker or celebrity fails to turn up	M	M
Bad service	M	L
Sued for damage	H	L
Power cut	M	L
Guest taken ill	L	L
Guest disruptive	M/H	L
Gatecrashers	M	M
Fire	H	L

2.5.3 Managing risks

Now you can start being more positive again, and look at what you can do to minimise the risk. Priority areas are those which you've marked as both high impact and high likelihood. If an area is marked as high impact but low likelihood, action is less urgent but you will still need to make sure you minimise the likelihood of the risk materialising. Low impact and low likelihood can be treated with lower priority, but should not be ignored. There may be a simpler way of dealing with such a risk, such as just being sure who the first aider is or having emergency phone numbers to hand, in the unlikely event that a guest falls ill.

Worked example: adding the actions to manage risk

Risk identified	Impact (HML)	Likelihood (HML)	Action to manage risk
Don't sell enough tables	H	M	Proper research regarding prices Proper marketing Check minimum number without losing money
Venue double-books	H	L	Double-check the booking nearer the time. Ensure contract is robust Use a recommended or tried and tested venue
Caterers go bust	H	L	Use recommended or tried and tested caterers Keep a list of emergency back-up contacts
Guests get food poisoning	H	L	Use tried and tested caterers Check standards of kitchens with them Check for safety certificates at venue and with caterers
Speaker or celebrity fails to turn up	M	M	Have a watertight contract Double-check booking closer to the event Have a back-up ready

Risk identified	Impact (HML)	Likelihood (HML)	Action to manage risk
Bad service	M	L	Use tried and tested waiting staff (with caterers) Be clear about standards expected
Sued for damage	H	L	Ensure all reasonable safety checks and precautions are taken Ensure public liability insurance is in place
Power cut	M	L	Check venue's back-up cooking facilities: generator, gas supply, etc. Is emergency lighting available (consider safety)? Can a feature be made of necessity – candlelit dinner?
Guest taken ill	L	L	Ensure that a trained first aider is present Have emergency numbers to hand Always err on the side of caution
Guest disruptive	M/H	L	Consider employing security staff, especially if there is open access to the general public
Gatecrashers	M	M	Ensure tickets have unique identifiers and there is adequate ticket scrutiny on registration Check the venue for entry-points, consider employing security staff
Fire	H	L	Check fire safety certificates Check that all fire exits are clear Brief all volunteers and staff on fire procedures

2.5.4 Unmanageable risks

There may be some areas where you simply cannot remove the risk altogether, for example if:

- tickets have not sold, despite your best efforts;
- the main entertainment calls off at the very last minute;
- the event is weather-dependent and the weather is dreadful;
- someone hurts themselves badly while at the event.

This is when you need to consider insurance. Check the insurance cover of the venue, entertainment and any suppliers – you may want more cover as they are likely to cover just their own fees and costs rather than any potential lost income from the event, or any liabilities that may fall to you (section 6.4 provides more details on different types of insurance.)

Risk assessment table

Risks identified	Impact (HML)	Likelihood (HML)	Action to manage risk

Dos and don'ts

Do think of as many possible risks as you can.

Do take professional advice, especially when entering into onerous risks or obligations through contracts.

Don't confuse an identified risk with an actual problem – you can manage risks.

Don't skip risk assessment – you will be better prepared.

2.6 Timescale and timing

Experience teaches us that all events take longer to organise than predicted. If you are starting from scratch, then you will need to start building from the ground up, which will involve allowing time to sort out your overall strategy, aims and objectives, undertaking any necessary research on your audience, the type of event and estimated costs, and getting senior support for your events strategy and specific proposed events. All this needs to be done before you even come to plan and put your specific event together.

If you do not allow enough time to plan and implement your event, it is likely to be both stressful and potentially disastrous. This section will guide you through some key considerations around lead-time, then looks at the key factors to consider about the timing of the event itself.

2.6.1 Allowing enough lead-time

Many major events need to be planned at least a year in advance. This may seem to be a long time, but organisations budget for their corporate hospitality a long way ahead, and a rushed event is not a recipe for success. A larger event is likely to take longer than a smaller one: if you have a major annual dinner or convention, you can allow yourself only a very short breather before you start planning next year's event.

Good venues are likely to be popular and booked well in advance, so to get the time and place you want, you need to know your budget, event strategy, the type of event, target audience, etc., so that you can identify and book the right venue. Similarly, top entertainment, celebrities and speakers will be in demand and have many other engagements, so will need early booking.

When you have a specific event in mind, settling the venue, speakers and entertainment well in advance will enable you to work back from this date to establish how long you need to allow for proper planning and marketing. Chapter 4 covers in more detail how to break down all the specific tasks that need to happen, and how to identify key milestones.

2.6.2 Timing is key

Using your audience research, consider whether a daytime, evening, weekend or bank holiday would be best for your event. For example, if you are targeting a large audience where the majority will be working, then daytime events are not a good idea. Consider also the impact of the seasons, school holidays and so forth on your audience and their likely availability to attend your event. Check for clashes with any local, regional, national or international events which are likely to attract your target audience: for example, if you are considering a charity celebrity rugby match, make sure it is not arranged on a Six Nations fixture date!

For outdoor events in particular, you will need to consider the weather. Will it be better to hold it in the summer, when at least you can guarantee longer daylight hours, if not dry or sunny days? The British public is quite 'gung ho' and prepared to face the elements armed with umbrellas and wellies, but you will need to have contingency plans in place and be prepared to cancel if it looks likely to be a real washout.

Consider both the start and finishing times of an event, especially if people are travelling some distance to and from it, or have come by public transport. Remember also that you will need to give people time to set up the venue, or to set up stalls and attractions before the public arrive (sometimes this cannot happen the night before, for various reasons). Similarly, allow time for taking down stalls and attractions, and clearing rubbish from the site.

Type of event	Ideal preparation time to allow
Dinner (200–300 guests)	9 months–1 year
Ball	18 months–2 years
Concert	1 year
Challenge event	1 year–18 months
Art or photographic exhibition	9 months (if artwork offered; longer if need to source or commission)
Picnic in the park	1 year

Top tips

Always overestimate the time things will take, especially if you have complex reporting lines.
— Teresa Greener, special events manager, The Royal British Legion

Don't plan an event with too little lead-time: it would be better not to run it at all.
— Caroline Chilton, PR consultant

Dos and don'ts

Do plan well ahead.

Do draw up a list of things that need to be done, working back from the event date, and allow a realistic amount of time for each task.

Do check key timeframes and deadlines, for example around publishing, publicity materials and programmes – often they are longer than you might think.

Don't fall into the trap of thinking, 'Summer's a long way off, I don't have to worry about that yet …'

2.7 Budget

However good the idea and the intentions, it will not happen if you cannot pay for it. Events can be very resource-intensive, so it is important to think and plan carefully at the start, in order to make sure that you are aware of all the different elements of cost (including staff time), and the realistic income to be achieved from the event.

2.7.1 Establishing a realistic budget

You need to consider both costs and income on a realistic basis. This means including all costs, based either on actual amounts spent before (allowing for inflation) or on detailed quotes, and making sure that income projections are based on likely figures of attendance and price or sponsorship per participant, rather than wishful thinking or those made up to match the cost figures. A classic example of this might be the Millennium Dome, where soaring costs tempted the organisers to project much higher attendance figures than they were able to achieve, in order to make the budget balance.

For most events, costs will be broken down into two main types: fixed costs and variable costs. You also need to consider indirect costs and hidden costs.

- *Fixed costs* remain the same and will have to be paid no matter how many people attend (for example, the cost of venue hire, marketing and promotion, audiovisual equipment, speaker and/or entertainment fees). Clearly, it is easier to project these costs and work out how many you need to attend as a minimum in order to break even.

- *Variable costs* are more difficult to project, since they depend on the numbers eventually attending the event. The main variable cost in any event is likely to be the catering, where you will agree a price per head. However, you may need to agree a minimum number for which you will pay, regardless of how many tickets you actually sell.
- *Indirect costs* can be overlooked, although they are a real cost to the charity. They mostly consist of staff time, use of other departments such as press and accounts and the cost of senior management attending the event itself.
- *Hidden costs* may vary from event to event, and every effort should be made to discover them upfront. Examples might include copyright fees for music, or overtime charges for staff at venues.

		100 participants	300 participants
Costs	Venue		
	Entertainment		
	Catering		
	Tickets, invites, etc.		
	Marketing		
	Insurance		
	Staff costs		
	VAT		
Sub-total cost			
	Contingency @ 10%		
Total cost			
Income	Tickets sold @		
	Raffle @		
	Programmes @		
	Corporate sponsorship		
Total income			
Net cost/ income (total or gross income minus expenditure)			

2.7.2 Forecasting costs

You may have an overall budget for fundraising events, or need to prepare a specific budget for an individual event. This will form an essential part of your project management (see Chapter 4). To ensure you capture and cost all the key stages of an event, write out the most important budgeting tasks and make sure you include the following:

- start-up costs – for example, deposit for the venue;
- marketing costs – mailings, brochures, leaflets, website, etc. to help you sell the event;
- management costs – your time and the cost centres of other departments supporting the event;
- research costs – for example, if you are carrying out a survey;
- replacement and repair costs of equipment you hire;
- closedown costs – for example, the time of accounts department staff.

Checklist: expenditure items

- Venue – includes the hire costs of venue, staff (reception, cloakroom, security), ticket sales, credit card commissions, performing rights, rehearsal time.
- Advertising and marketing – includes 'piggyback' mailings, mailing houses, agency fees and media advertising.
- Printing and design – includes artwork, posters, flyers, press and sponsorship packs, invitation and reply cards, stationery, menus and programmes.
- Performers, artists and celebrities – includes fees, travel expenses, accommodation, meals, refreshments, rehearsal time, any additional performers such as backing groups, pianists, etc.
- Catering and drinks – includes food, drinks (and corkage if you supply your own wine). Remember to allow for your own staff and volunteers in the headcount.
- Personnel – includes any additional secretarial assistance, security, programme sellers (unless using volunteers).
- Physical equipment costs and hire – includes audiovisual, projectors, sound systems, tables, chairs, decorations, flowers, balloons, marquees, linings, heating, electrics, flooring, portaloos.
- Travel – includes charity staff and volunteers' travel expenses and accommodation as appropriate.
- Committee costs – includes refreshments during meetings, travel, etc.

- Prizes – ideally these should be donated, your committee should be able to source these items.
- Postage – includes any costs pertaining to the event.
- Consultants – include these if the event is too large or time-consuming for your charity to do without specialist help.
- Insurance – include this if you need special cover (see section 6.4).
- Photographer – a useful addition to an event, this will provide a photographic record of the event for publicity and future marketing of events.
- Contingency – always add a 10% contingency to your budget.
- Management costs – include your time and that of any members of your organisation who help before the event. This may include press and PR and your director, chief executive or any other staff who may attend the event. This is a real cost to the organisation, and should be included to get a true reflection of how much the event costs.
- VAT – it is advisable to check on all the items listed above to ensure that the charity is not liable for VAT (see Chapter 6 for more details).

2.7.3   Estimating income

Doing your research on your likely audience, and the most appropriate type of event (see sections 2.3 and 2.4), should give you a certain amount of information and evidence to enable you to anticipate income from an event. However, it is easy to fall into the trap of overestimating income in order to make it look as though costs will be covered. Be realistic, and calculate both the best and the least acceptable case scenarios.

Checklist

Income items:
- ticket sales
- merchandise
- corporate participation
- sponsorship
- franchising
- food
- wine

Added value:

- raffles
- auctions
- promotions
- collections
- dual tickets – if you share your event with another charity
- donations – it is always worth including in the invitation an opportunity to send a donation if invitees cannot attend (remember Gift Aid – see section 4.10)
- celebrities and members of the royal family – if they are attending, the added value they bring to your event should be reflected in the ticket price.

2.7.4 Using and controlling your budget

A budget should be a living document, something you update with actual expenditure and income on a regular basis. This will enable you to monitor progress against the plan, and to report back regularly to trustees or senior management. It is important to keep on top of costs and in control of your budget. Manage the event budget, do not let it manage you. As an integral part of the project management process, there are six main aims of budgeting:

- plan – your budget should follow a systematic and logical process that adheres to a long-term strategy; it should form a rolling three to five-year plan;
- coordinate – the budget should help you to coordinate the activities of the various parts of the organisation and ensure that they are consistent;
- communicate – it will be easier to communicate the opportunities and plans of the business to various stakeholders if there is a clear budget;
- motivate – your budget should provide motivation for managers and individuals to achieve their goals;
- control – the progress and cost of activities can be monitored against the original plan, and adjusted accordingly;
- evaluate – your budget provides a framework for evaluating the performance of an event.

2.7.5 Return on investment ratios

Everyone will have their own view on what the right level of return on investment ratios should be. Most charities try to work on a cost ratio of at best 4:1. For some the absolute bottom line is a 40:60 return – that is, for every £40 spent, £100 should be raised with £60 net return. Obviously it is better for your charitable cause, looks better and is easier to justify if you have a better return ratio: if you can raise £100 by spending just £20, then you should. Your charity may have a policy on return on investment ratios – and if it does not, you should be clear what kind of return would constitute success.

Having clarity about your return ratio will help you to control costs, and may help you to encourage corporate sponsorship of the event. For example, if a company sponsors the event for £10,000, and you expect a profit of £40,000, they will be reassured and impressed that the event is not only going to be a financial success, but has been professionally planned and managed as well.

You are likely to find that you need a higher investment ratio the first time you put on a particular event, and that this should improve once the event becomes more established. Be aware of where you are in the product life-cycle, and use the Boston Matrix (see section 2.1.4) or similar review process to keep an eye on progress; if an event appears to have a worse investment return every time you put it on, this may indicate a problem you need to investigate.

If you have a portfolio of events and other fundraising activities, inevitably some income streams will have better and worse return on investment rates, which should balance each other out across the overall fundraising activity. However, do look at individual activities to consider whether they are still worth doing.

Top tips

Always underbudget for income, and overbudget for expenditure.

Never budget on 100% ticket sales: there is always someone who has to have a freebie!

> — Teresa Greener, special events manager, The Royal British Legion

---

Dos and don'ts

Do set a budget and review and revise it as the event progresses.

Do make sure that you have written agreements with suppliers covering costs and terms of payment.

Do check all invoices against written agreements.

Do agree who has the authority to sign off on invoices.

Do take control of agreements and contracts, and take action if necessary.

Do record actual costs and compare the actuals with budget.

Do keep aware of cashflow, and be aware that it often turns out worse than you planned.

Do ask plenty of questions – what if?

Do update your budget if any costs change.

Do talk to your finance department before drawing up the budget, in order to avoid surprises when the final audit takes place.

Don't just guess at costs. Look at what you have paid in the past, and get some quotes.

Don't sign off any invoices until you are totally satisfied.

Don't assume that everyone will keep to their terms about payments.

Don't forget VAT.

2.7.6 Budget templates

The sample templates in this section will help you to design your own spreadsheet for an event. The expenditure is self-explanatory; the income is designed to include individual sponsorship if you do not succeed in getting total sponsorship. Modern spreadsheets incorporate a facility for formulae to use in the financial columns, therefore all the totals, profit/loss, etc. will be updated automatically as you add in new figures. Finally, you should discuss the spreadsheet with your finance department, so that it agrees with the format.

Top tip

Remember to update income every time you receive it. Do not record income until you have the money in your hand: do not go on promises such as 'The cheque is in the post' – wait until the cheque is received and cleared.

Figure 1: Charity corporate golf day

EXPENDITURE			ESTIMATED INCOME		
	cost	sub total		Estimated income	Actual income
Venue hire			Ticket sales teams x 4	£	£
Staff costs					
Credit card commissions			**Corporate sponsorship**		
		£_____	Overall event	£	£
Advertising and marketing					
Piggyback mailings			**Individual corporate sponsorship**		
Media advertising			Golf pins	£	£
VAT			Brunch	£	£
		£_____	Refreshments during play	£	£
Printing and design			Reception	£	£
Artwork			Dinner	£	£
Posters and flyers			Champagne/wine	£	£
Press and sponsorship packs			Prizes	£	£
Invitation/rely cards			Programme advertising	£	£
Stationery			Scorecards	£	£
Score cards			Merchandise	£	£
Menus			Photographs	£	£
Programmes			Donations	£	£
VAT			Gifts in kind	£	£
		£_____			
Catering			**Total estimated income**	£_____	
Main meals					
Reception			**Total actual income**		£_____
Refreshments during play					
Staff meals, refreshments					
VAT					
		£_____			
Personnel					
Management costs					
Additional administration assistance					
Security staff					
Photographer					
Travel and accommodation					
VAT					
		£_____			
Physical equipment hire costs					
Sound system for speakers					
Flowers, table decorations					
VAT					
		£_____			
Committee costs					
Meeting expenses					
		£_____			
Prizes					
Event insurance		£_____			
Bad debts		£_____			
Contingency @ 10%		£_____			
Total estimated expenditure		£_____	**Total estimated income**	£_____	
Total actual expenditure		£_____	**Total actual income**		£_____
Net profit		£_____			

Figure 2: Template budget spreadsheet

EXPENDITURE			ESTIMATED INCOME			ACTUAL INCOME
	cost	sub total				
Venue hire			**Corporate sponsorship**		£	£
Staff costs			Overall event		£	
Credit card commissions						
		£_____			£	£
Advertising and marketing						
Piggyback mailings			**Individual corporate sponsorship**			
Media advertising					£	£
VAT					£	£
		£_____			£	£
Printing and design					£	£
Artwork					£	£
Posters and flyers					£	£
Press and sponsorship packs					£	£
Invitation/reply cards			Programme advertising		£	£
Stationery					£	£
VAT			Merchandise		£	£
		£_____	Photographs		£	£
Catering						
Staff meals, refreshments			Donations		£	£
VAT			Gifts in kind		£	£
		£_____				
Personnel			**Total estimated income**		£_____	
Management costs						
Additional administration			**Total actual income**			£_____
assistance						
Security staff						
Photographer						
Travel and accommodation						
VAT						
		£_____				
Physical equipment hire costs						
VAT						
		£_____				
Committee costs						
Meeting expenses		£_____				
Prizes		£_____				
Event insurance		£_____				
Bad debts		£_____				
Contingency @ 10%		£_____				
Total estimated expenditure		£_____	**Total estimated income**	£_____		
Total actual expenditure		£_____	**Total actual income**			£_____
Net profit		£_____				

2.8 Review

There is a huge temptation to collapse in a relieved heap once the guests have gone, the bills have been paid and the money has (hopefully) come in. You may consider it a measure of success to have simply survived the process. However, reviewing the success of the event is a crucial stage in the planning process. There is no point in establishing aims and objectives if you do not look at whether you've achieved them! This is your opportunity to look at whether your event has been successful, and whether there are things you could do better next time.

2.8.1 What to review

You will probably want to review both the outcomes of your event (that is, whether you have met your targets) and the process of organising, so that you have a full picture of what went well and could be repeated and where the problems were, so you can try to avoid them next time around.

2.8.2 Collecting information

There are various ways of collecting the information you need to review.

- *Your own experience.* You may find it helpful to keep notes as you go along, to remind you of the good, the bad and the ugly, what caused you sleepless nights, what opportunities were missed and which ones you made the most of when they arose.
- *What did you hear on the day?* Listen to staff and volunteers as you move around the event, and also listen to attendees and participants. Volunteers and supporters tend to be very forthcoming when asked for their opinions. If possible, arrange a debrief with staff and volunteers at the end of the event to capture their views on how things went. Consider phoning supporters the day after the event to ask for views while they are still fresh.
- *Formal feedback forms.* The nature of the event will dictate whether it is appropriate to ask participants or attendees to fill in forms, but it may be possible to ask for feedback along with a thank-you letter. Most supporters tend to prefer the personal approach, either at the event or by telephone. You may want to find out opinions about the venue, the entertainment, the impression they gained of your organisation and the overall enjoyment and success of the event from the participants' perspective.

- *Formal evaluation meeting.* At the start of the planning process (see Chapter 3), timetable a meeting of key people to review the event and identify learning points.
- *Statistics.* You should have a record of attendees or participants so that you can see whether you have met your target. In addition, you should have a method of capturing how much was given as a result of the event.

2.8.3   Reviewing against aims and objectives

Refer back to your original aims and objectives for the event. Do focus on reviewing your achievement towards your primary purpose, but also remember to look at how well you did with your secondary purposes and how you dealt with unexpected opportunities and obstacles.

2.8.3.1   Bottom line and finances

Review the actual spend: where did you go over and under budget? Why and what difference did it make? What could you do differently next time?

Review actual income: have you met or exceeded your targets? From what sources? If not, why not? What could you do better next time?

Review future income: plan reviews for one or two years further on, if you set this as an objective. Make sure that a good follow-up with attendees or participants is planned, to make the most of the 'feelgood' factor following the event.

2.8.3.2   Profile

Review the articles and press coverage that you received. Did this meet your targets? Could you have done more? What could you have done differently?

2.8.3.3   Process

Look at the pressure points which occurred during planning and implementation. Why did they occur? Could you do things differently to make it run more smoothly? Did something work really well, and could you replicate this in other areas of the process?

Look at how you dealt with the unexpected. Capture these things and put them in the project plan next time. There will always be things you do not plan for, but hopefully they will be different next time.

2.8.4   Ongoing review

As part of project managing each individual event (see section 3.2) or an overall events strategy, you should have a plan and be aware of how you are doing against that plan, so that you can see if you are ahead or behind schedule, and spot any problems before they become critical, putting the whole event at risk.

It may be worth scheduling specific review sessions at crucial stages throughout the project, in order to check that you are on track and to decide what changes you might need to make to account for changing circumstances.

The product life-cycle

Just like any other product, events tend to follow marketplace rules in terms of a life-cycle: at the planning stage of a new event, you will spend more time and money putting it together, then it will gain its own momentum, popularity and success. However, as with all successful products, interest will tail off and it will become boring unless you spot the right time to change or tweak it in some way.

For example, let us consider the car market: a functional car has all the same components – engine, wheels, body, windows, etc. – but manufacturers change the design and the name on a regular basis in order to refresh the brand whenever the market is becoming stale. In essence, the car is more or less the same vehicle, but from the customer's perspective it is a brand new car.

Similarly, events need to change and develop over time in response to customer needs, competitive activity and perhaps legislation; few (even good) special events will last forever, and most will benefit from regular refreshment. There are four phases.

1. *Introduction* – launch and conception. At this stage you will need to spend more time and more money to get the event off the ground. You will be taking some risks and trying out new ideas and will need to put a lot of effort into raising awareness and support.
2. *Growth* – an established event. Event objectives are achieved, awareness has increased, and the event is perceived by supporters to be an excellent event, giving good value for money: 'the place to be'.
3. *Maturity* – the event is in demand. Everyone who wants to attend has difficulty in acquiring tickets. Tickets go without too much marketing, more via word of mouth. Objectives are overachieved.

4. *Decline* – too many other charities have jumped on the bandwagon and are copying your charity's events. The event is no longer the novelty or the 'place to be'. Tickets are still selling, but with difficulty. More time and money is being spent on promotion. Objectives are not quite achieved.

The time to change the event is just before maturity: begin to tweak a few elements, then in the following years make a further change (as the diagram below illustrates). Alternatively, you can drop the event altogether and do something completely different. Your loyal supporters should have faith in you in order to produce another excellent event. Never try to resuscitate an event once it is going down the back slope of the illustration.

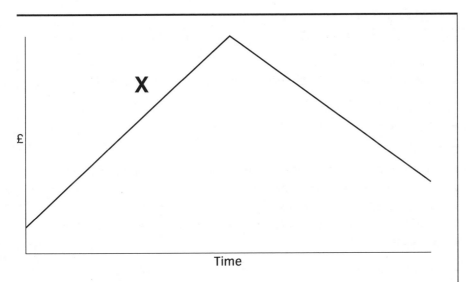

X marks the time to change or tweak the event.

Dos and don'ts

Do review the event as a team to capture wider experience and ideas for how to do better next time.

Do use your review.

Do be honest and critical.

Don't use the review as a 'blame game' exercise.

Checklist

1. Why do you want to hold a special event:
- is the purpose fundraising, raising profile, engaging supporters?

2. What type of event does the charity wish to hold?

3. How does the event fit with the organisation's aims:
- how does it address the charity's fundraising objectives?
- how does it provide non-financial benefits for the cause? (Use the Remember to be SMART list.)

4. What is the expected net income:
- gross income less expenses: amount of sponsorship needed to offset costs; expected return on investment?

5. Initial finance needed:
- remember to include VAT, your time and overheads, travel.

6. Performers:
- do you have contacts with agents, celebrities and performers?

7. Audience:
- what type of audience does the charity wish to attract?

8. Sponsorship:
- is there a list of contacts that can be approached for sponsorship?
- what are the benefits for sponsors?
- will they enhance their marketing or strategic objectives?
- what are the risks and benefits of sponsorship to the charity (other than income)?

9. Resources needed:
- will it be necessary to recruit a new committee or chairperson?
- is the committee available to run the event?
- what other resources are needed to stage a successful event, and are they available?

10. Equipment:
- what is required? Include technical equipment, transport, printing and other material costs.

11. Planning time:
- when does the event need to take place?
- how long will it take to plan, prepare and stage the event?
- do you have sufficient time?

12. Permission and licences:
- what permits or licences are required for each event?

- how much time is required to apply for and secure the necessary permits, licences or insurance?

13. Celebrities, VIPs, royals:
- does the charity need any of these people to support the events within the programme?
- are there good contacts with them or their agents?
- are they available on the day required?
- are they charging for their appearance or speaking fees, or donating their time?

14. Publicity:
- who is responsible for publicity, media contacts, photographers, etc.?
- what publicity is required to ensure the event's success?

3 MAKING IT HAPPEN

Having established your overall strategy, worked out the basics of what sort of event you are putting on, what the primary aims are and who your target audience is, you now need a plan of action. Events have to be thought through and planned to make sure that the right things happen at the right time, and that everyone involved knows what their responsibilities are. It is a team effort – you need to make sure you have the right mix of different experiences, skills and knowledge to contribute, and that everyone knows their role and has ownership of the plan.

A good project plan will provide a road map that everyone in the team can follow, covering all the tasks and who has responsibility for what, and mapping timings and dependencies (see section 3.2) to a realistic timescale. It will enable you to keep track of progress, make sure that critical elements are delivered on time and make changes as you go to ensure that the event is successful. No matter how large or small the charity, whether national or regional, whether catering for 50 or 700 people, the same planning principles will apply.

This chapter will take you through the planning process and introduce you to some useful tools and models. These can be used either manually (using flipcharts, lists, Excel spreadsheets and wallcharts) or by various project management software programs which can be very helpful, particularly when reviewing and updating plans. However, before investing in software, it is vital to understand the underlying project management skills so that you can use the software effectively and do the key tasks required.

Some of what follows may seem complicated and daunting if you have not come across it before, or if you are keen to plunge straight into looking at venues, booking entertainment and so forth. However, it is well worth the effort to invest the time in planning at this stage, as it will save a great deal of time in the long run and may well avoid a crisis.

3.1 Putting a team together

Most of the time you will not be working entirely alone. This section is about taking time out at the start of the project to consider the people you need to help you: how to find them, how to make best use of the people you have, and how to get them pulling together towards the same goal, in order to achieve the successful event.

Your team may not just be the people you work with on a day-to-day basis. Different people will perform different functions over the course of a project, and it is worth considering who they are and what their roles are in relation to your event, and making sure that they are available and willing to participate.

3.1.1 The special events organiser

Whether you are already a special events fundraiser looking to appoint somebody, or want to develop your skills to enable you to move into special events management, it is worth taking a step back to think about what is actually involved and what qualities and skills are necessary.

People come into fundraising from various backgrounds: some choose fundraising as a first choice directly from university, while many others have had a range of experience in the world of commerce. Some experience of the wider world is important to generate a healthy environment and a range and mix of skills and experiences in the fundraising team. It is often worth looking beyond the direct line of work of someone's previous career or study and seeing whether a potential fundraiser has gained experience through voluntary fundraising activities.

A special events organiser may have to work on their own, or be fortunate enough to be part of a team. They may be a general fundraiser, with events a part and parcel of what they have to do to achieve their targets. Every situation will be unique, and may require a different emphasis or mix of qualities and experience, so do take time to consider what is right for your organisation.

3.1.1.1 Marketing

This is an essential skill. Fundraisers are in the selling game, and for special events fundraisers, you are not only trying to gain support for your cause or charity, but also may be literally selling tickets for the event. You need to be able to promote it internally, recruit and support volunteer groups, secure corporate sponsorship, entice celebrities and high-profile patronage, and secure attendance and participation at the event itself.

3.1.1.2 Organising

As a special events organiser you must be able to manage strategically, and plan and work towards long-term goals. You need to organise and coordinate teams of people and suppliers to ensure that everything happens in the right order and comes together at the right time. You need to be able to control budgets and have contingency plans to cope with the unexpected in a structured way. In addition, you will need to be organised and meticulous in keeping records, both to ensure proper accountability and to learn and progress with every event you manage.

3.1.1.3 Leadership

You will be dealing with all sorts of people, including senior members of your organisation, staff, suppliers and volunteers. It is essential to have the skills to bring them together to achieve the shared goal of the event, to be able to motivate and encourage staff and volunteers, delegate effectively to use available skills to the maximum and help staff and volunteers to develop, as well as manage expectations and control external relationships (particularly finance and delivery).

3.1.1.4 Enthusiasm

You will need to demonstrate resilience and drive, not only to keep yourself going but also to motivate the whole team. It is important to keep a fair balance between the enthusiasm needed to deliver and sell an event, and the need to retain credibility, so you will need to communicate effectively and manage expectations carefully in order to ensure that you avoid the extremes of total doubt and excessive optimism.

3.1.1.5 Ideas and creativity

Thinking creatively is vital to keep your events fresh and interesting, to enable you to cope with unexpected situations, and to be flexible while working within your plan. As a manager you need to have your feet firmly on the ground, but you need to be able to recognise a good idea when you see it, whether it is your own or you have others around you to make suggestions. You also need to have the creativity to find ways to inspire others to support your event and cause.

3.1.1.6 Communication and networking

The main resource available to organisers of special events is people, therefore it is essential that you can communicate effectively. You will need to listen to staff, volunteers and fellow fundraisers so that you know exactly what is going on, and whether tasks are happening on schedule. It is vital that you communicate clearly what the goals and key milestones are and what you expect from individuals on the team.

3.1.1.7 Research

You may want to outsource your market research or undertake it yourself, but you need to be able to analyse and make decisions on the results of that research. It is helpful to have an outlook which makes you aware of the possibilities in various experiences, and to absorb useful information in this sort of informal research.

Do not worry if you are not equally skilled at everything on the list. However, it is important to look at ways of improving areas of weakness, and you should look at training opportunities, either through in-house programmes or experience, or through external training bodies.

Example: job description and person specification

Event fundraising manager, WaterAid

Job description

Job title: Event Fundraising Manager

Team: Corporate and Events Fundraising Team, part of the broader National Fundraising Team

Salary: Grade 3

Location: Vauxhall, London

         Note: this post involves travel within the UK and possible occasional visits accompanying supporters overseas. Also working some unsociable hours when required (evening and weekends).

Reporting to: Development Manager – Corporate and Events

Managing: Event Fundraising Assistant and volunteers

Income target: Annual income target of c. £420,000 in 2007/08

Resources: Annual expenditure budget of c. £55,000

Purpose

This is a new role which has been created to develop and implement an events fundraising strategy for WaterAid. Currently the main activities are the Flora London Marathon, other running, triathlon and cycling events and the volunteer presence at Glastonbury Festival as well as music events, water-related events, extreme sport and overseas challenges.

Description of main tasks

1. To evaluate the current events programme, looking specifically at issues such as return on investment and time resources required. In consultation with the Development Manager – Corporate and Events, develop and implement an events strategy which focuses on those areas most beneficial to WaterAid and identifies any potential new areas for growth.

2. Effectively manage the events fundraising budget and work with the Development Manager – Corporate and Events in the preparation of annual budgets. Monitor, evaluate and report against plans.

3. Ensure all events comply with legal requirements, health and safety regulations and Institute of Fundraising codes of practice. Provide advice and support to other fundraising teams on these areas.

4. Ensure that the team provides friendly and professional support to our event participants, ensuring that they meet their fundraising targets and receive appropriate levels of support.

5. Line manage the role of Event Fundraising Assistant. Recruit appropriate volunteers to support specific events and provide general support to the events team.

6. Work with the regional fundraising development managers to ensure coordination between the teams, for example with the events which take place in the regions and through water companies.

7. Working closely with the Corporate Manager who manages our Glastonbury relationship, provide support by managing WaterAid's volunteer presence at the Glastonbury Festival (c. 150 volunteers).

8. In partnership with the Communications Services Team, produce targeted fundraising and publicity materials for all events fundraising initiatives and ensure any events or event participants using our brand are doing so within the guidelines of our Communications Team.

9. Working with our Media Team, coordinate the PR for all events.

10. Identify and implement opportunities for event sponsorship, liaising closely with the Corporate Team.

11. Identify and implement opportunities for celebrity endorsement and opportunities to become the selected charity for events, e.g. runs, triathlons and third-party events.

12. Manage the event volunteer needs of the Corporate and Events Team, including those people volunteering for Glastonbury, the London Marathon, etc.

13. Contribute to the development of WaterAid's fundraising strategies; develop effective and workable annual planning documents and, if requested, take the lead on specific national and international fundraising initiatives.

14. Undertake any reasonable tasks requested by the Development Manager – Corporate and Events or the Head of National Fundraising.

WaterAid person specification

Job title: **Event Fundraising Manager**

Reporting to: **Development Manager – Corporate and Events**

Experience

Essential	Desirable
• Proven experience of events management • Experience of mass participation events and supporting large numbers of event participants • Proven experience of writing successful fundraising letters and applications • Proven experience of managing and coaching staff or volunteers day-to-day • Experience of managing information on fundraising databases (WaterAid uses Raiser's Edge)	• Experience of events management within a charity • Experience of devising, monitoring and evaluating annual plans and budgets

Knowledge and skills

Essential	Desirable
• Proven excellent verbal communication, written communication and numeracy skills • Confidence and ability to present a cause and detailed project information to supporters, and to network and represent WaterAid at donor and other hospitality events • Ability to analyse and understand budget and project reporting information • Strong administrative and wordprocessing skills required in a self-servicing post	• A good understanding of international development

Aptitudes

Essential	Desirable
<ul><li>Ability to recognise and develop new fundraising opportunities</li><li>Willingness to work some unsociable hours when required (evening and weekends)</li><li>Commitment to WaterAid's stated values and working principles</li><li>Ability to work effectively with other managers within the fundraising team and with other key internal and external contacts at all levels</li></ul>	<ul><li>Willingness to travel overseas with supporters</li></ul>

3.1.2 Trustees and senior staff

It is likely that these people will be in place already, and may have appointed you or asked you to put on the event. As discussed in Chapter 2, you need their commitment to support you in planning and organising your event, and they should have signed off the overall event fundraising strategy.

You may need their contacts and networking skills, either to find a celebrity to appear at your event or to ensure good attendance and participation in it. They will need to be kept informed at key stages in the preparation of the event, and they should be fully briefed before the event itself, so that they know the aims and messages for the organisation, what to expect at the event, and any VIPs they are hosting.

3.1.3 Events committee

This is usually a voluntary committee which has overall supervision of and responsibility for an event. It is desirable to have a committee for each individual event rather than one special events committee: this means that you can match the knowledge, skills and interests of volunteers to appropriate events, ensuring that their enthusiasm and motivation is retained. It is recommended that you separate the business or planning committee from any ticket-selling committee – each will need a different set of skills and focus, and those keen on selling tickets may not want to get involved on the planning side (and vice versa). Small is beautiful: it is preferable not to have too many members on your special events committee; approximately no more than eight people ensures that it is workable.

Choosing the right people is vital to ensuring that this committee is a genuine asset, adding value to the event organising process, rather than being an obstacle to the event itself. Often, committees are composed of 'people we know' or 'people like us' – this may be fine, but the risk is that it will be 'cliquey' and less dynamic and imaginative than a more thought-through committee. It is worth thinking about the skills you need on the committee and trying to represent all areas of need, looking not only for good communicators and enthusiasts but also people with contacts, creative thinkers and people with organisational experience, a passion for the cause and some financial knowledge. In some cases, it will be enough to find people in a wider circle of acquaintance who have the necessary skills, but larger charities are looking increasingly at some form of advertising to attract people from a wider section of society.

Ongoing research is essential: keep spotting (and making a note of) people whom you may need, even if it is not for some time. Look out for future committee members at events themselves or at business meetings, other activities within the charity or socially. People like to be asked – they feel flattered that you have confidence in them.

Top tip

When asking someone to join a special events committee, make the approach special. Rather than relying on a casual telephone call, arrange to meet them for tea or coffee, or a drink after work. Tell them what you want them to do and when, and why you are asking them.

The key person to find is the chairperson: they need to have experience in managing a team of people, specifically volunteers; they need a commercial understanding of the charity and the importance of corporate partnerships; and knowledge of committee procedure would be an important added advantage.

Make sure you are clear about the role description and the time commitment you are asking for: while the old adage 'If you want something done, ask a busy person' may hold true, you do not want someone without the time to give to make the event a success. If the person you approach does not realistically have the time, it may be better to give them a smaller volunteer role helping out on the day itself – they may be enthused by this to make more time next time.

Take time to prepare an induction for special events committee members: brief them on the charity and the purpose of the event. Introduce them to the work of the charity if possible, and to the members of staff who will be their main contacts. Make sure they have a keyworker contact within the charity to maintain continuity, if the special events manager is not doing this themselves.

Once a committee has been established, the first and last rule to remember is to communicate. As a volunteer committee, the members are likely to be very busy people – it is important that you keep them informed about progress. In addition, effective and well-run committee meetings will help to ensure that everyone feels they are making the best use of their time, and achieving progress from meeting to meeting.

Making the most of meetings: how to hold effective committee meetings

- Plan all meeting dates for the duration running up to the event (and the debrief immediately after the event) at the start. Dates should be agreed at the first meeting.
- Check that the meeting venue is convenient for everyone, with public transport and parking available.
- Check that the time of the meeting is appropriate, and stick to that time and venue for all other meetings, if possible. It will help busy people to remember and keep these meetings in their schedule.
- Decide the agenda well in advance with the chairperson, and be clear what items are for reporting back, discussion or decision-making.
- Ensure that everyone receives the agenda, briefing notes and a time plan in advance of every meeting, so that they are fully prepared and can focus on the decisions they need to make at the meeting.
- Start meetings on time.
- Work with the chairperson to keep meetings short, to the point and at a good pace, sticking as far as possible to the time plan.
- Check that everyone fully understands the implications of what they have agreed to do and is happy with it.
- Ensure that all action points are agreed on; including who will be responsible for them with timescales for completion, and that they are minuted.
- Ensure that minutes are taken by the staff keyworker – this ensures that you can keep a watching brief on the progress of the committee, and

provides valuable administrative support for the volunteers, ensuring that pace is maintained.

- Ensure that minutes with clear action points are circulated well on time – aim to send them shortly after the meeting, rather than shortly before the next one. This ensures that people are reminded of their action points in good time.
- Keep in touch and ask how things are going, but do not check up on committee members – it defeats the object of having delegated in the first place.

3.1.4 Event staff team

Depending on the size of your organisation, you may have fundraising staff or even a small team specifically dedicated to organising special events. It may be that this is a developing area of activity, and although you have not had dedicated staff before, you may need to recruit a team as an investment in a future programme of fundraising events.

Think about the scale of the event(s) and whether the overall programme would merit a staff team to work on it. Section 3.2 will look at the process of developing a project plan: this will help you to identify the various tasks that need to be done. You need to be realistic about what can be done by one individual in the time available, and work out how many people you will need to realise the project. While many tasks can be done by volunteers, if the event is large-scale it may be better to allocate some important tasks and responsibilities to members of staff, for example, volunteer management, raising sponsorship, developing corporate relations and managing invitations and ticketing.

3.1.5 Other staff

It is worth considering and identifying others in your organisation who may be involved in some way in making your event a success, even if they are not in the events or fundraising teams. We have looked already at the importance of getting 'buy-in' to your plans from senior staff and trustees, but you need to make sure that everyone in the organisation understands and supports your event. You may need to involve those in press, communications and marketing, in which case you will need to meet early on to ensure that you build your event into their schedule and make the most of the opportunity that the event provides. You may need the advice and help of human resources, accounts and finance staff as you enter into contracts or apply for upfront funding of the event, or need expert eyes to check your forecasts and process the funds raised.

Furthermore, make sure that you maintain good and close relationships with operational staff – they are doing the activities that you are raising funds to support, and should be a mine of inspiration and information to provide good stories or ideas about key themes and achievements that you can use and celebrate in your event.

3.1.6 Volunteers

Volunteer fundraising has been the bedrock of all charities. Volunteers raise money, give their time freely and manage local groups and shops. They act as ambassadors for the charity, spreading the word. They create and run local fundraising events, shake the tin during charity week, and often when you ask what they do, they reply: 'I am just a volunteer.' Despite their own modesty, they are not to be undervalued; without this army of volunteers, most charities would find the widespread awareness of their cause diminished and their funds depleted.

Do not think that donors and volunteers are two separate categories. Very often donors can be volunteers, whether on special events committees or helping out in other ways to ensure the success of an event (for example, parking wardens, staffing the ticket desk or a stand or helping to set up). Many volunteers started out as donors or can become donors when they are more familiar and engaged with the work of the charity.

Working with and through volunteers is a skill in itself; the fundraising manager must be sensitive to people who are giving their time freely and without payment other than the reward of supporting something in which they believe. For many people who volunteer, it is an opportunity for them to develop skills, increase their confidence and self-esteem, and perhaps acquire a source of social contact and friendship which was lacking in their lives.

3.1.6.1 Recruitment

Identify the various tasks you need volunteers to do, and think about how many volunteers you need for each task. Consider the skills that volunteers will need, depending on the task you'll be asking them to do. In addition, consider where you will best find the people who will match the skill you need. You could approach existing supporters or the local university or make an appeal on your website. Some websites act as 'clearing houses' or 'matchmakers', matching potential volunteers to charities that need them to find people with professional skills (see Appendix 2 for more information).

If you have an existing pool of supporters willing to volunteer for you, consider undertaking a simple skills audit – you may be surprised at what they are willing to offer, and can match better the tasks to the abilities and interests of volunteers.

3.1.6.2   Induction and training

It is important for volunteers to know what is expected of them, and to be given the necessary tools to do their job. Often, the best method is to produce a guide to volunteering or induction pack, which includes the following:

- an introduction to the work of the charity;
- what the values of the charity are, and what expectations there are in terms of behaviour of anyone working for, or on behalf of, the charity;
- what is expected of them as volunteers – include a role description, covering what you need them to do and when, and how that fits in with and contributes to the overall plan;
- what expenses will be paid – this is important, and it should be made clear to all volunteers that they should claim back expenses. Those who wish to can always donate the money back, but those who really need reimbursement of expenses should not be made to feel guilty;
- what support, guidance and training is available, including contact details.

New volunteers who know little or nothing about the charity they are going to support should receive a face-to-face induction if at all possible: this will give them an understanding of the charity and the opportunity to meet staff and those who will be their main contacts.

3.1.6.3   Managing

Managing volunteers can be very difficult. You have people giving up their time for you for no reward except the feeling that they are doing something good. You may need to keep them motivated, even under pressure, and you need to make sure they actually do what you expect them to do in order for your event to run smoothly. Communication is key: make clear what you expect and how this contributes to the whole. Provide a key contact with whom they can raise any issues, questions and concerns. Remember to thank and praise them, and listen to their ideas and comments.

3.1.6.4 Pitfalls to avoid

Be careful that the relationship does not become *de facto* that of a contracted employee. Accidentally creating an employer–employee relationship can be problematic, as it will lead to various legal complications.

Because there is no contract, there is always a risk that key volunteers may not turn up on the day. If you have generated a good positive atmosphere and team spirit, this is less likely to happen. If you have a good open relationship with volunteers, hopefully they will come to you in advance if there are any problems. However, be prepared to ask some volunteers to step into the breach at the last minute to fulfil a different role.

Remember to be clear about what you need from the volunteers you select, and try to be selective in order to ensure that you have people with the necessary skills to do the job, otherwise you may spend a lot of time managing someone who is not really up to the task. By all means consider whether there are other ways to harness the goodwill which has led that person to volunteer, but remember that they should be providing a net benefit to the charity, and if that is not happening, you may need to end the relationship.

3.1.6.5 Template for volunteer skills audit

This form might be helpful when recruiting new volunteers for events support. However, do use it with caution and according to the circumstances and people you are approaching. As mentioned previously, a more informal, convivial approach may be best for some, and you do not want to appear patronising or unaware of the skills that a volunteer may be able to offer. However, it can be a helpful tool when used with a larger group of people in a club or society situation, where it can save some time and enable consistency in collecting information about individuals without them having to share it with the whole gathering.

What I am able to do (give details of experience)	What I would not do	What I would like to do with training or coaching

3.1.7 Professional event organisers

It can be expensive to use external professional events organisers, and many charities will not have the budget to do so. However, there can be good reasons for employing such professionals in certain circumstances if you can afford to do so. You may not have enough staff or time yourself, and it may be more efficient to use your budget to bring in experts on a temporary project basis. They should be specialists with plenty of experience, so they should not be making beginners' mistakes or learning as they go. They should have ready-made contacts and ideas for venues, caterers, entertainment and so forth.

There are many ways of sourcing professional events organisers, through adverts in trade magazines, the internet or Yellow Pages. However, a recommendation from someone who has used them before is worth its weight in gold, so it is worth asking fundraising colleagues in other charities, or people who have organised events through work or in other circumstances, whether they know of any company or person they could recommend. If you are paying for their services, you need to be sure that they will deliver and will not let you down.

Do be very clear what it is you want and expect them to do, and make sure you have a good, clear contract with them (see section 3.7). You need to be especially careful to be clear whether you are employing them to run an event, or whether you are employing them to raise a certain amount of funds through running an event – if you are employing them to raise funds, then they are most likely a 'professional fundraiser' in the legal sense, and you need to make sure that you comply with the Charities Act 2006 requirements for professional fundraisers (see Appendix 2). The Institute of Fundraising has a Code of Best Practice with guidelines on contracting with professional fundraisers, which is worth consulting (see Appendix 2).

3.1.8 Checking and vetting

There has been a huge amount of publicity regarding criminal record checks. Charities are finding that there is great access to information regarding people who want to work on a permanent basis or to volunteer, and are increasingly concerned about whether they have to make Criminal Records Bureau checks for everyone who works for them, or just for some people.

Not everyone can access Criminal Records Bureau checks, but organisations such as charities that work with children and vulnerable adults are likely to be entitled to ask for such checks. The Charity Commission offers extensive advice on the scope of these checks and when they are appropriate in the context of checking the potential trustees of charities (see Appendix 1) and further advice is available on the Bureau website (www.crb.gov.uk).

Criminal Records Bureau checks

The Criminal Records Bureau was established under the Police Act 1997 and launched in March 2002. It has widened access to checks for organisations with staff and/or volunteers who undertake work involving children and vulnerable adults.

Organisations wishing to use the service can ask successful job applicants or volunteers to apply for one of two types of check, depending on the nature of the position or work they will be doing. These are the Enhanced and Standard Disclosures, for both of which there is a fee for employees (£36 and £31 respectively at time of press), but no charge for volunteers.

Standard disclosures

These are primarily for posts involving work with children and vulnerable adults, and may be issued for people entering professions such as accountancy and law. They contain the following:

- details of all convictions, cautions, reprimands or warnings held on the Police National Computer;
- information from the Protection of Children Act 1999 list (see Appendix 2);
- information from the Protection of Vulnerable Adults Act 2004 list (see Appendix 2);
- information held by the Department of Children, Schools and Families under section 42 of the Education Act 2002 of those considered to be unsuitable for, or banned from, working with children.

Enhanced disclosures

These are for posts involving a greater degree of contact with children or vulnerable adults, such as regularly caring for, training, supervising or being in sole charge of individuals or groups. Examples include teachers and scout or guide leaders. In addition, enhanced disclosures are issued for statutory purposes such as gaming and lottery licences. They contain the same information as the Standard Disclosure, but include local police information considered relevant by the chief police officer(s).

If volunteers are likely to be in unsupervised contact with children and/ or vulnerable adults, the charity should use the checking system wherever it can. However, if the events committee itself is unlikely to come into direct contact with children or young people, then Criminal Records Bureau checks are unlikely to be necessary. It should be a decision of the trustees and senior management as to whether this check should be made for volunteers and members of the events committee.

Nonetheless, it is advisable to ask for and to take up references for events committee members. Volunteers should provide the contact details of two referees, neither of whom should be a relative. Always take up references, and if in any doubt, speak to the referee on the telephone. The type of questions you need to ask the referee are as follows.

- Does this person have the ability to work in a team?
- Do they have the ability to support a special event of the type we are staging?
- How long, and in what capacity, have you known them?
- What strengths do you believe they have?
- Would you say, to your knowledge, that they are honest and trustworthy?

Dos and don'ts

Do consider at the start the realistic level of support you will need in terms of staff, volunteers, etc.

Do communicate with volunteers, staff and trustees.

Do be clear what skills you need to do specific tasks.

Do take up references.

Do provide thorough induction, briefing and training as necessary.

Do be clear what you expect from volunteers and check that they can meet these commitments.

Don't accept just anyone who comes along – check that they will be a benefit, not a burden.

Don't create employment contracts inadvertently.

3.2 Project management

With the strategy setting the overall direction, and a specific event decided upon and agreed, you now need a project plan to map out the details and put it into action. You need to invest time in making sure that you and your team know exactly what you need to do and when, and how you will do it to reach your goal. Therefore, project management skills are key to a successful event.

Project management is a field of study and training in its own right, and there are many specialist books and training courses on the subject. This section does not pretend to be as exhaustive or detailed as a specialist book might be, but offers an introduction to the basic principles, some useful tools and signposts to further resources if you want to develop your knowledge and skills.

3.2.1 What is a project?

A strategy will set the direction for a number of events, perhaps over a number of years. A project is more concrete and finite – each individual event could be viewed as a separate project. The main elements of a project as far as special events management is concerned are as follows:

- it has a clearly defined start and finish;
- it is unique;
- it involves time, costs and resources;
- it is usually the responsibility of one person or a small team;
- it brings together a wide range of resources and skills;
- it has a specific objective;
- it results in something tangible being delivered.

The overall scope of a project has three key elements:

1. time – the project is completed within a set timescale and by an agreed date;
2. cost – the project is completed within an agreed budget;
3. quality – expectations of outcomes are defined, agreed and fully met.

The three elements are usually interdependent: if you have less time, the cost rises and/or the quality suffers; if you want higher quality, you need to spend more or take more time; if you want to cut costs, you may need to take more time or compromise on quality.

As with setting the overall strategic objectives in Chapter 2, you need to use SMART principles when you set objectives for each individual project or event. Check back that your event objectives will contribute to, and fall within, your strategic objectives.

3.2.2 The life-cycle of a project

Whether large or small, a special events project follows this process:

- agree on the objectives of the event;
- plan the project teams (event committee, staff, volunteers);
- identify all the tasks and activities, resources needed and budgets required;
- work out how long each task will take, and whether some are dependent on others being completed first;
- establish an overall timescale for the event, with key milestones identified;
- communicate the project plan to the events team (and/or line manager, if you are working alone);
- agree and delegate activities to staff and volunteers;
- manage, motivate, enable and keep communicating with teams (staff, volunteers, management);
- review progress, adjust budget, activities and delegations as necessary and communicate this to all teams (staff, volunteers, management);
- complete the event and any necessary follow-up;
- review and report on success and performance;
- praise and thank teams, support staff and volunteers;
- record learning points for the next time.

3.2.3 Identifying what needs to be done

The first stage in effective project planning is to think through and list all the activities that have to be done to complete the project. Do not worry at first about having everything in the right order – just capture thoughts as they come. You may find it helpful to do this by brainstorming with your team or events committee, thinking through all parts of the event, and writing all ideas down on a flipchart or Post-it notes. If it helps to think through the process in chronological order, then by all means do so, but you can rearrange and sort out timescales and sequences later – the main thing is to have all tasks and activities identified.

Top tip

Find somewhere where you will not be interrupted, and take time to identify all the work needed to stage the event. Once you have thought it through carefully, leave it, go away and do something else to clear your mind. Then come back to it and look at your list afresh. Get others to look at it too: discuss it with your team, line manager or even friends and colleagues. Different pairs of eyes and perspectives may spot something you have missed.

Example: a list of tasks and activities required to arrange a dinner dance

- Set objectives
- Identify audience
- Get senior sign-off
- Brief other departments (PR, finance)
- Book senior staff to attend
- Establish event committee
- Find a venue
- Find a band
- Find entertainers
- Arrange caterers
- Visit venue
- Visit venue with band
- Visit venue with caterers
- Check safety certificates
- Book first aiders
- Book photographer
- Agree menu with caterers
- Hire necessary equipment (sound, lighting, piano)
- Source sponsor
- Write programme for evening
- Undertake risk assessment
- Write budget
- Design invites
- Decide invite list
- Decide on decorations
- Order decorations
- Decorate venue
- Decide table layout
- Set up venue
- Source wine
- Send invites
- Collate responses
- Sell tables
- Review number of tables sold
- Print tickets
- Send tickets
- Confirm booking and numbers with venue
- Confirm numbers with caterers
- Confirm booking with band or entertainers
- Arrange necessary insurance (public liability, cancellation, etc.)
- Arrange security for money
- Put guest packs together
- Get maps of venue and car parks
- Print menu or programme for guests
- Put press pack together
- Contact local media
- Contact national media
- Write and send press releases
- Source celebrity magazines for attendance, articles and photos

Mind-mapping is another useful tool to brainstorm and capture all the activities you will need to plan for – it helps to break the project down into sections while maintaining an overview of how those sections can link together and contribute to the whole event.

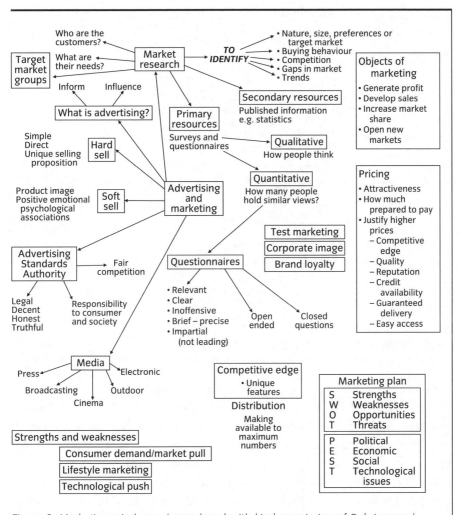

Figure 3: Marketing mind map (reproduced with kind permission of Bob Lamoon)

Now you can put the activities you have identified into logical groups and chronological sequences. You may want to split them into subsections which can run in parallel, for example, venue, entertainment, publicity and marketing, internal communication. This can be done by either ordering your list into subheadings, or using a work breakdown structure like this:

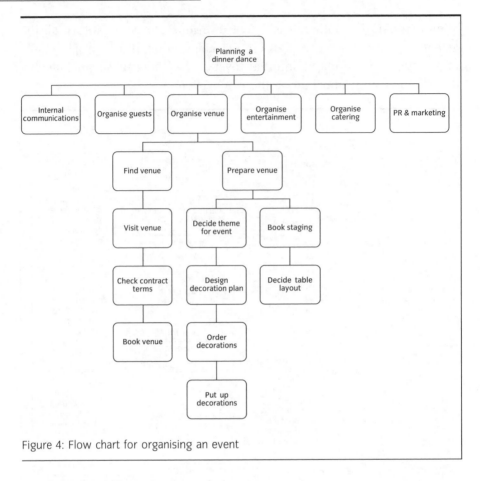

Figure 4: Flow chart for organising an event

Whichever method you use, it is helpful to break down each stream of activity into individual tasks to which you can assign an estimated duration and start and finish time. In addition, it is helpful to assign numbers along the lines of chapter headings, so that you can refer easily to different activity streams and individual activities within them. (NB: The example above is not meant to be an exhaustive list of activities; when you do this for yourself you are likely to have a much longer list, especially as you read through other parts of this book which provide more detail on specific areas to maximise the success of your event.)

Now you can draw a network diagram of these activities and dependencies. This involves identifying sequences and dependencies in a graphic form which you can add time estimates to later. There are different types of dependencies, but the most common is that B cannot start until A has finished: for example, invites cannot be sent out until they have been printed.

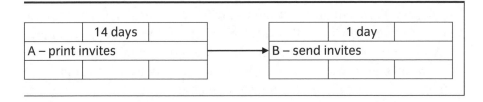

Another is that some activities can start at the same time, in which case they can be drawn side-by-side and the diagram continues from there:

	3 days					
Identify audience						

	7 days					
Find a venue						

The key with a network diagram is to decide what can be done first, and to follow a logical schedule. Do not be too bothered about detailed resources at this stage.

In this example, you are likely to start with establishing an events committee, first setting objectives and getting senior sign-off, but you could make a start on finding the venue, entertainment and caterer in parallel with finding a sponsor and setting a budget. Actually booking them should be dependent on agreeing the budget.

There are likely to be several viable ways of working the project, so do not worry too much about whether you have the right network diagram. The key feature should be to ensure that there is a logical progression from start to finish, and that nothing is in the network where it should not be logically: for example, sending out invites before they have been printed. It is advisable to write out the network diagram on paper before entering activities into a computer program – the program will not necessarily spot logical mistakes.

Add time estimates for each activity. For some this will be quite clear: for example, the printers may need two weeks from receiving final proofs to complete the print run, and they may need to be booked ten weeks in advance to secure the slot. However, you may want to build in some buffer time to allow for mistakes to be spotted and another print run before the deadline for sending invites or tickets. When allocating time for other activities, always allow a little more than you initially think. Experience shows that usually, we are optimistic about how quickly something can be done. Do make sure that you use the same unit of time throughout the network diagram (for example, days or hours rather than a mix of the two). Remember to identify when things need to be signed off, and to allow time for this. Also, include time for meetings and review points to check progress.

Now you can establish the critical path for the project. This involves working through the network in both directions to find the key activities that will dictate the completion time of the project (that is, if X is not done by a certain time, Y cannot start and the project will run over time). When assigning dates to the start and finish of the various tasks, use the time estimates you allocated above, but remember to allow for weekends and identify any bank holidays, holidays and other breaks in the schedule that will impact on deadlines. There are computer software programs that will make these calculations for you and spot critical paths, but it is useful to be able to do it yourself so that you can identify any logical errors – the computer is only as good as the information with which you supply it.

For each activity in your network diagram you should have a box, describing the activity, the duration of that activity (D), the earliest start time (ES), the latest start time (LS), the earliest finish time (EF) and the latest finish time (LF). The remaining field is to identify the float (F) – that is, the difference between the earliest and the latest time that the task could finish – this indicates that the task has a buffer in the schedule, so that if it overruns it will not throw out the rest of the timing. If an activity does not have any float, it is seen as being critical – that is, it must finish on time or else the overall timetable will slip.

ES	3 days	EF
Design invites		
LS	F	LF

ES	14 days	EF
Print invites		
LS	F	LF

ES	1 day	EF
Send invites		
LS	F	LF

You can work out the earliest start and finish times by doing a forward pass through the network diagram. Start with the first activity and assign it a realistic start date. If you are using a computer program, it will add the duration of that activity to arrive at the earliest finish date.

Then the earliest start date of the next activity will be the day after the earliest finish date of the preceding activity – or if several activities have to be completed before the next activity can start, the computer will find the last activity to finish and make the next activity start on the following day.

0	3 days	3		4	14 days	18		19	1 day	20
Design invites				Print invites				Send invites		
LS	F	LF		LS	F	LF		LS	F	LF

In this example, the earliest finish time of this part of the project is 20 days. Of course, this needs to be converted into real calendar dates, allowing for weekends and bank holidays – most computer software will do this for you.

If you complete the forward pass throughout the whole network diagram, you will find the earliest possible finish date: that is, the earliest possible date on which your event could be held. However, it is vital that you also make a backward pass through the network, to identify the latest possible start and finish times for each activity. This follows the same process as the forward pass, but starts with the latest possible date for the project (the event) to be finished. In effect, this charts your worst case scenario. For each activity, working backwards from the end, you take the latest finish time and subtract the duration of the activity to find the latest start time in order to complete the activity. You calculate the latest finish time for any preceding activities based on the earliest of the latest start times for the following tasks.

In this example, we assume that the invites must be sent on the 30th day, and work back from there:

0	3 days	3		4	14 days	18		19	1 day	20
Design invites				Print invites				Send invites		
10	F	13		14	F	28		29	F	30

The float is the difference between the latest finish time and the earliest finish time, which in this case is ten days for each activity.

You identify your critical path by looking for those activities which do not have a float: therefore, if they overrun, they impact on the overall schedule of the project. Again, the software available will help to identify the critical path and update it, should you need to change any of your time estimates.

The reason for identifying the critical path is to enable you to focus on crucial areas; not that you ignore other activities, but you know that they have some built-in flexibility. If a critical activity is threatened, either by a previous activity overrunning or because it is taking longer than expected, you will need to manage the issue tightly, usually by pulling out all the stops and putting in more resources (for example by marshalling volunteers or working overtime). This is all the more reason to impress upon staff and volunteers that any float identified elsewhere should be kept for unforeseen emergencies, and that they should work as hard as possible to meet schedules. The risk of having a buffer is that people relax or wait until the latest possible time before starting that activity – and then the buffer is not there when it may be needed.

3.2.3.1 Allocating activities

Make sure that each activity is allocated to somebody in the team. Make clear who is responsible for that activity and whether it needs supervision or sign-off, and identify all the people involved. Remember, you may need to check with and book the time of people in other departments, such as PR teams. If you have several activities running in parallel, and they are allocated to the same person, do check that there is a realistic amount of time for it all to happen, or see whether some tasks can be delegated (for example, if there are three activities running in parallel, each of which takes two days, and three people available to take one activity each, the total time allowed before moving to the next stage would be two days. If you are responsible for all three activities, you will need to allow for six days – that is, assuming that all three need to be completed before moving to the next stage).

3.2.3.2 Communicating your plan

Once you have checked your plan, you may need to have it signed off by someone more senior, who is acting as a supervisor and supporter of the plan (that is, by signing off they are agreeing to make the resources available as identified in the plan). Then, you should communicate the plan to everyone in the team and support teams. Each individual should understand their role and how it fits into and impacts on the wider plan. They should 'own' the plan – that is, they should agree with it and feel able to fulfil the expectations of them as outlined within it.

3.2.3.3 Keeping the plan under review

The plan is not likely to be set in stone: the unexpected will happen, from suppliers dropping out to staff falling ill. Keep lines of communication open, identify any problems as early as possible and keep the plan under review as it progresses. If any major updates are necessary (such as changes to dates, with any knock-on effects or changes in personnel and lines of responsibility), update the plan and make sure that everyone is kept informed.

3.2.3.4 Contingency plan

A contingency within a budget is about preparing for the unexpected and ensuring that you have allowed enough money to cover this. Contingency planning in project management is about looking ahead, thinking of alternative options and allowing time if activities change or resources cannot be found. Unlike an ongoing review and update of the project plan, a contingency plan should be prepared in case there is a major problem which will jeopardise the ability to hold the event at all.

Examples of what could seriously impact the viability of an event include:

- unexpected budget cuts
- lack of commitment by the charity (minds or aims changing part-way through the project)
- lack of commitment by the events committee
- time estimates too optimistic
- budget out of control.

As you will have seen in the previous sections, if you follow the correct planning process, most of these will be kept under control, managed and minimised, and should not come as a surprise to you mid-way through the project. However, given that the charity's reputation could be at stake, it is worth keeping a record of possible problems and what you will do to prevent them from happening, or what you can salvage to ensure that a professional event of some description takes place, even if it is not at the scale which you originally planned.

Furthermore, you should consider in advance when you would be better off cutting your losses and cancelling the event altogether. No one wants to be in that situation but unfortunately it does happen, and it may be better in some cases to cancel and prepare properly for the next event, rather than to push ahead with an event doomed to failure.

Project definition form

Event name	
Event description	
Objectives	
Expected results or benefits	
Risks	
Key staff or committees	
Resources required	
Critical success factors	
Stakeholders	

Dos and don'ts

Do invest the time at the start to plan your event project thoroughly – it will be time well spent.

Do allocate all activities to individuals, and make sure they all know for what they are responsible.

Do identify critical dependencies.

Do build in some buffer time where possible.

Do use your project plan once you have made it – check to see if you are still on track.

Don't underestimate the time it will take to do each activity.

Don't forget to allow for weekends and holidays.

Don't expect everything to go to plan. Be prepared to be flexible and to use contingency plans.

3.3 Finding the funds

It is a simple fact that events cost money to stage, and if you have planned and budgeted properly you should have a good idea what the upfront costs will be and what your expected return on investment is. However, the chances are that you will need to make a substantial investment upfront in order to finance the event before any return at all comes in – the event will not happen if you cannot source the funds at the start.

This section will look at various possibilities for obtaining the funding to run the event, but will focus mainly on the potential for corporate sponsorship and how to go about securing it in a competitive marketplace.

3.3.1 Reserves or fundraising budget

If you have the luxury of having 'spare' money which can be released from reserves or a healthy fundraising budget, then this is without doubt the easiest way to finance your event. However, you need to be very confident that your event will be successful in terms of a good return on investment, otherwise essentially you are spending money that would normally be used for the charity's cause and beneficiaries, and reducing rather than increasing the impact that the charity can make.

It is likely that any salaried staff, travel and accommodation expenses will come out of a fundraising budget in any event, and best practice in terms of accountability would look at whether this cost was being recouped properly in terms of the income that the team can bring into the charity, whether from general fundraising or from special events in particular.

For major event costs such as venue hire, catering, equipment, prizes, auction items or entertainment, it may be more responsible to look at the possibility of covering these costs from other sources, perhaps as gifts in kind, even if there are sufficient funds in reserves. Anything donated to enable the event to occur frees up the charity's funds to be spent on other projects which perhaps cannot find external support as easily.

3.3.2 Corporate sponsorship and partnership

Often, corporate fundraising is seen as a speciality in its own right, and so it is; there are many publications and training courses devoted to the subject. However, there is a lot of potential cross-fertilisation between event management and corporate fundraising. Events are an attractive way for companies to get involved with your cause. Therefore, it is important to know the basics, so that you can use this as a guide when negotiating directly with companies yourself, or in your discussions with your corporate fundraising colleagues when working jointly on an event.

3.3.2.1 Is it for you? Pros and cons of engaging with corporates in special event organising

Your charity may already have a policy regarding entering into relationships with companies. If so, you should check what that policy is, and make sure that you comply with it when considering whether and how to approach companies to become involved in your event. If there is no existing policy, it is worth taking a step back to weigh up the benefits and risks of engaging with corporates, and whether there are any ethical criteria appropriate to your charity. You may find that some forms of connection with companies, or some types of companies, are not appropriate for your charity – it is best to be clear about this from the start, and will help you to have a consistent approach.

Pros	Cons
• Access to funding for an event • Access to expertise or resources (PR, marketing, etc.) • Raising the profile of charity and event by linking with a well-known sponsor • Starting or helping to maintain a longer-term relationship with a corporate partner • Gifts in kind – the corporate partner may be able to provide a venue and catering (if not for the event, then perhaps for meetings of event committees, volunteers, etc.); it may be able to produce high-quality programmes or provide other services to assist the event • Access to the company's staff, directors, customers and other networks through payroll giving, staff lottery, being 'charity of the year', etc.	• Does the company fit with your charity's aims and ethos, or compromise them? • Does it want you to run an event for it? That is, where is the balance of control over branding, who attends, who benefits the most? • Is the company's expectations of what you can deliver too high? • Is it jumping on your bandwagon? Is it getting far more out of being connected with your charity brand than you are getting from the company? • Is there a risk of a scandal involving the company which could have a negative knock-on effect on your charity's reputation? (Remember, if the company wants to check that your charity is well run to protect its reputation, you should have a similar interest in how well run the company is.)

3.3.2.2 Why do companies sponsor?

Understanding the underlying motivation of companies and what they really want from their relationship with your charity will enable you to write an effective proposal and negotiate a deal which reflects the value that the company will get out of the relationship.

So, why do companies sponsor? Unlike charities, companies are not set up for public benefit but to make a profit for their shareholders. Sponsorship of a charity event is unlikely to be a purely altruistic decision motivated by goodwill, but in large part it will be because of the perceived benefits to the company, which are equivalent to the value of its sponsorship. Being the sponsor of a special charity event is often a strong marketing tool for a company – it demonstrates the company's social responsibility and is an opportunity to have its brand and logo seen in a positive light by the audience at the event, who will be seen as potential consumers by the company.

You need to put yourself in the shoes of the company and consider what benefits it wants and would get from sponsoring your event. Many sponsorship proposals fail because the benefits are not emphasised sufficiently. You also need to give thought to why it should choose your charity and not one of the hundreds and thousands of others who approach it every year. This is a highly competitive market, so you cannot afford to be complacent about your proposal. Try to discover what the company really wants from the relationship. Research into the company will help you to determine what motivates them.

Checklist

Companies are likely to be motivated to sponsor an event if:
- there is an association with a worthy charity or cause;
- they can see the PR benefits that they will gain, and are confident of good publicity before and after the event;
- it will have a positive impact on their existing and prospective clients;
- the event will give them access to celebrities, VIPs and royalty;
- the event will give them access to other decision-makers, senior managers in other areas and potential customers;
- they are confident that you are professional and positive in your approach;
- they are seen to be supporting a successful event;
- it will motivate their employees, both through participating and enjoying the event itself, and the 'feelgood factor' of supporting the cause;
- it will make them more attractive to new recruits;

- they can see the event as an occasion and audience for them to launch a new product;
- they can gain profile and community approval;
- they can gain tax benefits.

3.3.2.3 Finding a suitable company partner

If you decide that it is appropriate to go ahead and develop corporate partners to support your event, you need to establish some key criteria and spend time researching the possibilities. Corporate fundraising does require a great deal of time and commitment and the ability to bounce back from rejections (which will happen). However, with some planning and research, you can maximise your chance of finding a partner who fits and is interested in working with you.

Your starting point should be the charity's aims, objectives and ethos, as you will need to identify the key potential partners that fit in with these. Think about the broad types of company which might have a natural affinity with your cause, style, beneficiaries or supporters: for example, modern, youth-focused technology companies may fit with a charity benefiting young people; financial companies may be interested in educational charities or those with an older supporter base (depending on their core clientele). The event itself will define which sector you should approach in order to pitch your proposal effectively. Try to match the event to the company. The type of participants who will buy tickets or be involved in a challenge will affect the company's decision: do they want to reach a youth market or target older people?

To identify a list of potential sponsors that might fit with the charity and the event, you need to undertake a great deal of research. This involves:

- background research through the media – by watching both general and specialist business programmes and reading the financial information sections in the broadsheets, you will be familiar with who is doing what, and when;
- checking specialist journals for likely corporate sponsors, for example *Campaign* and *Marketing Week*;
- attending business networking groups, marketing groups or the Chamber of Commerce – apart from developing useful contacts, this will give you an insight into how these people think and speak;
- discussing opportunities with the corporate department within the charity – do not forget colleagues who deal with suppliers, and your trustees and senior management;

- looking through the many directories that give information on companies – *Hollis, Crawfords, Jordans, BRAD (British Rate and Data)*. All are available on CD-rom and regularly updated. If your budget is small, your local library will have them in stock;
- check the contacts and networks of the trustees and directors of your charity, and cross-reference them in *Who's Who* to see if there are other companies with which they are involved.

You may be fortunate enough to have a company actively approaching you with a view to discussing further participation. Usually it will have been involved in some way with your charity already, through payroll giving and donations, or via a member of staff with a particular connection with your cause. While this is a stroke of good luck rather than something you can plan for, do not get carried away with the flattery of being approached – you still need to determine what the company wants from the partnership, what it can offer and whether it is a suitable company with which to be involved.

If the company asks for a meeting to discuss further involvement with your charity, do try to find out before the meeting what sort of area of involvement interests it. The company will probably say 'events', as this is one of the more high-profile ways of getting involved, but you will need to explore this more at the meeting to find out what it really expects and whether you can meet the company's requirements. (I have found that a number of companies have no idea what type of event they want to support; alternatively, if they have an idea, it is something on a very grand scale.)

The first meeting should be focused largely on finding out what the company wants, rather than agreeing or committing to anything. Find out why it wants to be involved with a special event. Does it want a big event as a thank you to clients or to launch a product? Once you have information about expectations, you can consider this against your own strategy for events and see where there could be a match. Then you can develop an action plan with several options in order to present it to the company at the next meeting. Do not disparage any grand ideas, but do manage expectations. You can scale down a proposal, keeping it in line with the company's objectives and budget and being careful to keep things positive. Use words such as 'What if we do this …' or 'I think this type of event will be in keeping with your company ethos and charitable intentions'.

Useful information: cause related marketing

Cause related marketing (CRM) is one of the many aspects of corporate development of building relationships between charities and companies. It started in America, and American Express is credited with the concept of CRM in 1983 to order to raise funds for the restoration of the Statue of Liberty. It became apparent that the public would support a company readily which was involved in good causes. Corporate social responsibility and the need to be part of the solution in the social problems of the day are now firmly embedded within the business.

The CRM concept can be summed up as 'a strategic positioning and marketing tool which links a company or brand with a relevant social cause or issue for mutual benefits', and is widely accepted as part of corporate policy. Business in the Community (BITC) says:

> It is difficult to give an accurate figure on how much money UK corporates spend, or how much the community benefits from CRM. BITC has projected that CRM spend equates to at least 0.5 per cent of total marketing spend in the UK. The total UK marketing spend in the UK is above £25 billion for the year. This gives a CRM figure in the region of £100 million, to give an idea on how much money is involved. These figures may be slightly pessimistic but what is beyond doubt is that CRM is now established as source of income to charities and easier to access than before. (Neep, 2001; see Appendix 1))

Corporate Survey 111 is valuable quantitative research into corporate attitudes towards and involvement in CRM, building on the previous Corporate Survey studies conducted in 1996 and 1998. Based on almost 400 responses from chief executives, managing and marketing directors and community affairs directors, *Corporate Survey 111* is the largest study of its kind in the UK. It looks at the growth of CRM, why businesses do it, how they choose partners, how they manage it within their organisations and business predictions for the future:

- 70% of chief executives report that corporate social responsibility is an essential issue to their business;
- 89% of marketing directors believe their businesses should be involved in addressing the social issues of the day;
- 70% of community affairs directors who participated in CRM in the last year indicated that it was important to achieving their community affairs objectives;
- 90% of marketing and community affairs directors appreciate the benefits of CRM in addressing business and social issues;
- 64% of marketing directors who participated in CRM in the last year indicated that it was important in achieving their marketing objectives;

- 77% of all respondents believe that CRM can enhance corporate or brand reputation;
- 59% of marketing and community affairs directors have carried out CRM in the last year;
- 58% of all respondents reported that CRM has grown in importance to their business over the last two to three years;
- 68% of all respondents believe that CRM will continue in importance over the next two to three years.

3.3.2.4 Building a relationship

Once you have identified prospective company partners, it is often helpful to establish a positive relationship before sending in a written proposal. You can test the water and learn more about your prospective partner in order to fine-tune your proposal. Time spent at this stage can help both sides to develop an impression of the other, and how the relationship would work (or not) in the future. If a positive relationship is developed, then your proposal will stand out from the many others that the company you are approaching may have to assess. If problems are identified in terms of ethical fit or approach, then either side can walk away at this stage without having invested too much in terms of preparing a full proposal.

Gain as much information as you can about the companies you are interested in, and distribute the names of their board to the charity's trustees, senior management team and event committee to see if anyone has any contacts. A personal introduction and endorsement will go a long way to ensure that your proposal is at least read, and hopefully received more favourably.

Look for opportunities to meet key contacts in the company in an informal networking context. Do not think the person you want to meet is too important, too busy or too rich to have time to speak to you. Remember: everyone loves a little flattery, and to feel useful and needed. Being told that you have heard good things about them, or that their skills and support would be very valuable and make a huge difference, can help to smooth the way. However, do be careful to avoid being seen as patronising. If there is something you can invite key contacts to attend, this is even better.

Bernard Ross, director of The Management Centre (see Appendix 2), gives a very good insight into developing the relationship with a new client.

Corporate fundraisers should view this as they would view a courtship: building relationships, promoting understanding and mutual respect and agreeing to partnerships where both parties are comfortable and content with their part of the agreement. Different relationships require different timings, approaches and energy levels. Each new partner should be viewed as if they were your first. VIP syndrome should be your care policy for all corporate partners, ensuring the very best care and attention your organiser is able to provide. Any contact within a company at any level should be treated as an important person – it is surprising how influential assistants and secretaries can be when it comes to making decisions on your approach, or whether it is ever to receive full consideration.

These are wise words indeed, as it is said to be ten times more difficult to acquire a new client than retain or upgrade an existing one. Maintaining contact with your corporate partners is paramount to ensuring that in the run-up to the event, and during it, there is a regular flow of information.

3.3.2.5 Making a written proposal

Whether you are approaching a company 'cold' or have established a degree of awareness and interest in your cause and event already, the company will be looking for a professional approach when you come to submit your proposal in writing. You will need to be persuasive, understandable, attractive and credible. What makes your charity and your event different from others? How can you demonstrate the impact of the event and put it in the context of the bigger picture in terms of what your charity does? Above all, you need a positive attitude: even an unpopular cause which is not deemed 'sexy' or high profile can be attractive if you demonstrate energy, enthusiasm and commitment in your approach.

Here are some points to consider.

1. *Be clear what it is all for.* To have an incentive to support the charity, the company needs to know where the money raised from the event will be going. You should have a robust business plan in place if you have followed the strategy and planning sections in previous sections, so you can adapt this to provide a simple but robust overview of what you intend to do in the event, how much it will cost and what you expect to raise from the event both in terms of money and awareness. If the funds raised are to be earmarked for one particular project or to launch a new project, this should be

communicated to the company, as well as providing an overview of the work of the charity for context. If the funds are for general funds, it will be helpful for the charity to have a shopping list or wishlist of what the funds will buy – it makes the impact of its support more tangible to the company.

2. *Include a history of the charity's events programme*. You should build up gradually a portfolio of events in which the charity has been involved. Include publicity, endorsements and photographs – this will help to demonstrate a positive track record and give a company confidence that entering into a partnership with you will yield definite results.

3. *Be specific about what the event is* – and what involvement or contribution the company could make.

4. *Outline all of the potential benefits for the company*. Remember that it is not going to be interested in pure altruism, so tailor your approach according to the mutual interests you have identified. Successful sponsorship must meet the objectives of both the sponsor and the charity. Do decide in advance what level of flexibility you can offer to suit your sponsor (for example, adapting the location or dates). Also, measure the benefits you are offering against the contribution for which you are asking.

'Selling the benefits': what to consider and include in your proposal

- Will the sponsor get title to the event?
- Will the sponsor get exposure on all promotional material? If so, what: will this be just a logo, the sponsor's house colours or a sponsor write-up?
- Will the sponsor be able to use the event on all its own promotional material? Will you have any say in the wording or presentation of this material? Determine how long this will apply for, and do consider how much your logo is worth when negotiating the corporate contribution to the event.
- Will there be opportunities for the company to have a promotional display, handouts and samples or literature at the event?
- Who is the market being targeted? Does this overlap with a group that the company is interested in reaching?
- Will the company have an opportunity to network and meet with other high-profile decision-makers at the event?
- What are the corporate entertainment opportunities?
- Decide at the concept of the proposal how many tables, tickets or seats are being offered for sole sponsorship.

- When offering sole sponsorship, ensure that the charity obtains appropriate added value from the exclusivity.
- Will there be genuine media coverage – TV, press or radio? Or is this just a hope?
- Do not make any promises if you cannot deliver: for example, 'Of course Elton John will come', 'Of course we will get full TV coverage'. These are hostages to fortune, so only say this in your proposal if you are really certain of it, otherwise your reputation and the chance of an ongoing relationship with the company will be damaged.
- Consider whether to offer several levels of sponsorship such as gold, silver or bronze, with progressively increasing benefits linked to increased sponsorship. It is often of benefit when offering this option to state to the companies that no one else from their sector will be involved.

3.3.2.6 How to present your written proposal to make an impact

Keep the covering letter brief – no more than one A4 page. You will need to be succinct but still include your key message, a summary of the project to be funded, some context, what involvement is required and what benefits there are for the company. Make it eye-catching, and consider smart presentation as well as the content of your proposal. Also, make it personal rather than photocopied or a blanket mailing. Try to include a reference which can be attributed only to that company.

Try to demonstrate empathy with the company and why it is well matched with the charity and the event (for example, if it is a sporting event, try to target and match to a sports promotional or health associated company). Talk the company's talk, not charity jargon. Get inside the company's head. Prepare by reading its advertising, website and other promotional materials to understand its own priorities.

Be precise and confident in your style. Do not use words like 'I think' or 'maybe'; use definite and positive terms such as 'we will', and keep all content relevant to the proposal at hand. Describe the opportunities that the sponsorship offers realistically, creatively and logically. Break them down into relevant packages. If possible, include a testimonial from the charity patron, president, the trustee with a contact in the company or someone who will make an impression on the company.

Address the letter correctly: make sure that the right person within the company is being targeted, and check that the personnel have not changed. Telephone the company's office to find out how your contact likes to be addressed, and whether they have awards or qualifications which they like to see after their name. The charity's chief executive, director of fundraising, chairperson or a trustee should sign the letter. If the recipient is known to the person signing the letter, then a postscript in their own hand will confirm that this letter is personal. Before you send the proposal, ask someone else to read it – preferably someone outside the charity who will be able to give you objective feedback. When it is completed, do not send it by email, rather by first class post, saying that you will contact them later – for example, by telephone in ten days.

Ten reasons why a proposal may fail

1. The proposal is not relevant to the potential sponsor's customers or clients.
2. The proposal is too bland.
3. Although the event is significant to the fundraiser, it is insignificant on a national or regional scale.
4. There are no tangible benefits to the sponsor (or these have not been made clear).
5. The proposal does not make clear what the company is being asked to sponsor or why.
6. The language is inappropriate, with too much jargon.
7. The benefits offered bear no relation to the sponsorship fee for which the charity is asking.
8. The event has not been thought through and is therefore not presented in a logical, relevant manner.
9. The proposal has been badly written – it is too long, unclear, has overused clichés and poor punctuation.
10. There is no evidence of the charity's record of accomplishment in special events.

3.3.2.7   Presenting your case

Once a company has accepted your initial proposal, it may be necessary for you to present your case to one or two senior management people or the whole board. Also, the company may wish to involve its PR company.

Preparation is the key to success. You need to discover what the company is expecting – not all will want an 'all singing, all dancing' presentation. Some may like you to have some PowerPoint images to add impact to your statements; others prefer a simple presentation followed by a discussion. Whatever the method preferred by the company, your presentation is likely to be the deciding factor on whether the company will finally accept the proposal. Your preparation in researching the company before the original approach should be helpful now: you should be familiar with the company's brand and style, and be well rehearsed on how the company and the charity can work to mutual benefit on this event. Prepare your presentation in advance, and deliver it to a friend or colleague who can be a critical friend, giving you honest feedback so that you can make any necessary changes.

Whether you go to the presentation alone or with a colleague or supporter is your decision. Sometimes a supporter or a team approach can add weight to your proposal, as well as making you feel more confident.

Top tip

With practice you will become more confident when making your case. However, even experienced performers say how nervous they are before a performance. Do not worry about it – a few butterflies in the stomach are probably a good thing to stop you being complacent and lacklustre. If you believe in what you are doing, this will show in your presentation and hopefully win them over.

Aim to arrive reasonably early so that you are calm and collected. Start the presentation off by smiling, shaking hands and showing enthusiasm. Remember, the people you are meeting are probably busy, so do not waste time. Keep the presentation brief and concise and speak slowly and clearly. If you have a number of people listening to your presentation, do not fix on one person, look at each in turn.

You do not have long, so you need to get your message across quickly. Make sure your message is simple and as brief as possible, otherwise you may find you have too much information to get across in the time available. Decide on your key message. Most people will remember what a person says at the beginning and at the end of a presentation, so organise yours into sections, building up a logical case, and repeating your key points at the end. The rule of thumb in most presentations is to:

- tell what you are going to say;
- say it;
- tell them what you have said.

Remember to emphasise the benefits being offered to the company. Never criticise the competition, but do emphasise your previous successes. Think in advance about any questions or objections they may have, and be prepared to take questions as they come – this is usually preferable to waiting until you have finished the presentation. Be prepared to answer questions about your experience as an events manager, and have a note of all the important data. However, be prepared for questions you do not expect – you may be able to think on your feet, but if you are not sure of the answer, do be honest and say that you will provide an answer as soon as possible. It is far better to do this than commit to something you cannot deliver.

Top tip

It is better not to read word-for-word straight from a script, but if you do need notes then small cards are useful. Number them and put a treasury tag through one corner, so if you drop them, they will keep in order.

Try to develop a rapport with your audience: make eye contact, smile, listen to what they are saying and be aware of their body language and whether they look interested. An element of discussion is likely to arise as they examine your proposal and respond to it; this can be very helpful in developing the proposal so that it better meets both the needs of the charity and the company. While you do need to be flexible and open-minded, you should think in advance about your limits as to what you are prepared to concede. Decide on your bottom line and what is not acceptable before the meeting, and keep emphasising the benefits that the company will receive from the relationship. At the same time, do not interrupt when they make a proposal, even if you find it unacceptable. It may be more diplomatic not to reject it out of hand – try and negotiate the point, or ask for time to consider it and get back to them.

Distribute handouts at the end of your presentation rather than at the start. This helps you and your audience to stay focused on what you are saying. The handouts should not only summarise what you have said, but also include additional information about the charity's work. Prepare a short portfolio of other events you have managed, plus any testimonials.

If you are using presentation technology such as PowerPoint, make sure you have copies of the slides in case something goes wrong. If you are presenting at the company's premises, confirm your requirements well in advance. However, do not overdo it with slides – keep them clear and simple, and make sure that the attention is on you and what you are saying. You are not there simply to repeat your written proposal, but to meet the company representatives and hopefully to build a relationship with them.

Top tip

This may seem like stating the obvious, but pay attention to your own image – it is an important factor. You should aim to be smart and professional, paying attention to the small details of what you wear. You may think it is wrong to judge people by appearance, but in the world of business it is important to look the part.

3.3.2.8   Sealing the agreement

There is a saying in selling techniques called 'making the close'. This applies to presenting your case, insofar as you need to know when to stop talking and listen. You are looking for key statements such as, 'That sounds interesting', 'I would like to hear more', 'Would your charity be agreeable to ...?' – here, you are looking for signs of agreement.

Broad agreement is probably the most you should be aiming for at this kind of proposal presentation meeting. It is rarely a good idea to launch into detailed discussion of who will do what and when at this point, unless this has been agreed beforehand and the right people are present with sufficient time allocated to do this. You should be thanking those present for their time and agreement to enter into partnership, and asking who you should be talking to about the details.

Of course, even with the best will and planning you will not be successful every time. Do not prolong the meeting with desperate bids – this will not make you any more popular. Once you have made your pitch and done your best, accept that there may be reasons why they do not want to support this event at this particular time. It may be useful to leave them with some information; they may change their minds once they have had a chance to think about it.

Finally, no matter how the meeting ends, smile, shake hands and agree on what further actions you or they need to take. Whether there is a clear positive outcome or not, remember that it is never a failure, it is all good experience and you will develop valuable skills in making your case. (I have gone away from making a presentation to a group of company directors feeling rather dejected, thinking that they were not going to be interested in offering sponsorship for an event. I returned to my office and within ten minutes received a phone call saying that they were going to take sole sponsorship for this event. They remained long-term partners with the charity for a considerable time.)

3.3.2.9 Maintaining the relationship: customer care

Customers can be defined as internal and external.

- *Internal* – do not ignore the development of the internal customers from other departments within the organisation. As mentioned in the introduction, special events fundraising is perceived by other people to be glamorous and glitzy. You need other staff members on your side; ensure that when you approach them it is well in advance of the event, if you require their time and services. Explain exactly want you need and how they can help you. The more you make yourself known to other colleagues and approach them in a friendly and courteous way, the more you will be able to state your case. They may be able to provide you with the important contacts you need.

- *External* – these are organisations that deal with the charity on a one-to-one basis; a company which is prepared to sponsor an event but with which the charity is trying to develop a long-term partnership. Customer care is very important: meeting the needs of the company is paramount, but it must be equal; the company should respect the aims and objectives of the charity and benefits should be equal. Charities must ensure that the bar is set at a sufficiently high level so that they do not sell themselves too cheaply. Remember, not all companies are the same and some will require different service. The aim is not to neglect them but to treat them with respect.

Customer satisfaction survey

The following information comes from a survey conducted in 1989 by Michael LeBoeuf, Professor of Management at the University of New Orleans:

A typical organisation hears from only 4% of their dissatisfied customers. The other 96% just go away quietly and 91% will never come back. That represents a serious financial loss for an organisation that does not know how to treat people and a tremendous gain to those that do. (LeBoeuf, 2000; see Appendix 1)

A survey of why customers quit found the following:
- 3% move away (house, job, etc.);
- 5% develop new relationships;

- 9% leave for competitive reasons (other organisations entice them away with better opportunities for recognition);
- 14% are dissatisfied with the product;
- 68% quit because of an attitude of indifference toward them by the owner, manager or another employee;
- a typically dissatisfied customer will tell eight to ten people about his problem;
- one in five will tell 20;
- it takes 12 positive service incidents to make up for one negative incident.

Seven out of ten complaining customers will do business with you again if you resolve the complaint in their favour. If you resolve it on the spot 95% will do business with you again. On average a satisfied customer will tell five people about the problem and how satisfactorily it was solved.

The average organisation spends six times more on finding new custom than it does to keep old ones. Yet customer loyalty is in most cases worth ten times the price of a single mailshot promotion.

Organisations having low quality service average only 1% return on sales and lose the market share at a rate of 2% per year. Organisations with high service quality average 12% return on investment, gain the market share at a rate of 6% per year and have a higher response from customers.

The major goal of any employee is to create and keep customers. There is a big difference in selling and helping people to give.

3.3.2.10 Your own corporate culture

There are several publications on how to develop relationships with donors, supporters and corporate partners. One is *Friends for Life: Relationship Fundraising in Practice* (1996) by Ken Burnett: an extract from the chapter 'Five Foundations of Relationship Fundraising' is reproduced here, which bears relevance to what we are all aiming to achieve:

Corporate culture is more than just an understanding of procedures or everyone going in the same direction. To make an organisation into a distinct and singular entity involves agreement on common work habits and forms of behaviour. It also involves respect for staff and respect for colleagues. How people deal with their colleagues mirrors how they will deal with donors.

An effective corporate culture also includes politeness, ways of speaking, telephone manner and so forth. It involves standard of dress (an area much underestimated by some fundraisers) and issues such as consideration of others, turning up on time in the morning, being punctual for meetings, reliability, and a range of behavioural aspects that come with true professionalism. Precise communication is also part of the company culture. For example, how many charities do you know have detailed published corporate identity guidelines but no behaviour guidelines? An organisation's culture also encompasses its quality and orientation, systems of quality assurance, systems for hello and goodbye, attitude for money and more besides.

We fundraisers should get serious about our corporate culture. Your organisation's culture is a key component of your ability to put relationship fundraising into practice. As most charities have so far overlooked this area, here's another chance for you to gain the competitive edge – to be 15 minutes ahead. So take a lesson from the world of commercial enterprise and make yours a strong one.

Dos and don'ts

Do be clear about your charity's policy and aims in working with the corporate world.

Do spend time researching potential partners.

Do move outside your own charity's language and present your proposal in a way that links with the company's priorities and interests.

Do be clear about the benefits to the company.

Don't undersell your charity – be aware of the value you have to offer in any partnership.

Don't promise what you cannot deliver.

Don't rely on verbal promises – get agreements clarified in writing.

3.4 Finding a venue

Finding the right venue is absolutely vital to a successful event. It really is all about location, location, location! This section looks at how to find unusual venues, whether indoors or out, and what the venue has to deliver to make your event a success.

3.4.1 How to find a suitable venue

3.4.1.1 What type of venue do you need?

You will need to consider the following aspects.

- Indoors or outdoors? If your event is outdoors, do you need an option to go inside in the event of bad weather (for example, a marquee or access to a building)?
- How big does it need to be? It needs to accommodate the number of guests or participants you intend to invite, any entertainment and supporters or spectators at a sporting event.
- What kind of image or atmosphere do you want to create: is your event formal or informal, modern or traditional?

3.4.1.2 Finding unusual venues

Always be on the lookout for unusual venues to make your event that bit different, special and memorable. Of course, it can be in a hotel or conference centre, and many can put on a very special event with great efficiency, but it may lack that something extra. Here are some ideas for slightly different venues you could explore:

- art galleries
- company and guild houses
- corporate partners
- car showrooms
- country houses
- charity partners (for example, the National Trust).

3.4.1.3 Visiting the venue

It is essential to visit the venue before you finalise the booking, even if it has been highly recommended to you or looks good on the website. Things do change under new management, and the best photos will not necessarily show wear and tear or whether things have become a little shabby since the last refurbishment. Nothing can replace actually being there, meeting the staff, checking the size and shape of rooms and the quality of facilities. It is best to go with a checklist already prepared so that you do not overlook anything vital.

Checklist

- Is the venue clean?
- Are staff friendly and helpful?
- Is the location easy to reach?
- Is it close to public transport?
- Is there sufficient car parking? Are there wet weather contingencies (if parking in fields)? Does the venue provide stewards to cope with traffic, or will you have to do this?
- Is there adequate disabled access and facilities?
- Is there an up-to-date fire service safety certificate?
- Is there enough space for all attendees or participants, plus any band, speaker or other entertainment?
- Is the space suitable for the event intended? Are the acoustics good and will everyone be able to see and hear?
- Are cloakroom and toilet facilities large enough for the number expected?
- Can temperatures be adjusted easily?
- What insurance does the venue hold (so that you know what separate cover you might need)?
- Are the catering facilities suitable and accessible?
- If you or the entertainers need special equipment (for example, a piano), can you get it into the venue?

3.4.1.4 Making the final booking

Make sure you know exactly what costs you will be charged, what is included in the charge and what will be extra. Also, make sure there is absolute clarity about when you will have access to the site to set up, and how long you will have to clear up before you are required to vacate the site.

Check that you are happy with amounts and dates for deposits, any advance damage deposit (and terms for return of the damage deposit if none occurs – make sure you have made a joint inventory inspection of the site), cancellation arrangements and charges and when final payment is due.

If all is within your budget and planned timescale, obtain any necessary sign-offs from within your organisation and confirm the booking. Good luck – you are now committed!

3.5 How to book entertainment and catering

3.5.1 When to book

Clearly, you need to know what type of event you want and what your target audience and budget are before you can consider what kind of entertainment and catering to find. In addition, you should be sure of your venue and preferably have a fixed date, so that when you go to performers and caterers you can check their availability and avoid them becoming double-booked.

There is nothing wrong with getting their agreement in principle, and if you have a good relationship with a big name, then it may be worthwhile liaising with them when you come to book the venue and finalise the date, to make sure that they are available to support you.

3.5.2 What type of entertainment?

Again, this is all about the atmosphere you want to create, and the audience at which you are aiming the event. Most events have some form of entertainment, whether it is a warm-up person with music at a sporting challenge or an after-dinner speaker at a charity dinner, or perhaps the entertainment is the main focus of an event, such as a charity concert.

Here are some types to consider.

- *Music* – pop, rock, classical, something for the background (live or taped, a pianist or jazz group) or something for dancing (for example, ballroom, disco, barn dance, salsa).
- *Comedian* – old school or cutting-edge? Do you want them to do a full set or just a few minutes before or after dinner? Do make sure they come recommended, and consider whether they are appropriate to the audience.
- *Speaker or lecturer* – this should not only be someone eminent in their field, but also a good raconteur, so that they are entertaining as well as interesting. Consider motivational speakers from different backgrounds, and make sure that they have a good story to tell – even better if it is linked to your cause.
- *Magician, acrobats or dance* – something a little unusual will make people sit up and pay attention, and leave feeling that they have really been entertained. If they remember the entertainment on the night, they will remember your charity event and tell other people about it.

3.5.3   What type of catering?

Think about the type of event and the overall atmosphere you want to create. Also, consider your audience and the price of tickets – people will have certain expectations based on how much they have paid to be there.

If it is an outdoor event, you may be looking at ensuring that a variety of stalls or stands are available for people to buy their own food and drink. However, the entrance price and the sort of audience you are aiming for will have an impact on whether you are looking for basic hot dog, jacket potato and burger bars or whether there is likely to be demand for organic local produce or, at the more expensive end of the scale, marquees serving meals at tables with champagne and cocktail bars.

For relatively informal events, where the food is incidental to the main entertainment, you may be looking at sandwiches, a buffet, or finger food with nibbles, canapés and so forth. For more formal events, or where the food is part of the event itself (a dinner dance or charity ball, for example) you will be looking at a sit-down meal with several courses.

When providing food, make sure there is a vegetarian option, and where the event is ticketed and food is served to individuals, you should find a way of ascertaining whether there are any particular dietary requirements (gluten-free, nut-free, etc.) and check that your caterer is able to meet them.

3.6   Negotiating prices

Events are potentially the most contract-rich environment in fundraising. By the time you have brought all the pieces together, the cost of engaging all the different providers can mount up. You need to keep costs under control and within budget, so it is worth having strong negotiating skills to ensure that you get a good price. Some people are naturals at getting good deals, but others may have to work harder at it. This section provides some tips on how to get the best value – after all, the less money you spend on the event, the more funds will be available for the charity's purposes.

3.6.1 How to negotiate prices

Always ask potential suppliers to give you a quote. If you say to them, 'I have a budget of £1,000 for X', then amazingly enough, X is likely to cost £1,000 or just that little bit more. It is essential to get at least three quotes wherever possible – this will help you to test what the market price is from the range of quotes you receive. Do make sure they are all based on the same specification, so that you can compare like with like. Remember that the lowest quote may not be the best option – will the supplier deliver the quality you hope for? Conversely, the most expensive will not necessarily mean better quality – check the supplier's products and standards for yourself, or make sure you have a recommendation from someone who has used it before.

If you change the terms of engagement after you have selected a supplier, you can expect the price to change from the original quote. Thinking things through carefully will help you get the right specification in the first place, but if you have to make changes, make sure you know the impact in terms of cost.

If you are getting a lot of something, ask if the supplier will do a bulk discount. At the very least you may be able to get it to waive any delivery costs. Equally, if you are going to do a lot of events, use this to negotiate for a good price – 'dangle the carrot' of using the supplier again on a regular basis to get the best rate.

3.7 Establishing contracts

When you have made sponsorship arrangements, and have found and confirmed a venue, engaged caterers and entertainment, you are likely to need to confirm agreements in writing to form a contract between the parties involved. For a large event, a whole sheaf of contracts may be needed with various suppliers. This section looks at what a contract is, why and when you need one, and advises on the key elements to include.

3.7.1 How to establish contracts

3.7.1.1 What is a contract, and why do I need one?

In its simplest form, a contract is an agreement by one party to do something for another party in exchange for payment or another service. A contract may be verbal and relatively informal, but it is better to get a clear written contract where a service is vital to your event, involves complex arrangements and/or a considerable amount of money.

A written contract should lay out all the key elements of the agreement, and therefore should provide absolute clarity for both parties about what is expected. This will help to avoid misunderstanding and disputes later on, and will ensure that you know exactly what you are getting from the agreement. In some cases you will be required by law to have a written contract with certain basic elements included: for example, where you are working with a professional fundraiser or commercial participator (see section 6.1.3).

Although a good relationship with suppliers and sponsors is vital, and you should avoid being overly legalistic and pedantic, the contract is there to back you up if things go wrong. It can be a useful tool to keep the relationship on track and to make sure that both sides deliver what they have agreed on time.

3.7.1.2   When is a contract appropriate?

You may have good or personal relationships with some suppliers, or be relying on goodwill to provide a particular service for your event, and it may seem awkward to try to transform that into a more formal written contract. However, unless it is something incidental to the success of the event, in most cases it is wise to have a written record of what has been agreed. This is all the more important when you are committing the charity to high levels of expenditure or to certain activities. You should consider taking legal advice before making binding commitments and check the level of authority you have in your organisation, since the contract may need to be signed off by a more senior person.

Contracts are usually drawn up after the substantial discussions about what is required have taken place. After all, you need to know what is expected on both sides in order to make sure that it is covered in the contract. Some venues and suppliers may have their own standard contracts prepared. Venues in particular may have very long and complicated contracts of their own. You need to read them (especially the small print), and may need to take legal advice. Do not hesitate to question items that you do not understand or agree with; quite often the venue management will have a blanket contract which covers a multitude of events, and you need to make sure that it is suitable for your own.

When you have more experience of events, you are likely to develop similar contracts for the various relationships that you are regularly involved in (such as venues or catering). A standard form of agreement can help to streamline the process, but it is always worth checking that it remains appropriate to each individual situation. You may find that you have less need for legal advice or senior sign-off if you have tried and tested contracts which you are confident are watertight.

3.7.1.3   What should be included in the contract?

The simple answer is: everything important! Of course, the precise details covered in a contract will depend on who it is with: whether it be a sponsor, venue management, equipment suppliers, caterers or entertainment providers. However, for all contracts, the principles remain the same; make it clear who is responsible for the following:

- who
- what
- where
- when
- costs.

To safeguard both parties, a contract with a sponsor should cover these key elements.

- Who exactly is entering the contract?
- Who owns the contract and the event? (NB: if the event belongs to the sponsor, with tickets bought from the sponsor and a subsequent amount given to your charity, the sponsor is probably a commercial participator by law, and there are more specific requirements for the contract and how the event is marketed; see Chapter 6.)
- Who owns any logo or trademarks, and for how long?
- What rights are there to any subsequent payments or royalties?
- What exactly is the sponsor agreeing to supply in terms of payments, publicity, staffing or other expertise and gifts in kind?
- When are these things to be delivered and to what standard?
- What exactly is the sponsor to receive or not? Specify benefits such as complimentary tickets, opportunity to display corporate branding at the event, on tickets or programmes.
- What is the approval process for promotional materials and advertisements? You may need to state such things as the relative prominence of corporate branding, depending on the ownership of the event as a whole and the level of financial support being received.
- Will the sponsor have exclusive rights, or is there an option for other parties to be involved?
- What are the cancellation terms for the event? Can either party terminate, and what penalties may be payable?
- Where do liabilities lie?

- What are the payment terms? Is payment to be made wholly in advance, or 50 per cent before the event and 50 per cent afterwards?
- What is the schedule, with key dates, for progress meetings, decisions, printing publicity, etc.?
- What terms should apply to the use of your charity's logo? Consider what this is worth to a sponsor and do not sell it too cheaply. You should specify how long the sponsor may use it in its advertising and promotions (subject to the level of sponsorship it provides), and have the right to check any materials before publication.

Venue contracts should specify the following:

- when you can gain access to the premises, and when you need to vacate (allow enough time for setting up and clearing away);
- who is responsible for security and who is covering what in terms of insurance;
- the precise premises to be hired – ensure that reference to this is consistent throughout.

Top tip

Beware of the term 'relocation' in a contract issued by a venue. It may appear innocuous, but it could have a serious impact on the event, if it were to be relocated to another less suitable venue. Make sure you know and approve any alternative locations and have them specified in the contract, especially in the case of an outdoor event.

Stallholders' contracts should specify:

- the times when they can start setting up and the time by which they need to be ready;
- how much space they are allocated and where;
- what they can bring in terms of equipment, and what will be provided on-site for them;
- times for the removal of the stall;
- stallholders' obligations to clear the site and leave it tidy when they go.

For a supplier of equipment, the following should be covered:

- what will be supplied, where it will be delivered to and when;
- whether staffing or expertise is included in the price;
- when it will be collected from the venue.

Check any equipment on delivery for any damage or faults, and record this so you do not have to pay for it on return. Also, check beforehand that the equipment is useable at the venue (for example, can you get it on site, is there sufficient power supply?).

A catering contract usually includes the following:

- the menu to be supplied and number of covers to be provided for (often charged on a per head basis);
- when catering is to be provided, and where;
- what equipment (tables, chairs, decorations, cutlery, crockery, glasses, etc.) is to be provided by the caterer, and what is to be provided by yourself or another supplier;
- what facilities will be supplied by the caterers, or whether they will have access to facilities at the venue;
- a final cut-off date to confirm final numbers;
- when they can access the site and facilities to prepare;
- when they have to vacate the site, and to what extent they should clear up afterwards.

Contracts with entertainers should state the following:

- the date and time of performance;
- the length of performance;
- the expected content of performance;
- what equipment they will bring.

You should discuss their equipment and support needs (lighting, sound, dressing rooms, food or dietary requirements) and be clear if they are bringing a support team, as you may need to arrange accommodation, food, passes, etc. for them.

For more detailed information on contracts and their content, look at the Russell-Cooke *Voluntary Sector Legal Handbook* (see Appendix 1), and the Institute of Fundraising Code of Best Practice (see Appendix 2).

3.7.2 Managing contracts

Once you are satisfied that the contract reflects the parties' desired relationship and expectations, it can be signed by both parties. Although the contract represents a useful legal backstop should there be a misunderstanding or dispute, it can also be a useful management tool.

Do not relegate the contract to a dusty shelf as soon as it has been signed; keep it handy so that you can refresh your memory about what was agreed, and keep in touch with the sponsor or supplier to ensure that things happen on time and to the quality agreed. You may need to exercise some flexibility – timings may not be 100 per cent in any project. However, at the end of the day the contract reflects what the other party agreed to do, and if delivery is crucial to the event going smoothly, do not be afraid to remind people of their obligations under the contract, and keep them to it.

3.8 Before the event

Of course, the whole process of planning and organising the event happens largely before the event, but this section looks in more detail at some of the key things to keep on top of in the few weeks leading up to the event, especially the last-minute checks and preparations you need to make the day before or just before people start to arrive, to ensure you are ready for them and that the long-planned event goes well on the day.

3.8.1　What you need to do before the event

3.8.1.1　Tickets, invitations and programmes

Six months to one year before the event:

- source sponsors;
- agree joint branding, develop the design brief;
- identify suppliers, if you are using external printers;
- book printing schedules, if you are using internal departments;
- develop a list of invitees, checking the contact data for accuracy.

Three to six months before the event:

- send out invitations;
- prepare for and start managing responses – who is coming, their access and dietary needs, etc.;
- develop programmes and any other materials for guest packs, book printing slots and allow sufficient time to proofread.

One to three months before the event:

- send out tickets;
- review response rates;
- proofread programmes and guest packs;
- finalise and order the final print run of programmes and guest packs.

One week before the event:

- check the arrival of programmes and guest packs – check their quality throughout the delivery rather than just the top copies.
- organise how these are going to be transported to the venue, and who will be responsible for handing them out.

3.8.1.2   Equipment

Six months to one year before the event:

- identify suppliers, check recommendations and references;
- check all safety certificates and liability insurance;
- confirm broad numbers or quantities required;
- book and get contracts signed.

Three to six months before the event:

- confirm more detailed needs – you should have a better idea of the numbers expected through ticket sales, and of site layout through the pitches sold;
- book the entertainment, enabling lighting and staging plans to be developed.

One month before the event:

- confirm the menu and other details;
- give clear instructions regarding dates and times for arrival and set-up on site, including access (where to park vans, etc.) and contact numbers;
- check whether the caterers are supplying cutlery, crockery and glassware or whether you are sourcing these;
- confirm instructions regarding clearing the site after the event.

One week before the event:

- confirm the final numbers with the caterers;
- depending on access and complexity, staging and marquees may need to be put up in advance.

3.8.1.3   Decorations, branding and signage

Six months to one year before the event:

- decide the overall theme of the event at a very early stage;
- factor in time to agree the design and branding of the event, especially if you are using external designers, but also with any in-house team – this includes time to agree a tight and clear design brief, for designers to present options and to arrange for more senior sign-off of the overall look. Ideally, you need to have the design

agreed in time to use a consistent look and message across all publicity, marketing, invitations, tickets and programmes.

Three to six months before the event:

- before ordering, check with the venue regarding what it is happy for you to do – there may be some limits on what or how you can fix things to walls or ceilings (for example, while you may regard a tonne of sand as essential for a 'Sahara' themed party, do not order it unless you are confident that the venue will be equally enthusiastic);
- source suppliers for signage and decorations – supply them with designs and specifications, and do not change your mind in the middle of the job as this will be more costly and may jeopardise deadlines. Ask to see samples to confirm accuracy and quality before confirming a quantity order;
- set delivery deadlines for one week to one month before the event itself, to build in a buffer which allows for delays or the need to reorder, in case of disaster.

One to three months before the event:

- keep on top of order schedules with suppliers;
- draw up final detailed plans for decorations, and ensure that responsibility is allocated to named individuals.

One week to one month before the event:

- receive and review signs and decorations – check that they comply with the brief and are the right size, quantity and quality;
- arrange for transport to the venue;
- ensure that there is a clear plan for where signs and decorations are to go, and that you have all the equipment necessary to put them up (ladders, fixings, stakes, string, etc.).

3.8.1.4 Safety and security

Confirm safety and security procedures at the venue: do you need to provide fire extinguishers, sand buckets, first aid points? You may need to contact your local St John Ambulance to ask for their attendance on the day.

Inform the police of your event if necessary – they may need to help to manage crowds or traffic, and they will be able to advise whether there is another large event in the area which may affect traffic or access.

Consider other potential security arrangements: does the event venue need fencing off (if it is a ticket-only event, for example)? Are crowd barriers required? If there is valuable equipment on site, the venue should be locked and attended, or equipment and valuable property should be kept in a locked safe overnight, if possible.

3.8.1.5 Developing a running order

At least a couple of weeks before the event, things will be beginning to seem more real, and the thought of it all coming together on the day may be a daunting and far-off dream. It is worth sitting down, perhaps with your events team, to go through in detail what needs to happen and when throughout the day. This should start before the public arrive: who needs to be at the venue to open it up, and when? When should stallholders start to arrive and by when should they be ready? When should caterers and speakers arrive, who will greet them and show them where they need to be?

You should develop an impressive list which breaks down what needs to happen on the day, allocates time to each activity and, most importantly, assigns responsibility to named individuals. This will be your masterplan for the day, so that everyone can see what they need to do, and you know who to approach if anything changes. You need to be flexible – things will not always run according to the plan, but you can still see at a glance what has to be done and how to rearrange other parts of the plan to accommodate change.

3.8.1.6 Setting up

Always allow plenty of time for setting up. Factor in an allowance for things not running smoothly, people not turning up on time and needing to make last-minute adjustments. Everyone should be given a clear timeslot for arriving on site and setting up stalls, signage and so forth. You should not be trying to do everything yourself: delegate various set-up tasks and be clear what you want, where and when; and supervise to ensure that all is going to plan.

3.8.1.7 Final walk-through

When everything has been set up, but before the public arrives, you should walk through the venue, preferably with the owner or duty manager, to check the following (where applicable):

- the area is clear of hazardous objects and litter;
- portaloos and indoor toilets are working, clean and have sufficient paper and soap;
- emergency exits are signed clearly, working normally and are clear of obstructions;
- the car parking area is staffed and well signed;

- all relevant signage and banners are in place (if you are using arrows to indicate the direction of parking or pedestrian routes, secure them well at both ends to avoid anyone turning them around);
- stalls and display stands are properly set up and well presented.

As you go round, imagine yourself as a guest or participant, consider whether you can find your way around easily and what impression the overall site gives.

3.9 At the event

All the planning has finally come to a head, the venue is prepared, volunteers, staff, caterers and entertainers are all there, the tape is cut, the doors are open and you are ready to welcome guests and members of the public to your event. You now run the risk of either feeling at a loose end or, more likely, becoming too involved in the detail on the day. This section looks at what your role as event organiser is on the big day, and how to make sure you continue to help the event to run smoothly without panicking or getting in the way.

3.9.1 What you need to do at the event

3.9.1.1 Your role

As the special event organiser, your role at the event itself is like that of a stage manager. You should not be tied down or involved in any activity that takes your eye off the ball and makes you unavailable where you are needed. This means that every activity that needs to take place must be clearly delegated to staff, contractors or volunteers. Equally, all staff at the venue and the volunteers and fundraising staff need to know how to contact you, the event organiser, if there is a problem and they do not know how to resolve it themselves.

3.9.1.2 Greeting VIP guests

Greeting VIP guests should not be your role, although you may want to be on hand in case there are any problems when they arrive. They should be met and welcomed at the entrance by someone given this express role, whether it be the chief executive, chairperson or director of the charity. Make sure that the greeter is fully briefed so that they know the background of these guests, when they are due to arrive and where they are sitting. As 'stage manager' it is important that you reconfirm the running order of the evening with any VIP actively participating, even if you have briefed them beforehand. This ensures that everyone is aware of the live programme (rather than working from previous versions), and gives you a chance to sort out any last-minute queries or problems.

3.9.1.3 Circulate

Do try and move about the venue whenever you get the opportunity. If you mingle with the guests, you will be able to get some immediate feedback about how things are going and whether there are matters you can deal with on the night, or whether you need to make a note of anything in order to make improvements in the future (for example, if the toilets have run out of paper you can chase that up straightaway; if there are lengthy queues, you will know to provide more facilities next time).

Your role is to observe and supervise: if you come across something that is not going quite as it should, try to avoid the temptation to pitch in and do it yourself, as it will pin you down and you may miss other more important things. Find the person responsible for that part of the event, and make clear what they need to do to put things right.

3.9.1.4 Keep calm

This is easier said than done! You will be under a lot of pressure at the event, on tenterhooks to see that what you have been planning for months will happen as you imagined it, and have to deal with all sorts of queries and issues that may not be going to plan. Try to keep calm and objective, to help you think on your feet. Does it really matter that the balloons did not arrive? It is probably more of a priority to make sure that guests are seated at the right time for the caterers to serve food.

Under this sort of pressure it can be easy to lose your temper, but keep hold of it at all times; it never helps to shout or humiliate someone who is not doing things perfectly. It is far better to take them briefly to one side and make clear what you expect or offer an extra pair of hands, if you can spare a volunteer from another activity.

3.9.1.5 Helpful things to have

Here are some useful things to have in place on the day:

- a running order – a list of everything that should be happening and when, with the names and contacts of key people responsible;
- a couple of runners – reliable people you can send off to carry out emergency tasks if necessary;

- a smile on your face – if you look worried and stressed, so will the people around you. Try to maintain a calm exterior;
- a mobile phone – so that you can be contacted in the event of an emergency. Make sure that all key staff and volunteers have the number, but be aware that you may need have it on silent mode to avoid any embarrassing interruption of entertainers or speakers.

3.10 After the event

The guests and participants have finally left, the music has faded away – finally the ball is over. Whatever the event, it is likely that you will be feeling a mixture of exhilaration, relief and exhaustion. However, the job is not over quite yet. This section looks at what you will need to do to finish the project completely, thoroughly and successfully, from clearing the site and learning from the event to managing follow-up and assessment of the overall success of the event.

3.10.1 What you need to do after the event

3.10.1.1 Clearing up

Whether indoors or out, you need to return your venue to as good a state as you found it. You should have established when booking whether the venue provides clearing up and cleaning services, and whether this is included in the price. If not, it is up to you and the helpers you can muster to make sure that stands are cleared away, food and rubbish are properly collected and disposed of, dishes are washed and returned (if you have caterers, they may be responsible for this, but it would need to be included in their contract to avoid any doubt), carpets and floors are cleaned, and so forth.

Be aware of any deadlines for vacating the venue – you may be able to leave the clearing up until the next day, or this may not be possible. Check your agreement with the venue, and make sure you have enough volunteers and staff on hand at the right time to help with the clear-up. If removal of marquees and skips is scheduled for the following day, it is important that you or someone delegated with that responsibility visits the site to ensure that this happens and that the venue owner is happy. If you are hiring a skip, make a note to arrange agreement for removal at the most convenient time with both the waste disposal company and the landowner.

When all is cleared, you should do a final check of the site, again preferably with the venue owner or duty manager, covering the following (where applicable):

- the site is clear of hazardous objects and litter;
- all signs of stalls and display stands have been removed;
- portaloos and waste have been removed – the company should have a designated time to remove and clear from site;
- indoor toilets are clean;
- all signage has been removed;
- marquees have been removed (either directly after the event or the next day, in agreement with the landowner).

3.10.1.2   Debriefing

You should have booked your debriefing meetings into the timetable – ideally, they should happen as soon as possible after the event. You may want to have one big debrief involving as many people as possible, or to split it into separate debriefs for volunteers, staff and the events committee.

It is essential to begin the debrief by thanking the volunteers and encouraging positive feedback from everybody. Experience suggests that people are more likely to accept any negative points if they hear positive ones first, so it is important to discuss all the good things about the event. What were the highlights of the event? What worked really well? Then move on to the negatives: what went wrong? What could have gone better? Remember to keep this part focused on the learning for the next time rather than using it as a blaming exercise. Think about how you phrase comments so that they are not targeted personally, and encourage others to be positive in their feedback.

Finally, remember to thank everyone for all their time and effort, without which the event could not have happened. Depending on the number of people involved, your budget and whether it is appropriate, you may want to offer a small token of appreciation to helpers, or at least to the chairperson of the events committee. In addition, you should follow up with written thanks and appreciation.

Another important debrief to arrange is a face-to-face meeting with any corporate partners. Again, focus on the positive feedback first, but listen carefully to any suggestions they make, and take on board any recommendations. Again, thanking them is paramount, and the meeting should be followed up with a letter of thanks, and feedback with regards to the success of the event in attendance, awareness and fundraising terms. If the event was a success, the meeting should be a celebration.

Hopefully, if committees and corporate partners have been selected well, then success will breed success and they will return for another event at a later date. However, be careful not to push any of these groups into another event too soon. Give them a well deserved rest, and stick to the overall event plan – do not rush into an unscheduled event or be pushed into another event without sufficient time to plan and stage it as well.

Do not forget to debrief yourself as well – keep good records, and keep all relevant information on a hardcopy file with notes to act as an *aide memoire* for future events.

3.10.1.3 Managing the money

Depending on the nature of the event, you may have varying amounts of cash donations or pledges to handle. At a dinner, ball or other entertainment event, the majority of funds raised will have been through ticket sales in advance of the event itself, and you will be able to calculate reasonably quickly how successful the event has been. However, you may have held an auction at the event, or had facilities for donations or pledges to be made. Any cash collected at the event should be counted (according to your internal financial controls, which usually means in the presence of at least two people), recorded and banked as soon as possible. You should ensure that you act in compliance with the terms of any insurance policies that cover cash, in case of theft at the event. It is to be strongly advised that no members of staff or volunteers should take money home; it is essential to organise a night safe or security collection. Cash should never be left unattended: a safe should be made available and money collected regularly from tills and stalls or from raffle sellers. All pledges should be noted and followed up politely but efficiently.

For sporting challenges, the biggest challenge perhaps is to gather in all the money given in sponsorship. There is a fine line between polite reminders and nagging for participants to collect and hand in the sponsorship they have raised, but bringing the money in is crucial to the success of the event. Increasingly, online sponsorship sites such as JustGiving (www.justgiving.com) help to smooth the process, as the amounts pledged are automatically collected via credit or debit cards without the need for the participants to go round after their challenge to collect money.

Make sure that you can account for all the money raised as a result of your event, whether from advance ticket sales, donations (or subscriptions) on the day, or pledges and sponsorship collected in the following months. You may need to set a cut-off date for collecting pledged donations in order to be able finally to draw a line under the event. Only then can you see whether the final figure raised, set against the costs of putting on the event, means that it has been a success in that it has added to the funds available for the charity's beneficiaries, or whether it has ended up as a burden on the charity's funds. Then you can review the feedback alongside the results, and go back to the start of the strategy and planning process to decide whether you can continue doing this type of event (but better, having learned from mistakes), or whether you should drop it and focus your attention elsewhere.

3.10.1.4 Follow-up

Keep in contact with all the supporters, participants or guests – thank them for their involvement, and keep them aware of how much was made, where the money is being spent and how the work of the charity is progressing. It is important not to lose touch: these people are likely to be the first ones you will approach for the next event, and it will be much easier following a successful event than an initial, cold approach.

4 MAKING THE MOST OF IT

Although your main priority will be to organise the framework of the event and ensure that it actually happens as planned and makes a return for the charity, there are various methods to add to the profile and value of your event. No matter how good and glittering the event, it will not be a success unless people know about it and come to it. This chapter will explore some of the key ways to add value to your event, make it more appealing, get it talked about and generally make the most of the event you have worked so hard to produce, maximising the potential benefits for your charity.

4.1 Publicity and marketing

Raising awareness of your event is vital to ensure that it is well attended and supported, and that it promotes your cause, even among those who do not come to the event itself. If your event is ticketed, you need to sell those tickets, so PR and marketing skills are key to the success of special events.

There are commercial organisations devoted to marketing, designing and managing campaigns, publicity and promotions, and you may want to use their expertise to market your event effectively. You may have your own in-house marketing and PR department to approach for help, or you may be managing the whole project on your own. This section will look at different methods of 'selling' and promoting your event and how to work effectively with a PR company. Whether doing it yourself or setting and managing a contract with professionals, the information in this section should provide a useful background and guide to managing a marketing campaign for your special event.

4.1.1 What is marketing?

Often, marketing is confused with publicity and promotion, but these are just a part of the concept. To ensure that you market events effectively, you have to encompass all the elements that make up the marketing mix: the 'five Ps'.

- *Product* – the products or services offered to your customers or clients – for special events, this is the event itself, something that meets both the customer's and the organisation's needs.
- *Place* (distribution) – how you get your products or services to your target market. Do you have the right venue to encourage your target audience of people to want to be part of that event?
- *Promotion* – how you communicate the features and benefits and endorse your products or services to your customers or clients.
- *Price* – the goal of making a desired profit margin.
- *People* – the value that your people bring to your business by providing a service to your customers and clients.

4.1.2 Planning your marketing

If you have followed the planning process for your event as outlined in the earlier chapters, you should have established three of the 'Ps' already – people, product and place – and have a clear idea about price. That leaves promotion: having the other 'Ps' in place will provide a useful framework for planning this, although it is a two-way process, as your promotional ideas may feed back into your product and price. Therefore, your marketing plan is not totally separate from your overall plan, and should not be a last minute add-on once everything else is settled; ideally, you should be thinking about marketing as an integral part of the plan.

The key steps to organising a marketing campaign are as follows.
1. Draw up a profile of your target market.
2. Identify your supporters who fit your target market profile.
3. Select the most appropriate methods of marketing the event.
4. Calculate the cost of your campaign.
5. Handle the response.

4.1.2.1 Profiling your target market

This is an integral part of the whole planning process, not just marketing. Section 2.4 looked at how to identify who you are aiming the event towards, and how to build information about them in order to create the sort of event that would appeal to them. The same information can be useful in thinking about what kind of marketing would reach them and where they would be likely to see it.

4.1.2.2 Identifying supporters who fit

These 'warm' contacts are likely to be the first people you would try to get involved in your event. You can add to this a list of names produced by the ticket selling committee, which should include the guests that the sponsors wish to invite. Because there is an existing relationship with your charity, you can use a more personal approach, address to correct names and addresses and give them priority access. In-house leaflets or invitations may be appropriate and sent out with charity newsletters, or you may want to include publicity in direct mailshots to supporters.

4.1.2.3 Selecting the most appropriate methods

For the wider target market, there is more of a challenge to gain interest without that personal connection you have with existing supporters. Often this means looking at advertising, which can be costly. Therefore, it is important to target your audience and be selective about what newspapers and magazines they are likely to read. In addition, you might consider getting local radio coverage, editorial in lifestyle magazines and using the venue's own 'What's On' advertisements (see section 4.1.3 for a more detailed discussion of different methods). Most venues will publish a 'What's On' programme, giving information on forthcoming events.

4.1.2.4 Costing the campaign

There is a difficult balancing act to maintain here. If you allow too little in the budget for promotion, the event may not be a success because no one will be there. If you spend too much, you could be eating into the return for your charity. Your event plan should contain a reasonable budget for promotion, based on the size of the event, who you are trying to reach and so forth. Once you have decided on your promotion plan, you should be able to cost it more accurately and check to see that it is within budget.

4.1.2.5 Handling the response

If your promotion works, you will get a response. It is important to be ready to respond to enquiries as soon as you run the promotion – there is nothing more off-putting than trying to book tickets and not being able to get through, or seeking information from someone who does not seem to know any more than you do. Lack of information and delays will reflect badly on your charity, so make sure that you are prepared with mechanisms in place to handle enquiries and bookings:

- brief all those who will be responding to telephone enquiries;
- post information, Q&As and contact details on your website (plus booking facilities if you are selling online);
- ensure that phone lines are working and staffed;
- check that booking systems and databases are working;

- employ a specialist direct mail company if the scale of the event cannot be managed internally, but remember that this will add to your costs;
- use theatre or conference centre booking facilities if they exist – they may be geared up better to handle large responses, and it may be worth your time to use them; again, this is likely to cost.

Top tip

If you are staging a large event and cannot cope with a big response, stagger the advertising, target one section of your customer group at a time, or employ a specialist direct mail company.

4.1.3   Methods for promoting and publicising your event

Whether you are doing this on your own or briefing a PR department, to obtain the maximum publicity to sell the event you need to combine several methods. This allows optimum penetration and one technique builds upon another. You may find that spreading your advertising budget over a range of media will be more effective than putting all your eggs in one basket.

4.1.3.1   In-house leaflets, newsletters, invites

You can produce some eye-catching A5 leaflets in-house, especially if you are adopting a more personal approach for existing supporters. There are various publisher software programs available to help you find a striking design and layout. Make sure that the event itself stands out, and that all essential information is clear: the venue, date and time any celebrity attending, the cost and how to book. You can add incentives for early booking to avoid disappointment, and include leaflets in newsletters to donors and supporters, or distribute them at conferences and meetings.

4.1.3.2   Websites

Most charities now have websites, and if you hold events regularly there should be a clear section for events so that people can find up-to-date information easily about what is on. In combination with email it is a relatively cheap way to use striking design and photographs, and provide all the information necessary to market your event – at least to those of your supporters who are internet literate. The additional benefit is that browsers can find out more about the work of your charity on your other pages before deciding to support your event. You can offer additional support for those doing challenge or sponsored events, such as training tips, downloadable sponsorship forms and fundraising tips. Furthermore, this can be a great way to recruit volunteers from among existing supporters. Give browsers the opportunity to sign up to regular newsletters informing them of other events, but do make sure that you offer an opt-out mechanism.

If you can, provide an online booking facility as well as information about the event, and give other contact details for making bookings, as not everyone is comfortable about doing so over the internet. Make sure that you have appropriate security on your website if you are inviting people to book: internet fraud is a problem, and you need to do all you can to protect your supporters and inspire their confidence. Paypal is a good online payment system to sign up to (www.paypal.com).

A good search facility is worth investing in, particularly if you have lots of events. Allow browsers to search by date, type of event or even location, in order to make it as easy as possible for people to find the event with which they are most likely to want to be involved. Make the most of the search and tracking technology that the internet offers: include your event description on your search information, and use web tracking to find out where people are coming from or routing into your site. Finally, it is worth looking at what others are doing in the event management field online, as you will gain some useful tips and inspiration for your own website.

4.1.3.3   Blogs and special interest groups

For a major event, you may want to set up a weblog (blog: an online diary) to describe the build-up to the event and, finally, report on the event itself. Your tone should be chatty and informal, and your content unswervingly honest at all times. Avoid at all costs stilted corporate speak – it simply will not work with this kind of audience. Above all, it needs to be interesting, rather than a dull list of tasks ticked off. Again, it is about the story, the highs and lows, remembering what the event is all about at the end of the day.

> *'If you try and overspin, people will find you out,' says Neil Major, an online consultant for August One, and part of an advocacy group that deals with non-media communications. 'Disregard these rules, and your site will be subjected to scorn or attack. If it is dry, dull and predictable it will be totally ignored. Your blog must also be new. To get people reading it needs worthy content. To keep readers coming back they need to be sure something worthwhile will have been added since last looked at.' (The Director, October 2005)*

4.1.3.4 Email

Email is a cheap and excellent way to keep in touch with supporters, and to send them colourful and eye-catching information about upcoming events. However, do give supporters an opportunity to opt out if they wish their name to be removed from an email list. Data protection principles apply to email communications as well as to other forms of communicating (see section 6.2).

You should avoid mass emailing (spamming) cold prospects, as this is poor practice, is likely to put people off and potentially will embroil you in the complex world of data protection law. It will do no good for your charity's reputation, and most likely recipients will delete the message out of hand in any case.

If you are using graphics or design elements in an email, be considerate. Think about the file size of downloads and images you use, and try to keep it as small as possible – it will not make a good impression if your email clogs up your prospects' inboxes. Asking supporters to spread the word about an event (via a 'pass-along' email campaign, where emails are passed on rapidly from person to person) is more acceptable: people will ask those they think will be genuinely interested in the event, and your event will be presented with the equivalent of a recommendation to a wider circle than your immediate supporter base.

4.1.3.5 Social networking sites

Social networking sites, examples of which include Facebook and MySpace, are a new development in the online field, and at the time of going to press it remains to be seen how effective they are in publicising events. However, all the components for success are there:

- the ability to provide details about the event;
- links back to your website and other booking contact details;
- the ability to have a discussion about the event with other website users, post photos and updates;
- the ability to get rapid reach to a wide range of people – that is, if you invite the right people in the first place.

Whether such sites will be any use to you may depend on whether you already have an established profile and a group of supporters signed up through this route. If so, you can use it as a hub for information and discussion activity, posting videos, asking for inspiration, sending invitations to events and PR purposes. Facebook groups offer the possibility of being a little more maverick than you might be comfortable with on your corporate site – only use it if you are happy with this and you feel confident in managing the site content.

4.1.3.6 Direct mail

You need to budget for a mailing if this is an integral part of your marketing plan. You may want to opt for a more professional design than an in-house leaflet, and your direct mail company may be able to advise and design a complete pack. Do make sure that it is relevant to the event, and that the mailing list is targeted: it can be very expensive to do a blanket direct mailshot. If you are adding something extra to a pre-planned mailing, consider the weight and cost implications when designing the enclosure.

4.1.3.7 Advertising

As mentioned previously, purchasing advertising space can be expensive, so if you use paid-for advertising, it needs to be targeted to the appropriate audience in order to maximise the chance of return on your investment. It is worth combining any paid-for advertising with a PR campaign: send out press releases and contact editors to see if you can get interviews, articles or features about your event. This is potentially free advertising for you, and provides the event with the context, the story about your cause.

4.1.3.8 Newspapers

Is there a local or a national news angle to your event – the first in a particular region, the biggest of its kind, raising funding for a particular breakthrough in your field? Approach the relevant newspapers and see if they are interested in running a story about the event.

4.1.3.9 Radio

Regional and local radio are often happy to do interviews with a local interest slant. Remember to get across the key contact details for those who wish to attend after hearing your piece. Follow up on this by offering to come back and report on the success of the event.

4.1.3.10 Magazines

Choose your publication carefully, as you want to publicise your event in a magazine that your target audience is likely to read. The angle may be less 'newsy' and more focused on the venue, the design of the event or the celebrity attending, but again, a good feature in the right magazine will give the event valuable publicity.

4.1.3.11   Venue

Venues are likely to have their own PR programme, with a 'What's On' diary at minimum. Look into this, and whether it will cost you extra to have your event listed with them. In this way you can reach the audience of the venue users as well as your audience of supporters. For example, if you are using a National Trust venue, or a museum or church with 'Friends', this could broaden the field greatly.

4.1.4   Designing materials

If you are working to a tight budget and have someone in-house with a talent for design and a good publishing software package, you may elect not to go out to a professional designer. However, do be aware of false economies: it can be worth investing a little more to get a better result, which in turn will sell your event more effectively.

4.1.4.1   Finding a designer

Many printers will have a design service available. Do your research at conferences – often the exhibitor section will have stalls for suppliers, including design and print specialists. You can check their previous work and perhaps talk to previous clients while you are there. As with most contracting, get several quotes and sample designs in order to judge the best price and what is the most eye-catching. Having a recommendation is invaluable, as you can check the designer's reliability and whether they deliver on time.

4.1.4.2   Preparing a brief

You have to be very clear in your own mind what you need to say to get your message across in your advertising and promotional literature for the event, then you need to communicate this well to your designer. Look at material which other charities have produced, and think about what you do and do not like about it: is it too fussy, too bland, is there enough information? Take the good ideas and change them to suit your event, and be clear about what you don't want in your literature.

Decide what form you want the material to take (for example, leaflets, adverts, invites) and how you want it to look. Be creative, and keep it simple and striking. Going over the top may alienate your supporters, by giving them the impression that you are spending a lot on glossy materials. Be aware that the more colours you use, the more it will cost. The more information you supply to the designers, the better the price, and do use their expertise – with the right information, they should be able to produce a few samples of design for you to select.

The information to provide in the brief should cover the following.

- *Corporate identity* – your charity should be branded, presenting an integrated and instantly recognisable image that is regarded in a positive way by your supporters and donors. The logo and corporate colours should be distinctive and used on all stationery and publications. Work the branding into the design for the event material.
- *Who is the audience?* What is the style of the event? Are you going for an overall formal, sophisticated event, or a more light-hearted, fun event?
- *What is the likely function and distribution of leaflets and posters?* What size will they need to be?
- *What size of programme?* Will it be just for distribution on the table, or a larger programme to be sold at the beginning of the event?
- *How many different types of material do you require, and in what quantities?* Sometimes there are minimum print runs, and prices can be discounted for greater quantities.
- *How much text will there be?* Consider who will write the copy, what you want to say, and what the deadline is for final copy.
- *Do you want to use photographs or a graphic design, or both?*
- *What is the typeface and font size?* You should incorporate the one used by your charity in all its written material.
- *What weight of paper do you want to use?* This could affect postage costs when sending out a mailing.

If you have a corporate sponsor, it may want some input, or at the least an opportunity to include its own logo and branding according to the agreement you have. Make sure the sponsor receives a draft of the design so that you can discuss it before it is finalised. In addition, you should decide how much freedom your designer should have. Show them some of your charity's publications and the designer should be able to produce something attention-grabbing. Remember: always confirm your requirements in writing.

Top tip

Allow time in case things go wrong. I once printed some programmes for a golf day and when they were delivered by the printer the top 20 or so were fine. I looked through the box of about 150 and some had pages missing, some were illegible. Back they went to be reprinted in a hurry. Fortunately I had allowed two weeks before the real deadline.

Dos and don'ts

Do allow time in your schedule in case of printing mishaps.

Don't give your designer/printer the real deadline.

4.2 Working with the media

The charity you work for may have its own press and promotional department, or you may have to go it alone. Whatever the case, having some understanding of the media world and what it responds well to will help you in preparing accurate and interesting briefings. Without good briefings and the right information, neither your press department nor the media outlet you are targeting will be able to react effectively and understand your needs. The following guidelines should enable you to deal with a press department or the media directly.

4.2.1 Writing a press release

A press release is a simple statement of fact to do with any subject you are publicising. The key point to bear in mind is to put the fact in a newsworthy context, thinking about it from the viewpoint of the audience. The people who read the press release need to be able to create a story, so the aim of the press release is to arouse their interest. They may not be familiar with you, your organisation or your appeal, or be aware of any background (a week is a long time in the media). They will not be interested to learn any more about the event if the press release is full of jargon and too much about the charity with not enough emphasis on the event being promoted. You have to make it lively, interesting and, above all, clear. For absolute clarity and succinctness, you need the 'five Ws':

- who
- what
- where
- why
- when.

There are also various ground rules which will help with initial presentation and any follow up that may arise.

Layout:

- use A4 headed notepaper on one side only, and type in double spacing;
- if you use more than one page, type 'more' on each page – do not continue a sentence or paragraph onto the next page. At the end type 'ends' so that they know there is no more copy to come;
- number each page and use plain paper for continuation;
- leave plenty of space at the top and wide (1.5") margins on both sides, so that editors can write alterations or typesetting instructions.

Content:

- always put a simple heading on the release, something catchy and a maximum of eight words;
- your first paragraph should state who, what, where, when and why;
- each paragraph following should be of lesser importance, so the story can be cut from the bottom;
- include at least one direct quote from a named person where possible;
- you can include more detail on your charity or other background information in the 'notes for editors' at the end of the press release;
- put the first and last name of the contact (someone who is mentioned in the press release, who knows about it and can provide more information if contacted), together with a telephone number for day and evening, email address and website;
- remember to make sure that the contact is available to take calls and understands the brief;
- if you want to include a picture, give a 'note to picture editor' at the end of the press release, giving details of when and where photographs can be taken (see below under 'photographs' for more information).

Other conventions:

- date the release in full at the beginning;
- when mentioning a day in the text, put the date in brackets after it;
- state whether you want an embargo on publication until a certain date, or whether it is for immediate release;
- when referring to people by name, use both first and second name in the first instance;
- avoid jargon – keep it short, snappy and to the point. Always keep a copy of the release you send out.

Template: press release format

Your Charity Logo

Media release
EMBARGOED until: 00.01 hrs, Day, Date, Month, Year

Snappy Title Here

This is the event in aid of this charity, at this place, time and date. These important or well-known people will be coming, and the money raised will go towards this important or much-needed cause.

Here, give 'a quote' from the chairperson, chief executive or VIP in support of the event, and why it is important.

Further information about the event – more details about what will be there: theme, support acts, entertainment, etc.

How to book tickets and find out more – web address and contact details

'A further quote' from another important person here about how wonderful the event will be, and the good work the charity will be able to do.

ENDS

For further information: Contact 1: number/email
                            Contact 2: number/email

Notes to Editors
1. More information about the charity and what it exists to do, including website address.
2. More information about the particular appeal and why it is happening.
3. More information about the venue, sponsors and entertainers.

Notes to Picture Editors
1. There will be opportunities for photographs as the celebrities arrive and by arrangement inside the venue during the speech or entertainment.
2. For arrival photographs, there will be a designated photographers' area to the left of the main entrance. Please contact Name Surname on number/email to request a press pass and more details about arrival times.
3. To arrange access to the venue, please contact Name Surname on number/email.

4.2.2 When to send your press release

Newspapers all have deadlines – that is, the last possible minute they have time to get the information written up and put in the paper. Find out when your local newspapers' deadlines are. There is nothing more frustrating than supplying a story at 5pm when a deadline passed at 4pm that day. Once you have found out when the newspapers go to press, you can time your press releases for the least busy time, just after they have produced their copy, well in time for the next issue. (Probable deadlines are 11 am for evening papers and two days before publishing for weeklies.) Avoid the end of the week if you can – Wednesday midday is Prime Minister's Question Time in parliament, and even regional newspapers could be overloaded with news.

If you can 'dripfeed' press releases leading up to the event, you may find that you have a better chance of succeeding in having at least one, if not more, included in the paper. Change the story each time, saving the key points and quotes until the last release.

4.2.3 Where to send a press release

If your charity does not have a press department and it is up to you to arrange publicity, you will have to decide to whom you should send the releases. There are several directories which list publications; they can be expensive to buy, particularly as they have to be renewed each year, so the internet or reference library would be a good place to start your research:

- *PR Planner UK* – this lists all national daily newspapers;
- *Pims UK Media Directory* – this lists all national daily newspapers, and it has a towns list under regional headings;
- *Editors* – this is published in six volumes.

If you work for a regional charity, you have a great opportunity to develop a relationship with the local media. Find out who you should deal with, so that when you send out communications, they go to a named person. Try to arrange an informal meeting with them, perhaps over coffee. However, the nature of the media world is that people move on, up and down, and the person you spoke to last time may no longer work in that department, so check each time before you send the release that your contact is still there. Note that a news item should be addressed to the Editor, and a story would be sent to the local reporter.

4.2.4   What happens next?

Once your press release has gone out, be prepared. Follow up with a phone call to see whether the paper has received it: the best time to call a paper is between 10.30am and 11.30am. If the paper likes the story it will ring you, and if yours is the contact name supplied, be ready to answer questions (see section 4.3).

4.2.5   At the event

Prepare press packs for any reporters you have invited. Make sure someone is tasked with greeting them as they arrive, to ensure that they receive their press pack. Usually, press packs are presented in an A4 plastic folder with the name of your charity and 'PRESS PACK' on the front. Include the following:

- a brief summary of your charity and the work that it does;
- a brief summary of how money is raised;
- on A4 headed notepaper, a précis of the event – who, what, where, when and why.

Any photographs should be captioned, and important names should be included in upper case. Also, include a selection of previous press releases (if any).

4.2.6   After the event

If no journalists turn up, send out the press packs to those invited and include a short account of the event, plus a couple of good photographs with captions. Keep a scrapbook of press cuttings with all the details of the event – it will be of help in the future for you to include in your portfolio when making presentations to companies, and can be used to good effect in in-house publications.

4.3   Interviews

Occasionally it is necessary for the special events organiser to give an interview. If you have a press or PR department, they should be able to provide you with a thorough briefing on how to handle interviews, and give you a chance to practise and get over any nerves. Media training is also available from various suppliers, and is useful if you are likely to be called upon regularly for interviews across different media.

It is natural to be a little nervous before an interview – it is a form of performance after all, and you may not have much time to get your message across. Thorough preparation is key: have the facts at your fingertips, anticipate questions (ask someone to play devil's advocate for another perspective on what the journalist might ask), and work out how to answer any awkward questions in advance.

Top tip

Never assume that a reporter is 'off duty'. You may believe there to be a difference between what you say in an interview and what you say informally, but the reporter will consider everything you say to be fair game.

4.3.1 Print media

For this kind of interview, the journalist may arrange to meet you at your office, at the venue or somewhere neutral, or they may conduct the interview over the telephone. They may record your conversation as well as take notes, so that they can listen back and pick out any quotes when writing up the article.

4.3.1.1 Preparation

What is the publication? Who reads it? What interests them? Get a copy if you can, so that you can see what sort of style is used, and what is likely to appeal. Try to find out what sort of angle the reporter is considering, and what type of article they are writing. It is especially important to get an idea of the length of the piece – if it's a little 'What's On' box, you will have time only for the basic facts, but a feature piece allows you to elaborate on the event and the cause for which you are fundraising.

Decide what you want to get out of the interview, and choose a maximum of three main points that you want to put across. The shorter the interview, the clearer you must be about what you want to say. Think about anecdotes and illustrations involving people.

4.3.1.2 During the interview

Remember the main points that you want to make and be sure to get across the essential information, do not wait to be asked. Ensure that words are not put into your mouth. Use lively, simple language so that the journalist will have plenty to quote you on – if you disagree with something a reporter says, or you think that they may have misunderstood you, say so. You may feel more confident if you have notes of your key points with you, but it is better to be really clear what the main points are, so that you can respond to questions more flexibly.

4.3.2 Radio and TV

For both radio and TV you may do either a pre-recorded interview (which usually is edited and used as part of a larger piece along with other interviews and reporters' comments), or a live interview. The pre-recorded interview may be less nerve-wracking, but you can never be sure what will make it to the final cut. There are no second chances on a live interview, but if you can keep your cool, you can make sure that your key points come across, and you will know exactly what the audience gets to hear.

For radio, you may be interviewed 'down the line' (over the phone). Make sure that you know which phone will be used for this, and try to take the call in a quiet place where you will not be disturbed. For TV, a small crew (reporter and cameraperson with handheld camera) may be sent to record an interview somewhere topical (your charity or the venue itself). If you have your charity logo or a clear brand for the event, make sure you have some materials available, as they are like to want to include it in the background. Alternatively, you may be invited to the studio.

4.3.2.1 Preparation

What is the programme, and what do you know about the type of audience that it reaches? Try to find out the purpose of the interview and how it fits into the programme. Find out if anyone else will be there (if so, definitely try to be in the studio if possible, because if you are down the line you cannot make eye contact with the reporter or presenter to indicate that you have a further point to make). How long will the interview be? Will it be live or pre-recorded, and when will the programme go out?

Talk to the interviewer in advance if possible, and find out the general line of questioning. Try to agree with them the precise form of the first question so that you can start with confidence, but do not be too thrown if they do not always go with this. If you let a helpful interviewer know what kind of points you want to get across, they will usually adapt their questions to allow you to do so. If there are any tricky issues associated with the subject, work out in advance how you will answer awkward questions, and stick to the party line. Decide what you want to get out of it, and choose a maximum of three main points that you want to get across. The shorter the interview, the clearer you must be about what you want to say. Think about anecdotes and illustrations involving people. You will need to be really familiar with your facts and have them at your fingertips – technically you can have notes when on the radio, but you have to be careful not to rustle, and to make sure you sound natural and conversational. You cannot refer to notes for a TV interview.

If you are going to appear on television, keep your dress code smart but simple – nothing too loud, stripy or garish that will detract from you and your message. Make sure you are comfortable in whatever you wear, so that you do not fidget. Check to see if you will be seated, and ensure that your hem length leaves you appropriately covered. If you wear make-up, put on the bare minimum: the TV station may offer to make you up in the studio, which may be advisable to accept, as they know what works under studio lights. On TV, try not to wave your hands around or point. Prepare to keep eye contact with the interviewer, and try to remember to smile, be bright and animated without overdoing it or appearing fake.

4.3.2.2 During the interview

Conduct the interview as if it were a chat between two people. Project yourself – inject more authority and vitality than in a normal conversation. Be positive, sincere and pleasant. Avoid taking apparently hostile questions personally, they are usually just a tactic to liven up the discussion. Respond positively and assertively: remember that only rarely will the interviewer know better than you about the charity or event you are promoting. If you do not know the answer to a question, admit it and say you will find out and get back to them, and do so promptly. You can disagree with the interviewer, but keep it cordial and never be rude. In group discussions you can cut across someone else's chatter, but only do so if you have a really strong point.

Speak clearly, and do not be rushed – it is better to make one point well than several badly. Give brief, informative answers to questions, and do not wait for the right questions; treat each question as an opportunity to get a key point across. You can make additional points or deflect questions if necessary by saying, 'That's a good point, but …' or 'But even more important is the fact that …'.

Focus on what your key message is, and make sure that you repeat telephone numbers and websites as contact points for more information. Speak slowly, as people will be trying to get this information down on paper. Prior to the interview, ask if the numbers can be put on the screen at the end.

Do not be embarrassed by mistakes. If the interview is live, simply apologise and continue. If it is pre-recorded, you can ask to do something again.

Getting the right chemistry: selecting and working with a PR consultancy

Guy Woodcock, chief executive, Montpellier Marketing Communications Group

Definitions of PR

> Public relations is about reputation – the result of what you do, what you say and what others say about you. It is the discipline which looks after reputation, with the aim of earning understanding and support and influencing opinion and behaviour. It is the planned and sustained effort to establish and maintain goodwill and mutual understanding between an organisation and its publics. (Chartered Institute of Public Relations; CIPR)

As you can see from the Chartered Institute's official definition of public relations, the process involves the building of relationships. So the process of choosing and working with a PR consultancy ought to take into account some of these very same considerations.

Let's face it, we cannot like everybody we meet in life. There may be something quite mysterious about why we happen to like one person and not another, or it might be more simple and obvious. Eitherway, chemistry as experienced on first meeting and in any dialogue prior to that invariably will provide a good hint as to what might lie ahead. Indeed, the bond that grows between you and your PR consultancy team eventually will underpin and shape much of the way that business is done between you. So, take time to get this relationship right by shopping around a number of PR consultancies, initially perhaps by phone and email, and then draw up a shortlist of those you whom would like to pitch for your PR business. If you can, go and visit these in their offices to get a good feel for their size, organisation and facilities.

Finding PR consultants

So, where do you look for a PR consultancy? Much depends on the job required to be done and the likely budget. The larger the job or the tighter the timescales, the larger the consultancy may need to be because they will have the resources. At the smaller end, you could look for a freelance PR consultant, for example on the CIPR website (www.ipr.org.uk). For a list of quality assured PR consultancies and their competencies, go to the Public Relations Consultants Association (PRCA, www.prca.org.uk). All members of the PRCA have to undergo a very thorough biannual audit of quality and procedures, very similar to the ISO mark, but tailored bespoke to the PR industry. As a result, you will be dealing with among the best-in-class PR consultancies in the UK. Not all of its members are large consultancies, so don't worry if you are looking for a smaller firm to deal with. Montpellier, my own consultancy (www.montpelliergroup.com), belongs to the PRCA and we have members of the CIPR also. One final thing: sometimes (particularly if the work involves dealing with a specific locality) get hold of one of two of the local media, such as the local BBC radio station and the main daily newspaper, and trawl them for a few names and opinions.

Preparing a brief

The better the brief you provide, the better the consultancies will be able to respond. It is your job to make it easy for them to understand what they are expected to do, and it is in your interest to do so because a flawed or lazy brief may lead to you making the wrong choice.

Your brief to the consultancies needs to include your target audiences, which often include intermediaries, stakeholders, your staff as well as your target customer group. What are the objectives of the PR programme and do you have realistic timescales? PR is not like advertising, nor is it a quick fix. Don't be too cagey about providing them with a guideline on budget; they need to be reassured that you are being realistic. Remember, for any consultancy, a pitch – which for them is purely speculative and unpaid – often requires them to commit many hours, even days of work. Therefore, the main thing is to be fair-minded and, of course, commercial. Finally, give the consultancies a reasonable time to prepare their responses – three weeks is fair. Explain to the consultancies if there are good reasons why this isn't possible, so that they can see you are a reasonable person, and they will be very straight with you about whether this is possible.

The pitch process

This is likely to take place as presentations in the boardroom. Allow plenty of time so that each consultancy can present and then answer or ask any questions. Have someone with you at this, such as your chief executive, line manager and maybe one other person. Put the consultancies at ease and you will get much more from the pitch process. (I have been on a few pitches over the years where the prospective clients have remained rather aloof and unfriendly from their rather superior and advantaged position, and it's so unnecessary and ungrateful. To be fair, most pitches that I have attended have abided by the best practice things I am talking about here.)

During the presentations, check and be assured that the people presenting are the people who will be doing the work. Think twice about the organisation that wheels in the big guns, 'wows' you with their amazing thinking but leaves the account handlers who'd be working on the account back at the ranch. It can happen.

Consultants at this stage should be able to confirm what they understand of you and your organisation, and demonstrate a carefully considered approach to serving your requirements yet additionally taking a view to the future of growing with you.

Making your choice

At the end of each presentation, satisfy yourself that it has demonstrated:
- an intimate understanding of your organisation, products or services;
- similarly, an understanding of your marketplace and the factors influencing market conditions;
- realistic timescales;
- an accurate and comprehensive knowledge or understanding of the charity sector media and general, national media that will be important to your objectives;
- evidence of the consultancy having done similar projects or achieved similar results to your requirements (and how long ago);
- a strategy for evaluating their programme as it goes along;
- a transparent and efficient system for tracking their time spent on your account;
- agreeable budgets (take time to check what is in the contract price and what might be 'extra');
- at the end of the day, does the programme meet your brief, and does it sound as if it is achievable with the team to whom they have introduced you.

Once you have made your decision, try and get back to the consultancies within a couple of days. In the case of the unlucky ones, prepare a grateful and graceful letter or email, as if you were at the receiving end. Good relationships make for good public relations, and in any case, if for any reason you fall out with your appointed consultancy, you may need to go back to them. This does not happen very often, but you never know.

Last, ensure that the contract between you and the consultancy is tight and outlines all the elements you wish to include within the programme or project with which you have tasked your consultant. It is key to agree sensible targets so that the relationship is based on reasonable, achievable and mutually agreed performance benchmarks. If you are dealing with a

PRCA member, they will supply a very thorough and robust contract to protect both parties.

As you start working together, do invest plenty of time in building the relationship. Think of your consultancy as a surrogate member of your organisation. Vitally, keep them regularly informed: even though you will probably establish a routine of monthly meetings, they cannot read your mind or know what is going on if you don't talk to them regularly and inform them of all developments that will influence their work. To be a good mouthpiece for your organisation, they need to be constantly in the know. The more time you spend briefing them and keep up to speed, the quicker and more accurate their work to represent your company effectively will be.

Having taken all into account, you ought to be able look forward to a harmonious relationship that hopefully will last for years, and with you both performing to a mutually agreeable objective and at your best.

4.4 Photographs

A good picture is worth a thousand words: it is the best way to increase your coverage, so do identify picture opportunities and build them into your event. Also, think about how useful these photographs will be to you and your charity in the future – could you use them in the charity's annual report or other publications such as newsletters?

4.4.1 Hiring a photographer

If you need to hire a photographer, the British Institute of Professional Photography will help you to find one in your area. You will need to look at the photographer's portfolio to decide whether their quality and style is what you want for your event, and work's budget for hiring them. Confirm whether they bill by the hour or as a one-off commission for the session. Also, see if there is a reduction if they sell photographs of guests to them personally (but make clear if you do not want them to do this).

You should brief the photographer thoroughly: be clear about what you want, whether you want to keep contact sheets, etc. Are there certain shots during the event that really need to be captured? Note that when you commission a photographer, you do not own the copyright to any photographs taken at the event. When you buy the prints, that is all you are buying. You will need the photographer's permission to reprint them and must include their name in publications under the photograph.

4.4.2 Getting a press photographer to your event

Send details to the picture editor of a regional newspaper as well as the news editor. On a local paper the editor is the correct contact for both news and photocall information. To get a paper interested in sending someone for a photocall, first find out whether the paper uses photographic coverage, then make sure that you give plenty of visual information and spell out the arrangements on the day. Give the exact date, time, place and a contact name. Ring to check that the information has been received and is in the diary. Send a brief reminder of the photocall the day before to everyone involved.

4.4.3 Doing it yourself

Newspapers may be unable to send someone along, but may still want a picture, so be prepared to take the pictures yourself or to get local students and amateur photographers to volunteer. It is always useful to have a back-up at an event in case the press photographer does not turn up, and by using a volunteer you will have a good collection of pictures you may want to use for in-house publications.

The majority of effective pictures require some stage direction to bring out the right pictorial and editorial qualities, but try to avoid pictures which look posed. Also, avoid the 'grip and grin' pose with a cheque.

4.4.3.1 Your camera

Digital cameras are great if you are doing it yourself, as you can take as many pictures as you wish at very little expense, and they can be emailed to the newspaper (see section 4.4.4 for technical information on sending pictures). Good-quality pictures require a camera with a resolution of at least four megapixels. If your camera has a low resolution the pictures cannot be enlarged without becoming pixelated. If you can set the resolution on your camera, set it to the highest resolution (finest). Also, adjust the picture size to the largest possible and set at 200 ASA.

All pictures that you see in a newspaper have been edited in some way, but you can leave that to the newspaper. Avoid using Photoshop or other picture editing software to crop, lighten, darken or sharpen – only use your best pictures.

4.4.3.2 Finding the right subject

Try to capture unique moments and be descriptive – a good picture should tell a story. Capture the mood, aim for simplicity and force and reflect the feelings and responses of those involved. Capture animation, whether it is action or the expressions on people's faces. Children and animals are almost always winners (note that parental permission is necessary to take and publish children's photographs).

Think about the wide variety of angles, positions and subjects offered by the big event; go for large group shots only if they say something about the people or the occasion. There is nothing necessarily wrong with clichés – presentations, prizegivings and so forth are the bread-and-butter of local papers – but try and get a slightly different angle. Talk to people as you take pictures, so that you get a more relaxed photograph which reflects the mood rather than a dead, featureless photograph.

4.4.3.3   Lighting

Lighting is crucial to a good photograph. Arrange to take pictures in brightly lit places if possible. Watch for shadows, particularly over faces. Faces are important, so watch out for hats and caps overshadowing them, or single overhead lights which do them no favours. Try to get people to face into the primary light source, but not so bright that they screw up their faces, and be aware of where your own shadow is falling. Try to avoid using flash, as natural lighting is always superior. If you must use flash, be aware that it has a limited range and will not light beyond 10 to 20 feet. In addition, flash can give your subjects red-eye: some cameras have a setting to reduce red-eye, but another way to reduce it is to get everyone to look at your right shoulder rather than directly at the camera lens.

4.4.3.4   Composition

A classic rule of picture composition is the rule of thirds: this means dividing the composition into nine imaginary squares and framing the important picture elements within those gridlines to achieve the right balance. Get in tight: faces are usually the most important element of the picture, and they need to be clear. Look very carefully through the viewfinder and really try to see the whole picture. Does one person have a lamppost growing out of their head? Avoid signs, names and logos in your picture, as well as car number plates. Take care over camera angles to ensure that you do not obtain an unfortunate or unflattering view of your subjects.

4.4.3.5   Tips on technique

You will need to be firm with your subjects but understanding of their feelings, and try not to keep them from enjoying the event for too long. The more people you have in the group, the harder it is to get them all doing what you want for your photo needs. It might take time to get everyone in the right place so that you can see all of their faces.

Many people do not like having their picture taken and you may have to persuade them not to pull strange faces. Try to make your subjects comfortable by talking to them while you take the shots. A high percentage of shots turn out poorly, even for the professional. Take as many shots as you can and while you do so, move slightly to the right and left, or try kneeling down to get a better angle.

I am indebted to photographer Bob Lamoon for this section.

4.4.4   Sending pictures to the newspaper

Caption photos clearly with who, what, where and when. Captions should be typed double-spaced on paper which should be taped to the bottom of the photo and folded over. If you can, send both a landscape and portrait version of the same picture: one may fit the space that an editor has, and could make a difference between being published or not. Digital images can be sent by email as JPEG (.jpg) files. Give the file a short, descriptive name (e.g. 'parker.jpg') rather than using the number that your camera automatically gives it.

All the people who are clearly visible must be named. If a group they need to be identified in the order they appear in the picture (usually left to right, starting with the back row. Specify in what order you are naming). Some newspapers will not print pictures if not all people are named. Check the spelling of names very carefully, and get permission to use the photo at the time of taking it. In addition, check the file size limit. Many photo editing software packages enable you to reduce the file size of your photos, but that this may reduce the quality of the picture. If you use Photoshop to save your pictures, then save as JPEG files at level 6.

If your camera has the ability to take pictures as RAW files, you can check whether this is the format that the newspaper would prefer. Scanned images need to be 10 x 8 inches at 200 dpi.

4.5   Gaining the edge: attention to detail

How can you gain the competitive edge? The challenge lies in finding a way to differentiate your events from your competitors'. Try to make full use of different techniques to give you the edge. Uncover not only the differences but also what your supporters value. Pay close attention to detail: it is often the little things that count. Giving added value may differentiate you from your rivals.

4.6 Treating supporters well

Consider the following aspects.

- *Keeping promises* – do you deliver at the right time to the right people? Do you live up to your word? It is better to underpromise and overdeliver than to let people down.
- *Communication* – do you ensure that you and your team have sufficient training in good supporter service and communication skills?
- *Administration* – do you and your team deal quickly with requests for information? Are you prompt and courteous? Do you acknowledge and rectify supporter complaints immediately?
- *After the event* – are you proactive in monitoring how satisfied your supporters are? Do you have a method that gives them the opportunity and encourages them to provide feedback? Will they attend another event? A positive experience provides an opportunity to develop a long-term relationship with supporters.

4.7 Internal promotion

You may have an internal marketing campaign to manage. Today, people who work in charities have a much better understanding of their colleagues' work on the whole. There is a better flow of communication, and the special events department is not necessarily looked upon as something unconnected with the 'real work' of the charity.

However, there may still be a climate of wariness or lack of awareness among your colleagues about how special events can play an important part in supporting other activities within the charity by introducing new donors, supporters and corporate contacts and raising the profile of the charity's work. It is up to you to ensure that the events you are staging are well reported to other departments of the charity. Produce a diary of forthcoming events, which can be circulated around the organisation and displayed on noticeboards. These can be included in the fundraising newsletter produced for volunteers to keep them up-to-date with the work of the charity they support.

4.8 Celebrities

Having a celebrity to endorse your cause and attend your event can be a major boon to your charity. They may bring increased publicity, possibly their own contact lists as prospective attendees, and will certainly make the event more attractive to their fans, providing the icing on the cake. However, the event must stand up on its own merit – a celebrity will not hide a poor concept or bad planning, and there must be a 'plan B' in case they pull out at the last moment. Conversely, celebrity involvement can be a liability, as any connection with the charity may involve negative coverage along with positive. Fame is fickle, it is not just about the A or B list; those who are on their way up may provide the added value to the event you need.

Therefore, involving celebrities is not something to be undertaken lightly. It will involve some effort in finding, booking and looking after them properly. However, if you get it right, having their backing and involvement can add the final polish to your special event.

4.8.1 How to find an appropriate celebrity

Some charities employ a specific member of staff as a celebrity liaison officer. Do plenty of research, keep in touch with the media and set up a database wishlist of potential celebrities you would like to approach. There may be a link with a celebrity and your charity's work – review your wishlist, then research their backgrounds thoroughly. As with corporate sponsorship, they will receive hundreds of requests, so do narrow down your list and only target those who are likely to have some sort of connection or desire to support you.

Once you have selected your celebrity (or preferably a shortlist of possibles), the most usual route to contact them is via their agent. The internet can be useful to help you source the agent. Your trustees and/ or the special events volunteer committee may know someone famous and be willing to make introductions, so make sure they all know that you are looking for someone to add that extra something to your special event. If you do get a personal introduction to a celebrity, make sure you contact their agent to keep them informed of progress and timetables.

Be aware of the agent who approaches the charity directly. It may be quite legitimate, but do not rush into an agreement without doing some research. Bear in mind that an agent is often responsible for rehabilitating a celebrity's reputation, so check for any bad publicity or whether the celebrity is involved in any legal action, drugs, alcohol, pornography or anything with which you would not want your charity to be associated.

It is worth bearing in mind an article in *Third Sector* magazine a few years ago (20 August 2003), which reported that the controversial PR consultant Max Clifford thought that celebrities were less than altruistic in their support of charities:

> *I'm willing to use a star to the benefit of a charity even though I know that in their heart of hearts they do not have a clue or give a damn about it. I'd say that half the stars I've known see charities as a quick fix to their image – and not just when things go wrong either.*

At the same time, he said that charities were becoming more savvy in their use of celebrities because they knew that using them often made a difference between the success or failure of an event. So, proceed with caution. However, I have worked with a number of celebrities over the years and the majority have been a pleasure to meet and work with; choose them well, and engage them positively – even if they began with selfish motives, you could win them round to being a positive ambassador for your cause.

4.8.1.1 Briefing your celebrity and agreeing terms

If you are going through their agent, keep your initial request short and to the point. Make it clear what you would like the celebrity to do and when, and provide contact details. Be prepared for the celebrity to contact you directly to find out more, and have all the information concerning the event readily available. Brief them about the media and publicity, be very clear what your contacts are, and be truthful about the coverage you expect to get. Whether cynically motivated or not, they are busy professional people and you have to consider the selling points from their viewpoint.

Do not assume that they will do it for free. Performers have to earn a living, so you must expect to pay them. Offer and expect to pay their normal appearance fees, and be prepared to offer and provide transport and accommodation. They may have others performing with them, such as musicians, so find out what their additional fees will be.

When full terms have been agreed, make sure the agreement is in writing. It doesn't have to be a formal contract (although if you are paying a significant amount for a service you may want to formalise the arrangement fully), but it should at least be a letter confirming the arrangement.

4.8.1.2   Celebrity maintenance

Before the event, it is only fair to orientate the celebrity properly, as they may be taking centre stage in a world they know little about, so provide them with the following information:

- a summary of the charity and its work (and where to find out more);
- a summary of the event and what you want to gain from it – e.g. money, new supporters;
- what you will be doing with the money raised;
- who the audience is;
- what you would like them to do.

Remember to look after them before and on the day. Make sure you communicate in advance about whether the venue is suitable – what equipment will they need or be bringing, what lighting is available, electrical supply, etc. During any rehearsals, celebrities and their support group will need sustinence: provide a table with food and beverages. Also, remember to provide for and thank the backroom staff as well as the celebrity.

Make sure they are greeted on arrival, shown the ropes of the venue and their accommodation as appropriate, and given timings for when different parts of the event are due to happen. It is often helpful to give someone the specific task of looking after them throughout the event. After the event, give them feedback about the outcome, and emphasise what a difference their appearance made (if it did, of course). Tell them where the money raised is being spent.

Keep in touch, but do not bombard them with other requests for events too soon. Keep a note of their performances, birthdays and send a card at Christmas. If you treat them professionally, this could be the beginning of a good relationship, and you will gain a positive reputation with their celebrity friends.

4.9   Added value: auctions

Additional requests for money during the event can be irritating and diminish the enjoyment for participants who have already paid for their tickets. However, if they are organised well as an integral part of the entertainment and advertised as such (so that people come prepared to spend more), an auction can be fun and can help to boost the return on the event. Never include such things as an afterthought or with the primary motivation of needing to make sufficient money to make the event a success. You should make sure that tickets are set at a reasonable price at the outset.

4.9.1 How to hold an auction

An auction has three vital elements:

- *good, interesting or unique items to auction* – such as experiences with celebrities. People have to want to own the items, and will feel that they have gained even more value from the event if there is an element of exclusivity about the auction – only they will get this opportunity, and only tonight. Charities occasionally receive donations of art, books and other items which are worth auctioning, if the donor agrees. This can be included during a dinner or a ball. Alternatively, hold a specific event, such as a lunch or a reception, with the auction as the focus. If you have no items suitable to be auctioned, another suggestion is to invite celebrities to donate a picture they have painted, or photographs which could be exhibited before an auction. If you can involve a magazine or newspaper to help you to launch this idea, you are likely to get a good response;
- *a charismatic auctioneer* – whether a celebrity or not, this needs to be someone who can inject energy and humour into proceedings, and who will not be afraid to drive prices up while making the process fun. If you need to hire an auctioneer, go to the professionals: a good auctioneer is worth every penny, especially if they have an entertaining personality. The National Association of Valuers and Auctioneers (NAVA – see Appendix 2) is worth contacting. If you have no personal contacts with an auctioneer, NAVA will give advice as well as recommending someone;
- *an audience with deep pockets, big hearts and competitive spirit* – they need to know in advance that the auction is happening, and at least the main items to be included, so that they come mentally prepared to spend. Also, they need to be prepared to spend over and above what they might at a 'real' auction, since the proceeds are for charity rather than private profit.

Here, the auction needs to stick to the rules. An auction in a private place for invited guests has the same legislation as an open auction for the general public. A person is empowered to conduct a sale and the item is sold to the highest bidder. Under Part VII, section 59 of the Sale of Goods Act 1979 (see Appendix 2), the law which governs commercial transactions, each lot is deemed to be the subject of a separate contract of sale and concludes at the fall of the hammer, although if the item has a reserve price which is not reached, there is no sale. The auctioneer serves as an agent of the seller, must act in good faith and get the best price for the item auctioned (see section 4.10.4 for more details on Gift Aiding donations made via auctions – unfortunately if the item is unique and not commercially available, the price paid at auction is deemed to be the value of the object, and therefore no donation as such has been made or can be Gift Aided).

Macmillan Celebrity Christmas Stocking Auction

Jenny Edwards, Head of Events, Macmillan Cancer Support

Figure 5: Celebrity chef Antonio Carluccio at the Macmillan Celebrity Christmas Stocking Auction (pictured with Tania Bryer and Neil Fox, reproduced with kind permission of Macmillan Cancer Support)

The following is an example of a successful auction which has run for some years. Macmillan Cancer Support improves the lives of people affected by cancer: it provides practical, medical, emotional and financial support and pushes for better cancer care. The aim of the event was:

- to sell 400 reception tickets;
- to raise £120,000 net;
- to raise awareness and the profile of the work of Macmillan Cancer Support.

Choice of venue and why

It was key to choose a venue in central London with good tube and bus access and in a location convenient for the City. The venue had to be smart, have two adjoining rooms which could fit 400 for a champagne reception and 400 for the seated auction, theatre-style. The price and value for money in terms of service and extras also had to be right. It is worth negotiating to get the best deal.

Key to the success of the event

The Celebrity Christmas Stocking Auction is now in its 10th year. As an existing event, it was one which has continued to grow and raise more money year after year. Celebrities have become increasingly important to create a glamorous, high-profile evening, and where this event is clever is that the actual ask of the celebrity is very small: all they have to do is write their dream stocking filler list. It is a simple idea that makes a substantial amount of money for the charity without the costs being too high.

Securing sponsorship

It is always difficult to secure sponsorship for charity events, but Macmillan has the most success through encouraging its committee to think about who they know at work and socially who could help.

Volunteer committees

A committee of approximately 15 people was recruited specifically for this event. It is predominantly made up of the chairperson's friends and contacts. Some members stay on the event committee year after year, which provides valuable experience and continuity, but Macmillan also recruits new members each year to keep ideas and contacts fresh.

Marketing

The event is always sold out; committee members work hard to sell tickets to their friends and colleagues. Macmillan also has a dedicated public relations team at head office which secures coverage in national newspapers and magazines across the board. The publicity 'hook' could be a celebrity, a product in one of their dream stockings, the presenters, a committee member or a prize, but Macmillan always uses these hooks as a way to talk about its work.

Debrief and follow-up

It is very important to learn from one's mistakes and to use feedback and experiences to improve next year's event. It is also important to have a fun debrief evening to thank the committee for all their hard work.

Dos and don'ts

Do consider one or two well considered and well organised added extras if they fit in with the overall programme.

Do tell people in advance what they can expect, so they can bring their chequebooks.

Don't keep pestering people for money throughout the event.

4.10   Gift Aid

The easiest way for any charity to maximise its income from donations is to increase the take-up of the Gift Aid scheme currently offered by the government.

Gifts of money made by taxpaying individuals to charities in respect of sponsoring charity challenges will attract 25 per cent tax relief under the Gift Aid scheme. If someone makes a donation to the charity of, say, £100, the charity can recover a further £25 from HM Revenue & Customs (HMRC). This used to be at a higher rate of 28 per cent until budget changes in 2008 reduced the lower income tax rate from 22 per cent to 20 per cent. However, in response to concerns raised by charities that this inadvertently reduced the amount that charities could claim, HMRC agreed to transitional arrangements whereby it will top up every 25p claimed by a further 3p per £1 given. These transitional arrangements will last until April 2011, so make the most of this opportunity while it lasts, and build up a higher level of tax-effective giving to compensate for the likely lower amount retrievable per donation in the future. Furthermore, if the person making the donation is a higher rate taxpayer, they in turn will recover £25 when they submit their tax return.

4.10.1   Gift Aid and donations

If you decide to give additional opportunities for donations at your event, think about how you can encourage donors to Gift Aid their donations – it can seriously increase the amount your charity will benefit from the event.

Cash collections (via buckets or collecting tins) can be the most difficult, by nature being a more *ad hoc* and fleeting transaction, with coins or notes given as people enter or leave the venue or via a whip round at their table. At the end of the day you will have to use your own judgement as to whether it is appropriate to enable cash gifts to be Gift Aided at your event. However, a little bit of advanced planning can help to enable Gift Aid without causing delays and traffic jams. Consider pre-printing Gift Aid envelopes and making them available at tables, in welcome packs or at collection points. Make sure there are plenty of pens available to help people fill in the details. Give people advance notice of the donation request ('After dessert, volunteers will be coming round with buckets – please give generously'; 'On your way out, if you wish to show your support for this cause, volunteers will be available with collecting tins') and advertise the presence of the Gift Aid envelopes ('We can benefit by up to 25 per cent more from your gift if you are a UK taxpayer and fill in the envelope before putting your donation in it'). This has the double benefit of giving people adequate warning of the donation request and increasing the number that will be Gift Aided. (Do make sure that the Gift Aid envelopes fit into your collection receptacles.)

You will need to keep auditable records of Gift Aided cash donations, so make sure that those responsible for counting the donations at the end of the day are properly briefed. A list of Gift Aiding donors will need to be prepared, and as each envelope is opened during the cash counting, the amount should be noted on the envelope itself and on the list of donors.

If you are giving out packs to attendees with more information about your charity, do include an opportunity to give both a one-off or a regular gift by direct debit. Make sure that you include Gift Aid information and the ability to make a simple declaration alongside the donation forms, so that you can maximise your benefit from this. The regular giving form should contain a note reminding people to update the charity if their tax position changes.

Do consult with others in your organisation who are responsible for administering Gift Aid in order to make sure that you use a compatible system.

4.10.2 Gift Aid and ticket sales

The basic principle of Gift Aid is that it is available on all gifts that are voluntarily made to the charity. If you have to pay a certain amount to gain access (to a museum, art event or special event), then this does not count as a voluntary gift and cannot be Gift Aided. Equally, if you gain a benefit that is more than 25 per cent of the gift, the whole gift is deemed to be disqualified for Gift Aid, as it is seen as the purchase of a benefit rather than a voluntary gift. So, if the value received by the purchaser of the ticket (the dinner, entertainment, etc.) is more than 25 per cent of the ticket price, proceeds from ticket sales will not be eligible for Gift Aid.

You could give people the option of 'buying the benefit' and Gift Aiding any donations over and above this. To do this you need to make clear what the actual value of the ticket is, and that the purchaser has the option of just buying the ticket and attending the event, then you can give them the option to pay more than the value of the ticket and to Gift Aid the additional amount as a donation. For example, a ticket to a dinner might cost £40. Someone who wants to attend can simply pay £40, which purchases their right to attend and benefit from the dinner and any entertainment. Alternatively, you can ask them if they would like to pay £50 – the additional £10 would be entirely optional as support for your charity, and they could Gift Aid this amount. Their £10 donation would then be worth £12.80 to the charity.

A riskier option is to invite attendees to an event without a charge, but with a suggested donation amount. The whole of that amount would be eligible for Gift Aid, but only if it was genuinely possible for someone to accept the free invitation at face value, and not pay at all for the event. Clearly, the risk here is that if too many attendees make no donations (or insufficient donations), the costs of the event will not be covered. However, if you have a 'safe' group of keen supporters of the charity, this may be an option to consider in order to maximise the benefit to the charity through Gift Aid.

4.10.3　Gift Aid and sponsorship

If sponsorship of charity challenges is made by UK taxpaying individuals, the general rule is that these are gifts of money to the charity which can be Gift Aided in order to attract 28 per cent tax relief under the Gift Aid scheme. However, only donations to the charity are eligible for Gift Aid. If the participant has to pay a registration fee or deposit, this is not a donation to the charity and cannot be Gift Aided. If the participant is required to raise a minimum level of sponsorship to cover the costs of the event, then this amount of sponsorship income is seen as a benefit to the participant rather than a donation to the charity, and is not eligible for Gift Aid. If the participant pays their fee and any minimum sponsorship level, covering all the costs of the event themselves, the payment they make is not eligible for Gift Aid, but all the remaining sponsorship is, since it constitutes donations over and above the actual cost of participation.

If any element of the sponsorship money is to cover costs of the event (e.g. a minimum sponsorship amount), sponsorship payments made by people connected to the participant are seen as conveying an indirect benefit to the donor – this means that they fail the donor benefit rules and are not eligible for tax relief under the Gift Aid scheme. A connected person is defined as the wife or husband, or relative – that is, a brother, sister, ancestor (e.g. mother) or lineal descendant (e.g. grandson) – the wife or husband of a relative or a company under the control of the donor or under the control of connected persons. If the participant pays both fees and any minimum sponsorship requirements, so that all sponsorship raised is effectively a donation, then there is no benefit arising from the sponsorship, and a connected person can Gift Aid their donation. (For more information, please refer to the HMRC website, www.hmrc.gov.uk, and enter 'Gift Aid' into its search engine.)

To maximise the benefit to your charity from sponsored events, sponsorship forms should include space for sponsors' names and addresses and a box for them to tick to declare that they are UK taxpayers and agree to Gift Aid being reclaimed from their donation. You should include information about when connected persons should not Gift Aid their sponsorship, and about the level of fees to cover the costs of the event. Do make clear to participants and on the form that it is the sponsor's home address that is required for Gift Aided donations; if a work address is filled in, Gift Aid cannot be claimed.

(For more information on how to encourage Gift Aid on sponsorship forms, see the Institute of Fundraising tax-effective giving website: www.tax-effective-giving.org.uk.)

4.10.4 Gift Aid and auctions

Most charity auction donations do not qualify for Gift Aid. All the Gift Aid rules apply to the payments made by successful bidders at a charity auction. In theory, it is possible for at least some of the price they pay to be treated as a donation and eligible for Gift Aid. However, in most cases the benefit that they receive (that is, the item they successfully bid for) will disqualify the payment from Gift Aid.

An auction lot may have a commercial value (that is, it is available elsewhere for a given price), and if the bidder pays substantially above that value because they want to support the charity, then their payment may qualify for Gift Aid treatment. However, more often the lots at a charity auction have something unique about them – they are signed or made by celebrities, for example – and the value is essentially what a bidder is prepared to pay. Since the value is unique to them, and cannot be compared to a market value, the successful bidder cannot pay more than the value of the item, so they benefit by the amount they pay and Gift Aid cannot be claimed.

There are very limited circumstances where a successful bidder can 'buy the benefit' and treat any amount above that as a Gift Aid donation. This only applies where the items being auctioned have a commercial value which has been made clear in all promotional literature, and where the bidder makes clear before payment that they wish to buy the benefit.

If you want to explore the possibilities further, you can check more detailed guidance on the HMRC website, by searching under 'Gift Aid' or 'charity auctions'. The Institute of Fundraising also produces some very helpful 'Did you Know?' briefings on its tax-effective giving website (see above).

4.10.5 Keeping records and claiming Gift Aid

If your organisation has other regular income streams from public donations, it is likely that it already has systems in place to record and claim Gift Aid back from HMRC. Speak to your colleagues who work in this area, and make sure that you take advantage of their knowledge to set up appropriate systems for your event fundraising. If you do not already have systems in place, you need to contact HMRC to register. To make a claim you will need to send in form R68 (Claim), which contains totals and headline information together with Schedule R68 (Gift Aid), which details Gift Aid donations. HMRC also provides guidance notes to help you fill in the forms. You should contact them if you have any queries, if you have a large amount of data to submit, and to specify whether you want the money paid to you by cheque or straight into the charity's bank account via BACS.

You need to keep your own records of Gift Aid donations and corresponding donor information (including the Gift Aid declaration) for six years for audit purposes. The legislation does not specify what form records should be kept in – they can be paper records, electronic, on CD or microfiche – the key criteria are that they should be accessible and that you should be able to obtain a legible hardcopy when necessary. If a Gift Aid declaration is made over the phone, you may keep either a recording of the phone call or a copy of the written confirmation you send to the donor.

4.10.6 Template/checklist

The Gift Aid logo is available to download in various sizes and formats from the Institute of Fundraising tax-effective giving website (www.tax-effective-giving.org.uk):

giftaid it

Insert charity branding here

Please Sponsor Me (name)

To (event)

Note to participant: While anybody can sponsor you, the charity may not be able to claim Gift Aid from all your sponsors, for example family members ('Connected Persons'), if you have received a benefit by participating. Please check with the charity or the Institute of Fundraising for further details.

Gift Aid

If you Gift Aid your donation, we will continue to receive an additional 28p. We can claim Gift Aid tax relief of 25p on every pound you give and HMRC will also be operating transitional provisions for Gift Aid donations made from 6 April 2008 until 5 April 2011, paying a Government supplement of 3p on every pound you give.

giftaid it

So just tick here to Gift Aid your donation. It's that simple!

To qualify for Gift Aid, what you pay in income tax or capital gains tax must at least equal the amount that the charity will reclaim on the donation.

Full name	Home Address (Please give your full address including post code or we can't claim Gift Aid)	Postcode	Amount	Gift Aid	Date Rec'd
Johnathon Fotheringham	289 Queen Elizabeth Road, Walthamstow London	E17 8QP	£10	X	06/04/08

Total Amount

Figure 6: Sample Gift Aid sponsor form

This model form can be downloaded from the Institute of Fundraising tax-effective giving website, www.tax-effective-giving.org.uk.

5 TYPES OF EVENT

This chapter goes into more detail about specific issues to consider with the various types of event you may be planning. It includes ideas to inspire you, and case examples to help you see how the theory contained in previous parts of this book works in practice to help you cope with different situations and different events.

5.1 Balls and dinners

As part of your decision to hold a ball or a dinner, you should consider the audience you are aiming to attract, and therefore what style the event should be. The style has to suit the charity: are you comfortable with putting on a glamorous glitzy event, with celebrities and high-level donors; or are you aiming for something more downmarket but intimate, building a relationship with local corporate sponsors and supporters?

5.1.1 How to organise a ball or dinner

5.1.1.1 Programme

The key elements to a successful ball or dinner are very much the same.

For a ball:

- reception
- dinner
- auction or raffle
- dancing and entertainment
- finale.

For a dinner:

- reception
- dinner
- speaker or auction
- thanks and finish.

5.1.1.2 Venue

If it is a major event, perhaps your annual headline event, one issue which may arise is whether to hold the ball or dinner in London or in the regions. In today's economic climate, holding the dinner or ball at a hotel in London is probably no more expensive than a major hotel in the regions. However, London can give it extra cachet, attract more people and have more convenient transport access. However, if venues outside London are good and accessible, they can still attract a celebrity based in London. (One of the most successful balls I ran was held in Birmingham for 1,000 guests – it raised a great deal of money with the added attraction of a well-known celebrity.) With improving rail networks and cheaper internal flights, cities such as Bristol, Birmingham, Manchester, Newcastle and Edinburgh are all increasingly accessible for major events.

Depending on the sort of atmosphere you wish to create, you may be looking at hotels, but also consider other venues such as country houses, guilds and companies, which often have grand banqueting halls and facilities. Other suitable venues may be the VIP facilities at racecourses and sports stadiums, or universities which increasingly provide conference and dining facilities outside of term time.

Having found your venue, spend some time there; take one or two members of your special events committee for another opinion. Do the surroundings create the right ambience for your event? Crucially, check the maximum number that the venue can cater for: this is of great importance for safety management and fire safety regulations. When holding a ball, ensure that there is sufficient room at the venue (whether inside or out) for entertainment as well as dancing, adding further value to the event.

Check whether the main venue is attractive, the right temperature and size. Are there other rooms available for holding a reception, or for your sponsor's entertainment of their guests before the main event? When holding a reception it is preferable to have it set apart from the main room for dinner; this will enable the caterers to put the final touches to the presentation before guests go in to dinner.

5.1.1.3 Charges

If you are holding the dinner or ball at a hotel, ask if it offers rooms at reduced prices for guests. Discuss with the banqueting manager whether the charge for venue hire is lower if you have a certain number of guests attending. The day of the week may make a difference to the price – consider this when arranging the date of the ball. (Using the same venue more than once has enabled me to cultivate a good working relationship with banqueting managers, which has resulted in a reduced rate. This is certainly one time you can ask if they have a special rate for charities.)

5.1.1.4   Catering

Food glorious food! This can make or break your ball or dinner. Do not cut corners in this area – employ high-quality caterers, which you cannot do on the cheap. Go on recommendation and keep a record of good caterers you have worked with before. Sample their food, whether using your own caterers or those provided by the venue (sometimes the venue insists on this). If you can, try to find a sponsor for the wine or champagne at the event. However, if you are using the venue's caterers, they may insist that you pay corkage, sometimes at an exorbitant rate. Be aware of this and factor it into your budget.

Discuss your requirements with the catering manager – this should cover both the menu and the service level that you expect. It is essential to know how many staff will be employed: how many to a table, what bar staff will be available and whether the caterer will provide an overall manager on the night. Check with the caterers to be reassured that the overall presentation of the tables and bar will be to your liking. Keep it simple (less is more). The table linen should be spotless, and the china, glasses and cutlery should meet the standard you expect of the event – above all, they must be clean. You should stipulate that the staff are properly presented, confident and efficient.

Inspect the overall effect before the event and make any necessary changes with the catering manager well in advance of the guests arriving. Remember: you are the customer. Poor food and bad service will remain a lasting memory for your guests, so take time to reassure yourself and your committee that everything will go as planned.

5.1.1.5   Presentation: arrival

Check that the entrance area is attractively presented and clean. If this is a general entrance to the venue, you may not be able to dress it yourself, so make sure that the venue itself makes a good initial impression. It is important that guests know they are at the right place and can find their way to your event easily, so check to see what you can do in terms of signage and meeting and greeting people.

5.1.1.6   Decorations

Keeping a coordinated theme through invitations, programmes and menus, and reflecting this in the decoration of the rooms, will make the event look special and professional. You may want to use the colours of your charity or sponsors; if you are holding a themed ball, tailor the decorations in keeping with the event (for example, black and white).

If you want to use flowers, check with local florists to see if there is a deal that can be done by way of promotion for the florist (especially if they are new and just starting up in the area), perhaps by leaving their cards on the table or giving them a mention in the programme. Remember to keep the flowers and other decorations low on dinner tables so that people can see each other. Be careful with candles – they may look lovely, but the venue may have strict fire rules.

Cost will be a factor in what you might do with decorations. If you are unsure or have very little budget, keep it simple and classy. A few posters and half a dozen coloured balloons will only devalue the evening. If you can afford to spend more, stick to one strong idea or theme – if you throw in every idea that comes up, you may end up with an overfussy mess. Keep a note of good ideas that do not fit with this event, as you may be able to use them in the future.

5.1.1.7 Music

Live music creates a real focal point for an event, but remember to be careful and keep it in balance with the event. Visit the venue with the band or group and discuss the type of atmosphere that you want to create, the music you require and the type of audience you are expecting. They should be able to advise you. Book the entertainment first and then build around it.

Music can be expensive. If you are not going for a big name, consider local groups (on recommendation – and try to hear them for yourself if possible). Also contact colleges' schools of music. Being musically trained, usually they can put groups together to play anything from jazz to the classics. Discuss with the music tutor and explain your requirements; even if a large band is required, this may not be a problem for them.

If live or recorded music is being played at the event, a licence to play music may be required – contact PRS for Music (www.prsformusic.com) and Phonographic Performance Ltd (PPL, www.ppluk.com) to check (see section 6.6.2). In some cases you may need a temporary event notice, although in most cases the venue itself may be covered under its premises licence (see section 6.6.1).

5.1.1.8 Tables

Do check the spacing of tables and seats to ensure comfort. People have to get to and from their tables, so it is a good idea to try and see the room set up before the event. Sometimes, maximum capacity can be rather cramped. Consider whether you will need a dais for any speakers, bands or acts, and what impact this will have on table numbers and layout. Will people need to be able to make their way from tables to the dais to receive awards or take part in entertainments planned for the evening?

It is advisable to have a table plan – put up several to make it easier for guests to see them on the way into dinner, and give a copy to each of the hosts tasked with ushering people to their places. Theme the tables for added interest, but keep it clear so that people can find which table they are placed at easily, and where that table is within the room. Have table sign numbers high enough for all to see – this will also help the waiters.

Clearly sign seats at tables, so that people can find their places easily and to ease introductions to each other. If some places are not filled, ensure that the waiters do not clear them away – your guests may arrive late for various reasons.

It is a nice gesture to provide a goodie bag for each guest at the tables: a number of cosmetic companies will give samples, and perhaps you could include small individually wrapped chocolates. You should include in each bag:

- some information about the charity (not too much);
- an opportunity to send a donation (plus a Gift Aid form);
- an option to receive further information about your charity;
- an option to receive a programme of future events;
- a Freepost envelope (if the budget allows), or include a Freepost postcard with the above options printed on it.

5.1.1.9 Theme

Assigning a theme to a ball can help you to make it special and stand out from all the others. This is where you can let your imagination run riot and be truly creative. Your events teams, both staff and volunteers, can come up with some really original and creative ideas, so have a fun brainstorming session and ask everyone to bring a prop to illustrate their ideas.

Here are some ideas to kick-start discussions and help get the creative juices flowing.

- *Glamour* – many people like the opportunity to go over the top with dressing up, and this is a theme that can be created whatever the age group of your guests. You can adapt the music according to whether you have largely young or older guests.

- *White tie and diamonds* – guests are asked to wear diamonds (or anything sparkly) and gentlemen come in white tie. Maintain the classy feel with cocktails or champagne as the reception drinks, and a pianist playing music from Fred Astaire movies sets the scene. Continue the theme with decorations in white and silver throughout.

- *Masked ball* – guests are requested on their invitations to wear masks. Depending on the audience, they may buy or hire Venetian-style masks or make their own; you may consider sending out a template and offering a prize at the end of the evening for the best, most flamboyant or creative mask. Keep the Venetian theme through the decorations, and consider contacting the Dante Alighieri Society for advice on Italian music to match (see www.italian.bham.ac.uk).

- *Caribbean night* – an exotic evening can be created with special lighting, tropical flowers (is there room for a few palm trees at the venue?) and a steel band. Depending on the venue and your budget, consider creating an indoor beach. You can take the same idea to visit other areas of the world, from Arabian Nights to the Wild West – as long as you can define a clear sense of place and atmosphere.

- *Valentine's Day* – a classic romantic evening with roses, hearts and flowers, with a band playing romantic music and a singer to serenade all the couples. You may need to pay extra attention to the sort of age group you want to attract, but a theme of 'old fashioned romance' could well appeal to all age groups.

- *Nostalgia or schooldays* – pick a decade: the 1920s through to the 1980s provide plenty of material for theming with music and decorations from the period. You could go further back in time (Elizabethan, Regency, etc.), but decorations and costumes are likely to be more expensive for the right degree of authenticity.

- *Film themes* – *Moulin Rouge*, James Bond, *Pride and Prejudice*, Bollywood and Hollywood nights all provide material for a sharply themed event. This is a deep well of source material, as there are many more films from which to gain inspiration. You may be able to source backdrops via the internet, but do check copyright and royalty rights. Similarly, music from the films should be readily available, and you should gain plenty of inspiration for decorations.

- *Sporting themes* – the Olympics (ancient or modern), Grand Prix or an Ascot-themed event are some examples. If you can get a sports personality to be the guest of honour, this will be an added draw. Consider whether table games or raffles can be themed to match, with virtual horseraces or car races and a cup or other prize for the winner.

- *Colour themes* – ask guests to include the colours of the evening's theme in their dress – red and white, black and white, pink and black, blue, and so forth. The room should be themed in these colours, and it can have quite an impact. People can dress as dramatically or as low key as they wish.

- *Seasons* – a spring ball, a midsummer night ball or winter nights – choose your season depending on when you are holding your event. Again, you can coordinate both decorations and music to create the right atmosphere.

- *Casino night* – equipment can be hired and guests given the opportunity to play using Monopoly money. Guests buy their 'gambling money', for example, £5 for £10,000 in Monopoly notes. They then play the tables, with the option to purchase further amounts as they go. The person who wins the most Monopoly money receives a prize, with funds from the purchase of the Monopoly money going to the charity.

Think laterally, and see if you can find a theme which has a connection with your cause or the specific project for which you are raising funds. If you can, find a celebrity that matches your theme, e.g. the actor who plays James Bond, or a band from the 1970s. However, unless they have a special connection with your charity they are likely to be far above your budget. Do not despair: consider tribute artists or bands, which have become increasingly popular over the last few years, covering both acts that no longer perform and newer popular bands and artists. (I have witnessed a number of events where lookalikes were performing and the audience was just as enthusiastic as if it was the real person.) As with other entertainers, there are good and bad tribute bands, so it is important to assess the quality of their performance, via recommendation and seeing their demonstration DVD or video.

Do make the dress code as clear as possible. Sometimes the theme will make this obvious, but at other times guests may appreciate more of a steer (e.g. will beachwear be acceptable at a Caribbean night? Are people expected to come in costume to the Olympics ball, or is it just a theme? No one wants to turn up in shorts and running shoes if everyone else is in ballgowns, or vice versa). If guests are expected to make an effort to blend in with the theme, consider encouraging their participation by adding a competitive element, with a prize for the best interpretation of the theme – the prizegiving can provide a good finale for the evening. To complete the effect, follow through the theme on the invitations, posters, flyers, programmes and stationery for the event. Avoid using a theme unless you are prepared to be wholehearted about it.

5.1.2 Additional entertainment

At a ball, having various entertainments available as well as dancing helps to add value and a greater sense of fun to the event. Ensure that there is sufficient room at the venue, keep in mind your target audience and what is likely to appeal to them, and of course your budget and whether to include the entertainment offered as part of the event, or to charge or invite further donations. Some ideas and options include:

- magicians – small tricks performed around the tables are popular with guests;
- photographer – guests appreciate a memento of the event. The photographer can sell photographs directly to the guests (a word of advice – do not get embroiled in taking orders for photographs). Consider whether to arrange for a percentage to be donated to the charity, but be aware that this will probably constitute a separate commercial partnership agreement, and you need to make the arrangement clear to guests;
- cartoon portraits – similar to a photographer, but with a more fun element. Arrangements should be made in a similar way;
- demonstration dancing – a professional display to show people how it is done, perhaps with a brief session to teach people some basic steps (tango, salsa);
- acrobats, juggling;
- raffle – either have a traditional raffle with prizes donated by local businesses or your trustees and other connections, with hosts selling tickets to each table, or consider novel approaches such as a money tree, with envelopes containing raffle prizes. Guests buy an envelope, and everyone gets to win something;
- auction – keep this small and exclusive as it has more impact. As previously mentioned (see section 4.9.2), a good auctioneer or celebrity should be able to drum up enthusiasm and keep it moving;
- guess the weight of/number of sequins on an object – match this to your theme, invite donations for entries and have a suitable prize available to award at the end of the event.

When hiring entertainment, make sure you go on recommendation, and check references and endorsements. The entertainers should be able to show you a video demo of their performance – you must see their material in order to assess whether it is appropriate for your event.

Check to see if they have any special requirements, and check with the venue to make sure that it is happy with and able to accommodate your choice of entertainers (for example, fire eaters may not be covered by the venue's fire and safety certificates).

5.1.3 Fundraising

By being realistic when pricing the tickets, the problem of bombarding your guests with too many moneymaking activities can be avoided. They want to be able to relax and enjoy the entertainment you have put on for them. On the other hand, they will know that this is a fundraising event, so will expect one or two opportunities to donate further. Have one good raffle or auction with a small number of really good prizes.

Another idea for raising money and breaking the ice at dinners is to play 'Heads and Tails'. It is probably more effective if the event is not too large. Each guest puts £5 on the table; they then choose either to put their hands on their heads or on their bottoms. The compere flicks a coin, and those who get it wrong sit down; those standing choose again where to put their hands. This continues until the last six standing, who are asked to come to the front to continue. The last person left is the winner, who takes the money from their table – the rest goes to the charity. It is a very quick game and good fun!

5.1.4 Master of ceremonies

If a large number of people are attending, or if there are several speakers or elements to the event (especially involving moving people from one room to another), you might wish to consider using a master of ceremonies (MC). It also gives the event a certain style, if the guests are high-profile.

The role of MC or toastmaster has been a tradition at royal and formal events for centuries. They have experience in dealing with formal occasions and will help to ensure the smooth running of events on the night, adding confidence and a calming influence on what can be a very stressful occasion for the special event organiser. The MC should be discreet (the focus of attention is not them, but the event or speaker they are introducing) yet able to be authoritative in gaining attention for grace, speeches and toasts, and moving people on to the next stage of the event (for example, from the reception to the dinner or encouraging people to start dancing). Agree in advance whether you will require the MC to meet and greet guests, and make sure they are given the information to enable them to introduce correctly the keynote speakers and celebrities. Some have experience of auctioneering, and their presence can certainly boost an auction. They may be able to fill in gaps and keep the guests amused if a speaker is delayed – do discuss this with them beforehand, though.

When considering a professional toastmaster, check that they belong to one of the local or national professional bodies such as the National Association of Toastmasters, Guild of Professional Toastmasters or Toastmasters General Council (see Appendix 2). Other professional bodies can be found through yell.com, under 'toastmasters'.

5.1.5 The 'wow' factor

Think about how you want your guests to react when they arrive at your dinner or ball, how you would like them to feel as they leave and as they talk about their experience to others in the following days. You certainly do not want them to be disappointed, or for things to go disastrously wrong, and hopefully with good planning this will not happen. But will you be happy if guests react with 'It was all right, an OK night out'? You should be aiming for the 'wow' factor, with guests not only feeling that they have had good value for the price of their tickets, but that they have had a great time, would be first in the queue to come back for more and will spread the word with enthusiasm about your charity and your events.

To achieve this, your mantra should be to keep it simple, but stunning. Follow a strong theme with conviction, but avoid overdoing it:

- start off gently, peak two-thirds of the way through the evening, and finish with a 'wow';
- do not pack in too much;
- do not include too many raffles or auctions – one quality one is enough;
- think of novel and entertaining ways of raising cash.

First impressions count in forming the overall opinion of the event. Make sure the entrance of the venue is well-presented and well-lit, with clear signs to where everything is. If guests have to show their invitations, have at least two reception desks (obviously this depends on the number of guests expected – you may need more for a larger event).

If there are several parts to the evening (reception, dinner, speaker, entertainment), make sure that there is a programme available – people will be happier if they know what is happening and when. If you use a toastmaster or MC, this will help to let people know what is happening and where they should be.

Have plenty of hosts, who will usually be volunteers or staff who have been well briefed on the evening as to where things are; they can welcome guests and direct them to cloakrooms, reception, their table, etc. At a corporate dinner, I have engaged sixth-formers from the local senior school to act as hosts; this went down well with both the guests and the school. Whoever you use, make sure they are well briefed and keep up the overall atmosphere of professionalism (in terms of dress and friendly but efficient demeanour).

You may want to have a short speech by your chairperson and any sponsors to welcome guests at the reception, but the highlight will be the speaker or celebrity guest. At a dinner, coffee time is usually the best moment for them to speak – people are not distracted, they will be relaxed and ready to listen. Check the sound equipment before the event, and have a spare microphone in case of breakdown. Let the speaker rehearse beforehand, and have someone sitting at the back to make sure they can hear and see them.

Before the finale, the volunteer events committee should be thanked in front of the guests and presented with appropriate gifts. There should be a vote of thanks by the chair of trustees or chief executive of the charity, thanking the speaker, the entertainer and the guests who have supported the evening so generously.

Try to finish with a 'wow'. You should find something that will clearly define the end of the event, and have guests leaving on a high note. If the venue has a park, garden or other suitable area, one dramatic way to finish is with fireworks. Pyrotechnics are potentially dangerous and must be used strictly in accordance with the manufacturers' guidelines. This is not a 'do it yourself' job: go to a recommended company that will advise you and deliver the display in complete safety. Consider the amount of time when commissioning a pyrotechnic organisation – after 12 minutes, interest begins to diminish, so five to ten minutes usually works best. The cost can be anything from £850 to £1,250 but, especially if you have sponsorship, this will be worthwhile. If fireworks are not an option, but you have live music available, then consider an appropriate last dance or tune. With a service band this might be a last post or beating the retreat, which can have quite an impact on guests.

Case study: Members' anniversary dinner

Adam Stewart-Koenig, alumni and development officer, Queens' College, Cambridge

Figure 7: Queens' College anniversary dinner (reproduced with kind permission of Queens' College, Cambridge)

I work for a college in Cambridge and my job as an alumni and development officer is to both fundraise and 'friendraise'. A major part of my working week is planning reunion events for members of college to attend: this can include anything from an informal drinks reception to a formal black tie dinner for 300 people.

Sit

I am sitting with the director of my department who is telling me about the event I am to plan – the Master wants an anniversary dinner for a group of students and guests, and I will need to present a proposal. The event is for the matriculation class of 1999. I work with our database manager to action a data run with the necessary information, clean the data and transfer it to an Excel spreadsheet to provide the source for our initial mailing run. The date needs to be set with the PA to the Master – we find a couple of dates for approval, and finally 24 May is settled on. College rooms are booked with the bursar and the date entered into the college calendar, so that all know that a formal function will take place on this date.

Six months to go – I have an early meeting with the catering manager, outlining the event and intended venue and ensuring things are pencilled in, with details to be confirmed later. I also meet with the head porter to discuss parking availability, as parking is very limited in the centre of Cambridge. We agree to confirm a number nearer the time.

From the initial spreadsheet, an advance letter is prepared informing relevant members of the anniversary dinner, and enclosing helpful information about hotels where I have negotiated a discounted rate. As this is a mailing of 400 members, I ask volunteers to come into the office that afternoon to help stuff envelopes, and within hours the letter is ready to be sent. I now ask the database manager to list the event on our website.

Five months to go – we update the spreadsheet with information from returned mail and emails from other members updating their contact information.

Four months to go – we send out the formal invitation to members: this includes a formal letter of invitation from the Master, a formal invitation card to the member and guest, and a proforma for any dietary and access requirements. We also enclose a form asking for details of work, hobbies, awards, etc. which will be published in a year 'Who's Who' for members on the evening, so that they can read up on what their contemporaries are doing now.

We are privileged to have a Michelin Star-rated chef as our executive head chef in college, and I meet with him for an hour to settle on the menu for the evening. Then I track down the wine fellows in college to ask for suitable red and white wines, with a claret to finish.

Proformas start to come back, listing requirements and sending apologies, and are filed in an A–Z folder with apologies at the back for reference.

Prepare

Three months to go – the seating plan is prepared, grouping members by subject of study, meeting specific requests to be seated next to other members, and mixing in fellows and college officers. A returning member is contacted to ask if they would say a few lighthearted words on behalf of their year and toast the college.

Two months to go – the content of the 'Who's Who' is compiled and the printer contracted to print and bind the document in time for the dinner on 24 May. The catering manager, chef and college barman are updated with attendance figures at this point, so they will have some idea of the numbers expected. Name badges including matriculation year are made up, place cards printed for the table and the table plan is made ready but not published.

One month to go – the 'Who's Who' is delivered by the printers and stored ready for the event. An event briefing is prepared for the Master, including the seating plan, A–Z of who is attending, the menu, the wine list, the person saying grace and the person making the speech.

Two weeks to go – final numbers are passed to the catering manager to ensure that the chef knows the numbers dining, and that there are sufficient waiting staff to cover the drinks reception and formal dinner; also, to the Master's housekeeper to ensure enough glasses are available in the lodge for the drinks reception.

Attack

The day of the event. Some last-minute changes are made to the attendee list – an event manager's nightmare, but we always prepare for a couple of extras. The seating plan is rearranged to ensure that there are no gaps. The 'Who's Who' is placed on each member's chair. Name badges and handouts listing who is attending the event are made ready in the Master's lodge. Those using disabled parking or staying overnight in college rooms are confirmed with the porters' lodge.

Three hours before the event – we all change into formal dress, walk the function route and make sure everything is correct and ready to go. The catering supervisor is told who is saying grace, who the speaker is, and where special dietary requests have been made.

One hour before the event start time – we gather in the Master's lodge. Fellows and college officers arrive and take their name badges and attendance sheets. Although the event is scheduled to start at 7 pm, someone turns up at 6.45 pm – they are invited in, issued with a name badge and warmly welcomed by the nearest fellow, with a glass of champagne in the Master's gallery.

As members arrive, they are given badges, attendance lists and glasses of champagne. When a gong is sounded, the Master welcomes everyone and asks them to head across to Old Hall for dinner. While the guests are greeted, I go across to Old Hall to give a final update to staff on any last-minute changes to attendance and dietary needs.

This part of the evening is an event manager's dream. People are going into a splendid hall which dates from the 1450s, with a large fire that sends a warm glow around it. When all are seated, a gong will sound and the dining hall supervisor will ask for silence for the grace to be said by a returning member or the college dean of chapel. The starter, main course and pudding will be served in turn, accompanied by wine waiters to pour the appropriate wine with the dish. Catering staff are well trained and organised, so that dishes are cleared and each course served with the minimum delay.

During dinner, the 'friendraising' begins as we inform members of the benefits available to them, from high table dining twice a term to using the college chapel for weddings, blessings, christenings, etc. Mental notes are made where follow-up would be appropriate, and business cards are swapped.

The gong is sounded again for the Master to ask everyone to stand to say the final grace. He will then call for the loyal toast, 'The Patroness', which refers to the Queen as patroness of the college. Cheese, biscuits and coffee follow, and claret jugs and port decanters will be passed along the tables by members and guests in the traditional anti-clockwise direction. When all are settled, the gong sounds again to announce the light-hearted speech by a returning member – five to seven minutes of reminiscences. The Master will thank them and present them with a small engraved gift.

The Master then addresses the event. First, he is welcoming back old college members as part of the college family. Second, he is providing an update on what is happening, particularly with regard to development, funding and the future of the college, and how we intend to fund these multimillion pound projects. Conversations continue over port or claret, with fellows and college officers reinforcing what has been said about college development. Some Members may indicate interest in further involvement with a project or fundraising idea. The event draws to a close around midnight, with the Master bidding goodnight and members and guests departing.

I thank the catering staff in person for the time and effort they have put in, and have a quick discussion with my director about how the event went, before we both head home at about 1 am. On the following Monday morning, a copy of the 'Who's Who' is sent to members who were not able to attend. Formal letters of thanks are sent to the speaker and the departments involved in the event. We discuss who was spoken to and who will follow up any member's requests. We discuss if anything was not right, note any adaptations needed for the future, and put a report on file for the next event.

Follow-up

The second part of the event begins. I mentioned before my dual role as 'friendraiser' and fundraiser – the 'friendraise' has just happened by bringing back old members for a splendid dinner in college, to meet old friends and have a laugh about how much weight one has put on or what happened to all the curly hair you used to have. Now we put together the data collected from the 'Who's Who', the business cards and conversations we have had, and draw up a list of potential prospects for us to contact to reinforce the statement by the Master about intended development and funding.

At no time do we ask for a set amount of donation, for two reasons: we do not want to scare members away or make them reluctant to attend an event because they will be asked for money; more importantly, why ask a millionaire for £5 when they would be more than happy to donate £50,000? I know of other cases in other development areas where this has happened, and the organisation has missed out on a potentially life-changing large donation.

Members are contacted and replies are awaited, always keeping in mind that people have different agendas in life – if it is not a good time for them to be involved in a donation just now, this could change in 18 months or even ten years. Therefore, we monitor when it might be right to contact them again to follow up the idea of making a donation to college.

Although it is nice to sit back and smile when you land a large donation, it must be remembered that the member who donates £50 should be thanked just as warmly as the member who is happy to pledge £1 million. With all these small amounts trickling into the account, it will soon grow into a healthy sum.

5.2 Royal events

If your charity has a royal patron, you may have the opportunity to invite them to attend a special event. However, there may be a member of staff responsible for arranging royal programmes and it is useful to know what is entailed.

5.2.1 How to organise a royal event

5.2.1.1 Submitting an application

The programmes of events involving the royal family have to be submitted at least nine months in advance. If your charity has a royal patron there will be a designated route to follow by making an application to their private secretary, usually in the form of questions and answers. Once approval has been given, there will be an embargo on releasing this information, and until this is lifted, the information cannot be shared with anyone, even the sponsors. (If your charity does not have an established patron, the same process applies.)

5.2.1.2 Approving the programme

Nearer the date, you will receive a request from the private secretary or equerry to meet at the venue to discuss the programme. You will need to time the arrival and submit a plan of all the proceeding movements until the departure of the royal family member: this has to be submitted in detail to the palace for approval; also, it will include the names and addresses of all those who are being presented.

Once the programme has been received and approved and the date agreed for the release of information about the visit, you can include this on the special event material and submit the invitations to the palace for approval.

5.2.1.3 Press and publicity

At this point, the press will come under the jurisdiction of the Central Office of Information, which will issue press passes and control the press on the day.

5.2.1.4 Dealing with lord lieutenants and local councils outside London

If the event is outside London, the royal programme will be under the control of the Lord Lieutenant's office. The same procedure follows and liaising on the programme will be through that office. You may find that the local council becomes involved, therefore it is important to note that it is the *charity's* event working with the Lord Lieutenant's office, and you may have to exercise control over those from the local council who wish to attend. This must be handled in a diplomatic and sensitive manner in order to avoid complications.

5.2.1.5 Site security meeting

Nearer the date, another meeting will be arranged in order to meet the personal protection officers and the private secretary on site. This is a good opportunity for you to meet those who will be involved on the day of the event. Guests will be required to present their invitations when attending the event and it may be necessary for car numbers to be notified.

5.2.1.6 Arranging the dinner menu

If the event includes a dinner, a menu should be sent for approval to the palace. Preferences will be given on food and drink. The member of the royal family will be accompanied by their lady-in-waiting if female, or their private secretary if male, plus two personal protection officers, who will tell you where they wish to sit (you should remember to include the costs of the meals in your budget).

5.2.1.7 Protocol on arrival

The member of the royal family will be received by the Lord Lieutenant if outside London; if the venue is at a royal palace, then the charity's chairperson of the board of trustees would be the most appropriate person to present the chairperson of the events committee to the royal, who will then present the sponsors and other special events committee members. The day or evening continues and will end with the timed departure of the royal party.

5.2.1.8 Protocol for being presented

All those being presented will be unduly nervous of the occasion and it is up to the special events organiser to put them in a position to be presented and try to put them at ease. Whoever is presenting them to the royal party will introduce them by name. The royal party then offers his or her hand to the person being presented, who either bows their head (if a man) or does a small curtsey (if female) and says 'Your Royal Highness'. Male royals are addressed as 'sir', females are addressed as 'ma'am'.

5.2.1.9 Managing the rest of the event

On the day or evening, you need to follow the same briefing procedure with your helpers as at all other events, except there may be additional points to remember. They will ask about dress: usually if it is a day event, lounge suits are suitable for men with equivalent dress for women; hats are not worn except at garden parties, and even then they are not obligatory. Evening dress will be dictated by the type of event. Cameras are not allowed, photographs can only be taken of the presentations and the photographer must be commissioned by the charity.

The following case study is an example of a royal event where the charity took advantage of having royal patronage to design an event to gain maximum promotion for a small children's charity with a specific objective to celebrate the opening of a hydrotherapy pool.

Case study: The Brainwave Centre

David Davies, chief executive, The Brainwave Centre

Figure 8: HRH The Countess of Wessex opens a hydrotherapy pool (reproduced with kind permission of The Brainwave Centre)

Brainwave aims to support children with developmental delay, whether caused by brain injury, chromosome abnormality or accident, and has a centre in Somerset which helps children from throughout the UK. This case study deals specifically with one event, which was to mark officially the opening of a new hydrotherapy pool – the culmination of a four-year capital campaign to build it – a difficult journey in the context of the ongoing struggle to manage cashflow and raise unrestricted funds to cover core costs.

The opening of the hydrotherapy pool was to be a royal event involving HRH The Countess of Wessex. A date had been allocated and it was now our responsibility to ensure that the day itself was memorable for everyone involved. The board of trustees had a significant input into the planning process and a steering group convened every month preceding the event for tasks to be allocated and reviewed. The event was to be managed in two stages – our royal visitor would attend for one and half hours, and following her departure our guests, many of whom would be visiting the centre for the first time, would be given the opportunity to see the centre's facilities.

The guest list was compiled with a view to ensuring that those donors who had committed significant support to Brainwave for this project should remain long-term supporters in the future. Their names were placed on an 'A' list. Others were to be invited because they had some status in the local community or were of lesser value to the charity and were placed on a 'B' list. This information was of course privy to the steering group, but we wanted to ensure that recognition was given where due, especially during the royal visit. The event itself was not intended to be a fundraiser, although equally the principal costs had to be covered. Local companies were offered the opportunity of being introduced to the countess in return for sponsorship.

A royal event is choreographed down to the minutest detail. Our intention was that the Countess of Wessex should be greeted by members of the council, as is mandatory on these occasions, before being introduced to Brainwave's chairperson. He would escort her into the main centre, where members of the therapy team would be strategically positioned in various rooms throughout the building used for different interventions. Families with children on the programme had been handpicked to attend and they provided the interest and insights which the countess was genuinely looking for throughout her visit. The tour was to conclude with the countess being shown the pool, where several children and therapists would be in situ.

If you are lucky enough to have the patronage of a member of the royal family and your charity receives a visit, inevitably the local press will be very interested. We prepared press packs to distribute as soon as the engagement became public knowledge and distributed them to journalists who attended on the day. These consisted of a press release, a disc with photos of the completed pool and at various stages of its construction. We prepared case studies of children who would benefit from hydrotherapy, including quotes from parents and a list of local organisations, including two special schools, whose pupils would enjoy the facility during term time.

The pool was clearly to be the focus for the media on the 'big day'. It was agreed with the press office at Buckingham Palace that our host photographer would be the only one to accompany the countess throughout the tour, giving the remaining press a chance to acclimatise their equipment to the humidity of the pool area before she arrived at this principal photoshoot opportunity.

Facilities for hosting a significant number of guests at Brainwave are limited. Of course, the weather can never be relied upon. A buffet lunch was to be provided and it was determined that, to ensure the best outcome, a marquee should be erected in the grounds. This was to be dressed with blue ribbon, and photos of children using the various facilities hung around the walls. One hundred guests plus staff were invited. Everyone was allocated to a group in accordance with their status and given a name badge which included the number of their group; this number also reflected their position in the marquee where they were to be introduced to the countess. Guests were invited to attend 30 minutes before the royal party's arrival, when they were served with wine and canapés and formally welcomed by the chairperson. He also briefed them on the proceedings.

We were keen to fill the site that day with children. It was an opportunity to make a statement about the charity's position both within the local community and as a national provider of home-based therapy programmes for children with developmental delay. The local special school, whose children were to use the pool, were invited to attend. We provided lunch and, recognising that royal events can be tedious affairs for that age group, hired a professional clown who entertained the children throughout.

After the arrival of the countess and during her tour of the facilities, the buffet lunch was served. At the agreed time, the countess joined our guests in the marquee, by which time the principal host of each group had gathered the group members together and positioned them in the appropriate area. While this may sound rather formal and staged, in fact it worked extremely well and ensured that everyone was introduced in a timely fashion. The small groups (those on the 'A' list) were given more individual time. A brass plaque had been prepared and mounted in one corner of the marquee. The usual curtain drawing ceremony was enacted and speeches of thanks and acknowledgements concluded the royal visit.

Each group was accompanied to a different facility, so by the end of the tour everyone had experienced the interaction in each room. While the royal visit was potentially the highlight for many of our guests, in fact the enthusiasm of the staff was commented upon very favourably and this was fed back to them in a comprehensive debriefing the following day.

The fundraising appeal for the pool in fact took five years in all, not four, but many of the names listed on the board of appreciation, which still hangs on the wall outside the pool, remain committed supporters of the charity. More than four years have elapsed since that event took place and the charity's finances are now much stronger. The opening of the hydrotherapy pool was in one sense a turning point in the charity's 24-year history. It has provided literally hundreds of children with their first true experience of independent movement.

The mountain was climbed and the final summit reached. Everyone who took part in that event remembers it as exceeding their expectations and it proved to be the springboard for ongoing appeals.

5.3 Sporting and challenge events

Figure 9: 'Would you sponsor me? I'll be walking from the television to the fridge' (reproduced with kind permission of *Private Eye*)

Sporting and challenge events have increased in popularity over the last ten years. The phenomenon began with sponsored runs and bungee jumps and has developed into worldwide challenges, cycling, climbing and trekking events. With increasing demands on the public for funds, new ways of generating income have had to be created. Charities have to excite their supporters, and challenge events are a way to do this. The appeal for these types of event is not confined to the younger generation; many older people have found a great deal of enjoyment in participating in sponsored events.

Risk plays a very important part in people's lives. We are all protected increasingly from risk, especially children, and yet a certain element of risk is appealing and perhaps vital for our development. With no other outlets, it is thought that some resort to crime for the adrenalin rush. Having been heavily involved in sport, I know from firsthand experience the pleasure that children and older people get from taking that risk and achieving success. It is no wonder that challenge events have grown in popularity. They are becoming more innovative, from trekking in Peru to cycling or walking the Great Wall of China.

For participants there is a high level of achievement which, for some, can be life-changing: hidden qualities and skills emerge, with an increase in self-esteem. For the corporate sector, it is a great way to improve technical skills, fitness and motivation. Companies are seeing a growing need to incorporate teambuilding for their employees. Introducing challenge events and giving support to a charity combine their corporate responsibility as well as building successful teams.

5.3.1   How to organise sporting and challenge events

5.3.1.1   Is it for you?

You have to decide whether running challenge events is a viable operation for your charity. You will need to evaluate carefully the costs, return and impact on staffing, as these events are very labour-intensive. Managing a challenge event in-house can take considerable time and effort. However, some charities are finding that this method of fundraising brings a good return on investment, and that it pays to set up their own departments to manage challenge events.

There are now a number of companies whose job it is to manage challenge events, including overseas treks for charities (see Appendix 2). If you do embark on this method of fundraising, weigh up the pros and cons. Speak to other charities about their experiences and take recommendations. Thoroughly inspect and examine any company you want to work with, to make sure that it is up to scratch.

5.3.1.2 Advantages and disadvantages to sporting and challenge events

Advantages	Disadvantages
• They attract a large audience	• They are labour-intensive and potentially costly – keep an eye on cost/income ratios
• They are suitable for a wide range of ages, incomes and both sexes. They particularly attract a younger age group (typically thirties to fifties)	• With activity and challenges comes a higher than normal degree of risk of injury to participants – make sure proper processes are in place to manage risk, and that there is suitable insurance
• For participants there is a high level of achievement which for some can be life-changing; hidden qualities and skills emerge and an increase in self-esteem	• Because the charity relies on generating income from sponsorship obtained by the participant, there can be problems when trying to collect money
• For the corporate sector, it is a great way to improve technical skills, fitness and motivation. Companies are seeing a growing need to incorporate teambuilding for their employees. Introducing challenge events and giving support to a charity combines their corporate responsibility as well as building successful teams	
• Once planning processes are in place, these events can be easily repeated using the same formula, if it proves successful	
• They offer opportunities to raise awareness for your cause	
• They can help to showcase the work of the charity, giving participants firsthand experience which makes them more engaged and a more enthusiastic supporter for life	

5.3.1.3 Type of challenge event

You need to consider your own organisational capabilities and the type of audience that you are aiming to appeal to in order to decide what type of event to organise. Some types are smaller scale and easier to manage as an entry-level event, to build up your experience and confidence before going on to more ambitious events. However, as will be mentioned in the case example below, even challenge events abroad can be accessed by relatively small or inexperienced charities, if you can obtain a place on an open event run by a reputable and experienced company.

Event	Audience	Venue	Issues
Family fun run	Families, those who do not participate in serious sporting activities, open to all	Park, racecourse, sports field, country house grounds – obtain permission from local council or landowners	Consider access, numbers in the audience, whether you will also be arranging food, drink, first aid services, toilets Will you need a PA and stage for a fun warm up, entertainment and announcing winners and special runners?
Sponsored swim	All age groups, from school to adult. All skill levels can be included. Good corporate team event	Local swimming pool, health club or school. Obtain permission and booking from owners	Health and safety issues, appropriate levels of supervision, access for both swimmers and audience, crowd control
Serious sporting challenge – triathlon, 'Iron Man', marathon	People who take sport and training seriously	Street, parks, docks, swimming pools. Will need permission of local council, landowners, and police if roads are to be closed	Make sure participants are aware of required levels of fitness and safety (drinking enough water, protection from the sun, etc.) Have first aid providers on hand Take advice from sports governing bodies regarding rules and regulations and how to organise events properly Consider the needs of onlookers and supporters – do you need to provide food, drink, toilet facilities?

National outdoor challenge: Three Peaks; national paths (Coast-to-Coast, West Highland Way, Ridgeway, etc.)	Various levels of fitness and training required, depending on the route and challenge	Footpaths or open access land. If private land, get permission of the landowners	Consider access and safety requirements Make sure participants are aware of required levels of fitness, orienteering and safety and survival skills and equipment Have emergency contact numbers, and ensure that team leaders will contact base to sign out when the challenge is safely completed. If no call is received by the expected time, have an emergency back-up plan Let mountain rescue and other emergency services know when your event is, and have a record of who is supposed to be where Follow the Institute of Fundraising Code of Best Practice in challenge events – do not have too many people descending on one peak, start too early or finish too late – think about the impact on locals
International challenge and adventure (e.g. trekking in Peru, cycling in the Atlas Mountains, canoeing, whitewater rafting)	Fit and adventurous people. Can be aimed at gap-year young people, but thirties, forties and fifties are likely to have more access to sponsorship	Various areas, usually focusing on a landscape feature abroad. Generally best to arrange permissions via an experienced company	Do a thorough risk assessment of activities and areas to be visited You need to ensure that you are not acting as a travel agent Ensure that appropriate insurance is in place

5.3.1.4 Finding and signing up participants

Your methods of marketing the event will depend on your target audience and the nature of the event itself. If you are organising a family fun run or your own sponsored swim, then you can produce mailshots and sponsorship forms cheaply in-house and market through a local paper, groups and schools.

For externally organised sponsored swims, participants can be recruited in the same way as well as targeting local health clubs, swimming and other sports clubs. You might approach local businesses which could enter a team (or competitive teams) as part of their involvement in the community. For national and international challenges, target your existing supporters at first. You can advertise nationally, but this can be expensive and is usually advisable only if you have an established programme of successful challenges.

Research your timings so that your event does not clash with another challenge or national event. You are likely to be aiming for the same market of keen runners, climbers or hillwalkers, so the added competition may deter entries from your event, particularly if the other is more established. If you are fortunate enough to have a 'golden ticket' for the London Marathon, you may find that keen runners approach you as their way to secure a heavily rationed place at the event. This is an opportunity for you to provide them with more information about your charity as they go through training and fundraising, supporting them on the day of the challenge. If you get this right, you could find that you have converted them into loyal supporters who will get involved in more events and fundraising in the future.

You are likely to have a practical limit on the number of participants you can have at any one event, and you need to consider in advance how you will decide who can take part, if you are oversubscribed. You may choose 'first come, first served' as the simplest option, or you may require pledges of minimum amounts of sponsorship to be raised. You need to decide in advance whether to charge an entry fee; this may cover your costs or you may need some of the sponsorship money as well. The important thing is to be absolutely clear about this area in advance, both with the participant and with any potential sponsors.

5.3.1.5 Providing information and support to participants

You will need to provide some information in advance of potential participants signing up, to make sure that they understand what they are being challenged to do, and to ensure that they are up to the challenge. Information should include the following:

- dates
- times
- accessibility
- realistic minimum fitness levels
- minimum and maximum numbers in any groups
- minimum amounts to be paid or raised in sponsorship.

Once the participants are signed up or have registered, you may wish to provide further information and support to help them get the most out of the event. If you can team up with professionals in the relevant sport to provide week-by-week training guides, this will help people to prepare themselves physically for the challenge. Make sure that any guidance includes advice on warming up and down, and what to do in the event of an injury (usually guide them towards their GP or sports physiotherapist).

For overseas events, be sure to obtain and pass on accurate information regarding tropical diseases and other illnesses, for example dehydration, and recommend that the participants receive appropriate vaccinations and take appropriate preventive and protective action (for example, not drinking local water, eating salads, ice cubes, etc; having appropriate clothing for the climate; using mosquito nets and repellents, etc.).

Since completing the challenge is only one part of the event, and raising funds is the focus for you, it is a good idea to provide some guidance, tips and encouragement for participants' fundraising efforts. Sending out packs with sponsorship forms and a basic toolkit of ideas, along with some guidance on what they can and cannot do (for example, with the charity's logo), would be a great help to those who may not know where to start. Placing advice in a section of your website is increasingly helpful, and you can include a blog or forum facility for those participants who want to share their fears, tips and triumphs.

5.3.1.6 At the event

The exact management of the event itself will depend on what kind of challenge you are holding. If participants and spectators are gathering in one place, you will need to consider the traffic and crowd control methods mentioned in previous sections. Consider whether you need participants to sign in or register on the day, or whether you can get them to do this in advance and issue them with running numbers which they bring with them. The track or course should be well signed and laid out, with volunteer marshalls positioned around the course to direct people, cheer them on and deal with any emergencies which might arise. You will need a PA system to keep people informed of the start times of various races, to tell spectators about finish times, and relate any particular stories about the achievement of participants. Consider whether you want to have a stage with fitness instructors leading a warm-up. You will need to have first aid or St John Ambulance points, and water and food available (whether free or paid for), portaloos and rubbish bins (although the site still needs to be cleared afterwards). Also, consider providing goody bags and medals for all who complete the challenge (usually sponsored by a variety of companies that provide tasters for the bags).

For a more dispersed event, you will need a central control centre, and ask teams or individuals to sign in and out, notifying them in advance of their routes. Make sure that you have contact numbers, and that there is a signal to reach them (the tops of hills in remote places may be fine, but the valleys may not).

5.3.1.7 After the event: dealing with the money

The key thing for the charity is to be able to bank the sponsorship money pledged. This is the purpose for which you have worked hard to arrange the event and support the participants to achieve the challenge; often the hardest challenge is getting the money in afterwards. Encourage people to use websites such as JustGiving (www.justgiving.com), where sponsorship is collected automatically and passed on to the charity. There is a small fee, and a contractual relationship which should be looked at carefully, as with all such arrangements.

Otherwise, along with your letter of thanks and congratulations to the participants on completing the challenge, remind them of the final stage – returning the sponsorship money. You may need to plan a couple of follow-up letters or emails at intervals of a few weeks, perhaps putting forward a deadline for all sponsorship to be in, encouraging participants with news of the amounts submitted so far.

Case study: challenge events – an organiser's perspective

Jeremy Gane, director, Charity Challenge and Secretary, Community Projects Africa

Figure 10: The Inca Trail: a distinctive challenge event location (reproduced with kind permission of Charity Challenge)

The history

More than ten years ago, NSPCC asked me to organise an ambitious fundraiser: a climb of Mount Kilimanjaro followed by a trek across the floor of the African Rift Valley in the company of Masai warriors. NSPCC was not only looking to raise money from its cause but also, by promoting such a high-profile event, it was able to gain a wider awareness of the charity's work. The expedition was a very big success; it was reported in *The Times*, and within a couple of years we were organising fundraising expeditions for many UK and Irish registered charities. Soon it became necessary to set up a completely new company to take on the management of charity challenges. Now, as a director of Charity Challenge, I help to organise more than 120 expeditions each year to destinations in every corner of the world. They have become an integral fundraising tool for charities in the UK and Ireland and raise millions of pounds every year for hundreds of worthwhile causes.

Which expedition should I choose?

In the early days, we thought that unusual expeditions might attract more participants, but in fact we soon learned that the 'Big Four' (Everest Base

Camp, Inca Trail, Kilimanjaro, Great Wall of China) were the most successful, and they fill up year after year. This does not mean that more alternative challenges do not work. Some charities work with clubs of cyclists, runners, kayakers, equestrians or other disciplines to design challenges which suit their members. At Charity Challenge, we offer open challenges such as horseriding in Mongolia, cycling in India and rafting in Mexico, in addition to the more popular challenge classics. Many charities have challenges designed to fit in with overseas project visits.

How do I start?

For most charities, it is hard to get a unique event off the ground and recruit enough people from their existing database to do one tour with one type of challenge and one level of difficulty in one country at one time of year. Some will want a softer challenge, some cannot get time off at the right time, some will prefer a bike ride, etc. So we advise any charity considering events for the first time to offer a range of open challenges (for example, www.charitychallenge.com), where supporters of several charities participate on the one expedition, and see what response they get. A leaflet or email mentioning dates for open events such as Kilimanjaro, Everest Base Camp and the Inca Trail would cost next to nothing and yet could raise valuable funds for your charity. One person climbing Kilimanjaro on an open challenge will raise at least £1,500 for the charity (net), and of course, open expeditions run year round, so that supporters can choose the dates that suit them best. If most of your supporters respond to one style or type of challenge, you will have some funds being raised to give you confidence to plan something bigger as an exclusive, and you will have the confidence that an exclusive event should work for your charity.

Check out the companies offering challenges. Do not necessarily go for the cheapest. Rather, go for the company that gives good service, does most of the administration for you, and can show you references from other charities which have used that company. You should aim to recruit most participants through your existing database of contacts; do not base an event on adverts in magazines, etc. – they can be very expensive and yield minimal response. Your existing supporters are definitely the first people you should be targeting.

How are the expeditions funded?

Generally, there are two ways that participants can fund an expedition.

- *Self-funder* – with this option, participants personally cover the full cost of the expedition (which includes a donation to the charity). This means that the charity receives an initial donation plus every penny that the participant raises thereafter. The full cost is made up of the deposit due at the time of booking, and the balance normally due about eight weeks before departure.

- *Minimum sponsorship* – with this option, the participant pays their deposit when booking the expedition and pledges to raise a minimum amount of sponsorship for the charity. They send their sponsorship money to the charity as they raise it. At least 80 per cent of the minimum sponsorship must be sent to the charity about ten weeks before departure, along with pledges for the remaining 20 per cent (which normally are due within four to six weeks of returning to the UK). If participants raise the necessary funds, the charity will then pay the balance of the expedition costs (which should not exceed 45 per cent of the minimum sponsorship target). The charity benefits by keeping the remaining sponsorship money.

For example, the participant pays the deposit at the time of booking the challenge (£300) and then commits to raise a minimum sponsorship in aid of the charity (£2,500). They must send 80 per cent of the minimum sponsorship to the charity ten weeks before departure (i.e. £2,000). At this time, the charity will pay the balance of the expedition costs (45 per cent of £2,500 = £1,125). The participant has to send the remaining sponsorship money to the charity within six weeks of completing the challenge. Typically, the charity keeps about £1,500 of the minimum sponsorship, and of course any monies which are raised over and above the minimum sponsorship.

What about the safety of supporters and money?

The top companies which organise these challenges are experienced in providing proper risk assessment, dealing with emergencies, ensuring health and safety precautions, making complex travel arrangements, managing environmental and cultural issues and being aware of the ethics surrounding fundraising for overseas expeditions.

The charity representative should grill anyone offering to organise a challenge and ask for a risk assessment, tour operator public and product liability insurance, ATOL licence or equivalent and, most importantly, a series of references from other charities showing that the expedition company is sound and well respected. Should the company be booking flights, then find out about its licence to do so and discuss which airlines it uses and why. Ask the company how it checks the quality and safety of the overseas companies it uses. Discuss rescue and repatriation procedures for supporters, should they become ill or injured.

Make sure the expeditions are supported by a good level of local leadership, medical support and so forth. Most expeditions will be risk assessed, carry first aid provisions, have first aid qualified staff and a satellite phone for emergency communication.

What are the risks to the charity that I should consider?

It is important to make sure that the charity is not legally liable if anything goes wrong, and so the charity should not be the party with which the participant is contracting for the running of the tour. All booking forms should be with the tour operator and the charity should be linked only through its fundraising requirements. The tour operator should comply with the relevant travel and charity laws, including the Package Travel, Package Holidays and Package Tours Regulations 1992, 1995 and 1998, the Civil Aviation Authority (Air Travel Organisers' Licence) Regulations 1995 and 1996, and the requirements of the Charities Act 2006, insofar as they relate to this type of fundraising adventure. Participants whose personal benefits exceed £500 in any year become a 'professional fundraiser' under the Charities Act 1992, and therefore must have a formal agreement with the charity confirming certain minimum terms. This relates to a charity challenge expedition where the charity is contributing towards the participant's costs.

Make sure that participants have travel insurance provided as part of the challenge, or that it is a compulsory element for people to obtain their own. Where possible, make sure that the insurance provided also covers the charity, should the charity be committed to paying towards the costs of the event through sponsorship monies. Insurance should cover at the very least medical emergency, medical evacuation and medical repatriation.

If you decide to organise an exclusive challenge, be aware of signing a contract, paying a set-up fee or committing to a 'minimum' number of people in order for the trip to run. Many charities make this mistake and lose money rather than raising it. You should not pay any kind of set-up fee unless you are asking the tour operator to do something unique for you.

What about the environment?

Environmental issues are increasingly a concern: both the charity and the expedition organisers must make serious (not token) efforts to offset their carbon emissions. For example, planting seven trees through carbon neutral programmes offsets the average annual carbon emission of one adult who has one annual holiday. Furthermore, as responsible travellers, we must minimise any impact on overseas cultures and environments.

There are great opportunities to work with helpers on the walk and local people to develop cultural tourism, which will provide an important source of income to enable people to retain their traditional lifestyles as well as giving a valuable and memorable insight to visitors. There are also opportunities for challenge organisers to work hand-in-hand to improve the way in which local helpers treat the environment (rubbish disposal, camp latrines, wear and tear on popular trails), their staff (salaries and work conditions) and their animals, such as mules for the trekking. Well run, environmentally responsible tourism can do so much good, not only to the charity receiving the funds, but also to the people's and the environment of the area where the challenge takes place. It is very exciting to help to plan and run such expeditions.

Can my charity claim back Gift Aid on donations made?

Basically, any outright donations (that is, not a deposit, fee or payment for any perceived benefit to the participant) can be given under Gift Aid to enhance the value to the charity. If some of the sponsorship is to cover the cost of the trip, then special rules apply (see section 4.10 and check the latest position on the HMRC website).

Challenge events really do work. In 1997, we sent 30 NSPCC supporters to Tanzania. By 2009 we sent more than 2,500 supporters from numerous charities to the four corners of the world.

Case study: WaterAid Sydney Regatta 2006–07

Alan Machin, national fundraising manager, WaterAid

Figure 11: WaterAid 'Sail for Water', Sydney, Australia (reproduced with kind permission of WaterAid)

WaterAid's vision is of a world where everyone has access to safe water and effective sanitation. WaterAid works in partnership with local organisations to help poor communities establish sustainable water supplies and sanitation, close to home. WaterAid also works to influence governments' water and sanitation policies to serve the interests of vulnerable people. Originally established in the UK in 1981, WaterAid has grown into an international charity which now operates as WaterAid UK, WaterAid Australia and WaterAid USA. The objectives of the event were to raise funds for WaterAid overseas projects and to launch WaterAid 'Sail for Water' in Sydney as an annual yacht event.

Planning process

The planning process for a regatta should start at least a year before the actual event. Organising a regatta is a mammoth task and there is a lot to be considered before taking on such an event. Here is a step-by-step process of what we did to get this up and running.

Step 1: volunteer committee – WaterAid is in a unique position where we have a strong member base of corporate supporters from the water industry. A corporate member who had a keen interest in sailing and who is indeed one of the top female sailors in Australia approached WaterAid to run Australia's first sailing regatta. After an initial meeting, it was decided that the concept of a regatta was a good one. A small organising committee of six people was set up to plan the event, using WaterAid's strong member base in the water industry. An email was sent to all WaterAid fundraising champions and contacts to ask if other Sydneysider members would be interested in being involved in the committee.

Step 2: secure the sailing venue and date – it is important that a good local club is chosen, one which runs these types of events as the norm. In this way you can tap into the club's expertise and event management. Most yacht clubs have many sailing events throughout the sailing season, and it is vital that an initial meeting is held to see when you can hold your event, to make sure that it fits in with the yacht club's other sailing events. Normally, this will have to be approved by the yacht club's board, which can take a few months. It is important to note that you cannot produce any materials until the date is signed off by the board, so confirm this as soon as possible, otherwise you may find yourself getting sponsorship brochures out with only two months to go.

Step 3: develop the sponsorship brochure – again, it is vital that the sailing club approves any copy for the brochure. For the 2007 regatta, we decided on having one major sponsor at AUS$25,000, two mid-range at AUS$10,000 and three supporting sponsors at AUS$5,000. The sponsorship list included a further list of running cost items such as photographer, band or cocktail function costs which could be sponsored at cost.

In 2006, we just approached water industry contacts for sponsorship, but for the second year we opened this up to the following markets:

- suppliers or contractor of our members;
- companies which have a vested interest in the countries we are working in, for example, a mining company working in Papua New Guinea;
- companies which are currently sponsoring other sailing events.

Step 4: secure donated yachts – two of the main areas that are critical to the success of a regatta are having yachts donated and securing teams for the yachts. What is critical is using skipper contacts and requesting that they do a lot of the legwork in finding yachts for the day. However, if this fails, building a close relationship with the sailing office at your venue is recommended.

Most sailing offices have noticeboards and send out weekly or monthly newsletters to their supporters. Writing a piece for this and ensuring it is circulated to yacht members is suggested. Make sure that you explain what your organisation does as part of this email, as your skippers will want to know what it is they are supporting. It is also worth requesting that notices are put up on noticeboards around the club, to add impact. It was worth WaterAid's while having a good relationship with the sailing office, as it is constantly meeting skippers as they come into the club, or maybe even conducting a presentation, so you have total buy-in from them.

Step 5: confirm teams – this was one of the biggest challenges that WaterAid Australia met when conducting our inaugural regatta. Many saw it as a day off work, or a little expensive to pay as a teambuilding exercise, so it was a real challenge filling spots on the boats.

We developed a beautiful brochure that was sent out to our contacts and members, but still did not get the response that we had hoped for: we did all the obvious marketing, emailing contacts, a direct mail with the brochure, but what worked best for us was actually calling our contacts. In this way we could allay any issues that they had with the cost, and it gave us the opportunity to talk about our work. This was important for WaterAid Australia, as we are a relatively new charity in the Australian market. (Many potential attendees also thought that they had to be a sailor to be involved, which was not the case, as the yachts donated also included a full crew.) Calling our contacts gave us a list of people who were interested but for one reason or another were unable to attend, yet wanted to know about next year's event. It is my plan to offer previous attendees and interested parties an 'early bird' entry fee for next year's event.

Most of our marketing activity is centred on our contacts in the water industry, sailing magazines and website. For a March event we plan to start communicating about the event to our WaterAid email list as early as eight months before. We also look at all the sailing magazines and put together a list of their publishing and deadline dates. Other marketing activity will be promoting the event via the Australian water industry's email list, putting flyers in other sailing clubs and on the Australian Water Association and WaterAid websites. It is also beneficial to make use of any high-value contacts you may have, those on your committee or those supporters who may be high-ticket value whom you have met throughout the year and invite to enter a team.

The agenda for the event looked as follows:

12:15 Arrive at yacht club for registration, including race gear bag – initially at our first regatta we had people arriving quite early. However, a later arrival is suggested, as we found that the people who got there early ended up hanging around unnecessarily.

13:00 Race briefing – this is carried out by the sailing club at the venue and is mostly for the skippers and sailing crew.

13:30 Go to yachts – as we provided lunch, many of the skippers decided to have lunch before getting on board. It is probably worth checking with the skippers if they are happy for the teams to eat lunch on the boat. Many of the teams were eager to get out on the open harbour and waiting took some of the excitement away.

13:45 Leave yacht club marina, tour of harbour – this is where the teams decide how much involvement on the yacht they want. They can decide to be one of the crew or sit back and relax and enjoy the sea air. For us in Sydney it was important for the skipper to do a tour of the harbour so everyone could get their photo taken as they sailed past the Opera House.

14:15 Race start (around the islands).

16:30 Race finish (approximately, depends on the wind).

17:00 Return to yacht club.

17:30 Cocktail party and award ceremony.

19:00 Close.

We were lucky that we had a good relationship with our yacht club venue. Sailing is dependent on wind and the class of boats that you have. Some travel faster than others, and if you have a strong wind you could find yourself with a room full of thirsty sailors! We were lucky in that the first yacht got in about 30 minutes earlier then expected, but as the cocktail lounge started to fill, our event crew were happy to put drinks out a little earlier than planned.

WaterAid Australia really wanted an event that people would want to come back to, so part of our party was providing canapés to add that extra edge to the day. Yachting is an expensive sport and you really need to take full advantage of the scenery, venue and eloquence of such an event. In addition, we felt it was important to present high-quality trophies, and we found people viewing the trophies prior to the event, hoping that their team would be the one taking that prize home.

There are many options open to a charity to stage sporting events; they do take considerable time to set up, and embarking on a major sporting or challenge event requires professional advice and support. However, the positive side is the amount of public awareness raised, and the increase in support, which can be very rewarding and beneficial for the charity.

5.3.1.8   Planning a sporting or challenge event

Checklist

- What audience are you aiming towards?
- What type of event do you want to run?
- Are you managing in-house or employing a challenge event company?
- Does the event need a designated route or venue?
- Is it insured?
- Has a risk assessment been conducted?
- How are you getting information about the event to participants?
- How will you register participants?
- Is there a limit to the number of participants?
- Will you have an entry fee?
- Will you have a minimum sponsorship level?
- What support will you offer to help with training or raising funds?
- How will you collect sponsorship from the event?
- Are there further opportunities to raise funds?
- Do you need to provide anything for supporters or participants (changing facilities, portaloos, food, drink, water, entertainment, goody bags)?

5.4   Musical and cultural events

A large number of events involve music in some way. Music brings people together; it creates an atmosphere of well-being and sets the scene. Music can be used as an unobtrusive background at a drinks reception and will cover any awkward silences as guests arrive. It is for you to decide whether music will be the primary focus of the event, a pleasant interlude or background.

The processes involved in staging musical events have much in common with the other types of event described elsewhere in the book. This section will look at the ideas and issues particular to musical and cultural events.

5.4.1 How to organise musical and cultural events

5.4.1.1 First or preview night at the opera or theatre

This involves working in collaboration with an opera or theatre company to obtain access to tickets which have an exclusive nature, such as a preview night, possibly combined with access to the artists after the performance or a backstage tour. You need to decide whether to have a reception before the performance, during the interval or at the end of the evening. My suggestion is to go for one or two out of the three, but no more – do not gild the lily. A reception at the beginning and the end is often ideal, particularly if there is an opportunity to meet the cast. In addition, it might be possible to include a dinner, but be aware of the practical implications of organising essentially two events in one (see section 5.1 on dinners), especially if you have to book a different venue for dinner if the preview venue is not suitable. Not all guests may find their own way from one venue to another, so you may need to consider hiring a coach.

Whatever your desired programme, you will need to make contact with a theatre or concert hall and work together on this project, once you have established a mutual rapport. As a partnership project, it is all the more important to establish in advance who takes responsibility for what, and to maintain clarity about division of responsibilities and financial return.

5.4.1.2 Singalong in a local church, hall or theatre

Singalongs have proved to be very successful for a number of charities. The basic premise of singalong is that choirs of all ages come together to sing. It is absolutely vital to have a good choirmaster or conductor to hold the groups together. The music can be anything from 'The Hallelujah Chorus' to Gershwin and songs from the shows or films – the list is endless, but consider your target audience and pick a strong and marketable theme. Most choirs jump at the opportunity to sing in a large group and perform pieces of music which normally perhaps they would not tackle. Choirs usually have a certain amount of time to rehearse individually, and are brought together for rehearsal only on the morning of the performance or perhaps the day before – make sure you agree with the choirmaster at an early stage what the rehearsal requirements will be, as you will need to factor this into your venue booking. If orchestral accompaniment is required, consider approaching local music schools or youth orchestras, which may be glad of the opportunity to showcase their skills in support of your event.

The audience for such events is usually made up largely from relatives, friends, supporters and the general public who love to hear this type of music. Therefore, word-of-mouth marketing is a very important part of the success of these events; as there is a large number of singers, this provides a good base for getting the audience in. However, consider targeted marketing in the relevant music press, local 'What's On' papers and online to broaden the potential reach.

You can either charge for a ticket and/or take a collection at the end. It would be nice to serve refreshments if the audience is not too large, the venue setting allows for this and your local volunteers are happy to do it. Again, either charge or at least give the opportunity for a further donation. An event such as this should be seen as an opportunity to network and raise the profile of your charity among the audience. Use the programme to provide more information about the charity, and provide opportunities for supporters to send a donation and offer their time. The programme itself could be funded by local companies, shops and businesses sponsoring an advert in the programme or local press – another opportunity to build relations for the future.

5.4.1.3   Picnic in the park with orchestra

A picnic in the park can be a very worthwhile and well-supported event. Throughout the UK during the summer, many stately homes and even corporate organisations with large grounds put on musical events of this type. This may be an opportunity to work in collaboration with one of these organisations, again following the guidelines mentioned earlier in the book about ensuring that division of responsibilities and financial benefit are clear and in writing to avoid any misunderstandings.

If it is impractical for your charity to enter into such a partnership, or you want a more intimate event, consider a smaller location where you could have an orchestra and guests come with their picnics to enjoy an evening of music with their family and friends. Local schools or universities may have suitable grounds, or you could use local parks, for which you would need the permission of the local authority.

Although picnics are outdoor events, usually the weather does not appear to be a problem. Normal UK summer weather is catered for by putting the orchestra on a stage with a cover to protect the musicians if it rains. The picknickers do not seem to have their spirits dampened by rain either – they usually come armed with blankets, large umbrellas and a cheerful determination to enjoy themselves, whatever the weather. That said, it is still worth making emergency plans in the event of truly awful weather – contingencies for alerting people in the event of cancellation, and insurance to cover any costs which may be incurred if the event cannot go ahead.

The guests will bring their own picnics and provide the necessary equipment themselves, so the main problem is organising car parking, marshalling arrivals and departures, and making provision for litter collection both during and after the event. Be aware that guests usually arrive well before the concert starts, to enjoy their picnic in daylight – be sure to give the time on the tickets when the gates open and allow the car parking attendants plenty of time to set up. Selling the tickets before the event will save you having to slow down cars on arrival. However, it may pay you to have an alternative avenue roped off for tickets at the gate.

For added income, you could franchise some outlets such as a Pimms bar, coffee and tea (welcome for guests if it turns cold during the evening), ice cream or pre-purchase of hampers and champagne. Again, consider selling a sponsored programme as a guide to the evening, an opportunity to let people know about your charity (and a chance to give further donations), and as a memento. Marketing such events may be done in partnership with the venue. Target your database of supporters, and remember to talk to local radio as well as advertising through flyers and posters.

Make the most of the occasion and the outdoor venue, and finish the evening on a high with your finale. If your budget allows, fireworks can be spectacular, whether or not teamed with an appropriately rousing piece of music. If fireworks are not appropriate, consider another way of both marking the end of the evening and sending guests away on a high.

5.4.1.4 Musical masterclasses

Masterclasses are perhaps more niche, but are popular. The three key elements are a musician who is able to offer tuition at a high standard, preferably someone who is well known in their field; apt pupils who will benefit from first class tuition; and an audience with an interest and empathy in this area of music – often the friends and family of the pupils, or other members of a music society or school which can provide pupils.

Use the information available from music schools, colleges and the internet, but recommendation is vital. Performers will have videos to demonstrate their ability, but you must be reassured that they have a strong empathy with the audience you are targeting. Remember that modern as well as classical music can be popular, and that children and young adults with learning difficulties, or those who are visually impaired, can respond well to music and should not be precluded from such an event.

5.4.1.5 Location

Whether indoors or out, when creating a musical event the most important factor is whether the audience can hear the performance. The musical director or a member of the group whose responsibility it is to check and install the sound equipment will assist with this. (The majority of musicians I have worked with have been very professional and go to great lengths in order to achieve the sound they want.)

5.4.1.6 Equipment and preparation

You may have to hire a piano, and there are stores which hire, deliver and tune the instrument. The piano is usually tuned on delivery and then again about an hour before the performance. You will need to book well in advance and arrange with the venue owner the best time for delivery, and whether there is suitable access to the building. If using a piano at an outdoor event, the owner will need assurance that there is suitable shelter for the instrument.

Most concert and theatre venues will have staging available for you, but you may need to hire your own, either to accommodate a larger choir at a singalong, for example, or to construct a complete stage with covering for an outdoor event. If you do not have a known or recommended supplier, you can source them on the internet (see Appendix 2).

If you have to supply your own sound equipment, microphones and speakers, then seek recommendations or source them from reputable websites (see Appendix 2), and get several quotes. Sometimes retailers at the sophisticated end of the retail market may be pleased to help, provided that they can gain from some publicity. The sound equipment companies should provide a detailed list of the requirements suitable for the venue. Once you have found a company that suits your needs, confirm all agreements in writing (such as ongoing technical support throughout the event) and be there when it is setting up at the venue.

Case study: Mozart on the Move

Celia Davies, MBE, trustee and artistic director, Heritage Music and Peckleton Arts

Background

This case study is an account of a series of three professional orchestral concerts in 2006 celebrating the 250th anniversary of the birth of Mozart.

The concerts were part of the 2006–07 season presented and promoted by Peckleton Arts, a not-for-profit organisation founded in 1994. One of the main aims of Peckleton Arts is to bring professional orchestral concerts to the market towns and rural areas of Leicestershire and beyond where, because of local rural conditions including zero public transport, communities are completely without this arts provision.

Funding

The cost of the three concerts together was roughly £21,000. This amount was raised by contributions from a number of different funders including Leicestershire County Council, North-West Leicestershire District Council, Charnwood Borough Council, Loughborough University, Eastern Orchestral Board, The Arts Council, private patronage, Peckleton Arts and, of course, ticket income. The Graff Orchestra of England, London Mozart Players, and City of London Sinfonia were engaged for these events; all were chosen because the orchestral managements could supply the number of players and the type of programme required by Peckleton Arts to make the event commercially viable.

Venues

Concert halls do not exist in rural areas, so other venues had to be found which would serve the purpose. There are a number of requirements which a venue must have before it can be considered viable for this sort of concert. These include toilet and refreshment facilities, heating, adequate lighting for both orchestra and audience, sufficient pews or linked seating for the estimated audience, the correct number of chairs without arms for orchestral players, nearby rooms where orchestral players can change and wait for their call to come to the performing area, a stage or raised area, confirmation that public liability insurance for the venue is in place, space for tickets to be sold and programmes distributed and, if at all possible, parking.

Acoustics

It will be noticed that no mention is made of the word 'acoustics' as one of the requirements for finding a venue suitable for a professional orchestral concert. More hot air is expounded on this subject, most often by people who have little experience or knowledge of acoustics, than on practically any other subject connected with music. Obviously, one must beware of a venue which is thickly carpeted and has a preponderance of thick velvet curtains. If you are unsure of the quality of the acoustics, just walk about the room and give a single loud clap in different places; unless your clap sounds very muffled, do not worry about the acoustics.

Sight and sound

Sightlines for the audience are very important, and if you are selling tickets for a concert in a church, it is wise to price the tickets with this in mind. You are sure to get complaints from members of the audience if they have paid the top price for a ticket and then find themselves sitting behind a pillar. Take care, too, that during the orchestral rehearsal and performance there is no other sound invading your venue. If you are using a leisure centre as a concert hall, it is sensible to check in advance that the activities of the local pop group or football team are not taking place in the immediate neighbourhood.

Overcoming problems and finding opportunities

In one venue, a church where the concert opened a local arts festival, the Graff Orchestra of England presented the first half in eighteenth-century costume and imported candelabras in order to create a festive occasion. Many churches are insufficiently lit for musicians to be able to read music, but this problem is easily overcome by introducing portable lighting. Another venue, a wonderful auditorium with a stage for the orchestra and raised seating for the audience, lacked catering facilities. It was too far away from the nearest pub for the players to go out and get a meal and get back to the auditorium in the time allowed between the end of the rehearsal and the start of the concert; this problem was overcome by bringing a microwave oven into the venue for our caterer's use. The third venue was the sports hall of a modern leisure centre. It was not equipped with either staging or audience chairs, but by hiring in this furniture, a Leicestershire village discovered that it had a concert hall on its doorstep.

Marketing

Marketing a classical music concert correctly is vital for the success of the event. If you have never been involved in marketing music, take advice. Spend as much as you possibly can on marketing; remember the Hollywood adage – if it costs 1 million dollars to make the film then, for success, spend 10 million dollars on marketing it. Provided you have planned the distribution of your marketing material, the mix of leaflets, posters, media notices and some newspaper advertising will be a good basis for success.

Websites and e-marketing are essential. Of course, as we all know, the best marketing tool by far is word of mouth.

In the end, folk spend money on buying a ticket to listen to a professional orchestral concert in order to have an enjoyable social time. They have invested their time and money, have driven through traffic and then searched for a parking place before they have heard a note of music. Audiences need cherishing. Get your team to be really welcoming when members of the audience arrive; have clear signs up so that it is easy to find toilet facilities; provide them with an interesting programme and refreshment in the interval. Above all, get them to go home thinking that they have had really good value for their money. Then they will come back for more.

5.4.1.7 Literary lunch

If you have a local author or a contact with someone who is reasonably well-known, a literary lunch can prove a very rewarding way of holding a special event. The venue can be a hotel or any suitable venue with good catering facilities. This is an opportunity to create an intimate experience. You may consider a women-only lunch and invite local businesswomen as a means of recruiting suitable event committee members, or it can be open to both genders, depending on the author, of course.

Once you have decided on the author and have his or her agreement to speak at a lunch, then you need to target the audience. You could ask existing supporters to bring a guest and then you could network after the lunch is over. It would be good to include an opportunity for your guests either to bring or buy the author's latest book and have it signed.

5.4.1.8 'With great pleasure'

Another suggestion on the same theme is 'With great pleasure', following the concept of the popular BBC programme. Invite a well-known personality to a lunch or an evening reception and ask them to speak about the books, music, and poetry that give them the most pleasure. They may require one or two people to read passages for them, but you should be able to source these from local theatre groups or the performing arts department at your local schools or colleges.

Case study: Shugborough luncheons

Geraldine Mannion, corporate functions manager, Acorns Children's Hospice

Figure 13: Shugborough tree planting with Lord Lichfield (pictured with Viscount and Viscountess Linley, reproduced with kind permission of Acorns Children's Hospice)

Without any doubt, the highlight of my career at Acorns Children's Hospice has been to organise a special fundraising luncheon at Shugborough in Staffordshire each autumn, hosted by Lord Lichfield, founder patron of our charity. Unlike other events in the Acorns calendar, such as Marquee Week with its committee of a dozen people, Shugborough was my sole responsibility. I had to deal with high-profile, often extremely wealthy individuals who expected discretion at all times and who appreciated the personal touch. Attention to detail was imperative and I spent many hours researching the background of all our guests and planning with military precision the programme for the day.

For this sort of an event, my action plan (in essence a function sheet) became the most important piece of paper in my file. It helped enormously that I was the only person dealing with the suppliers, and they too were given a copy of my action plan, which highlighted very clearly what everyone had to do. The wonderful staff at Shugborough were given a copy, and I had several meetings with them before the big day, finally walking through the whole programme with the house staff and the key suppliers about a month in advance.

Lord Lichfield always invited one special guest who was a personal friend to help him to host the event, and our chief executive, chairperson and executive directors also acted as co-hosts on the day. Over the years, we have enjoyed the company of Viscount Linley and his wife; the author Frederick Forsyth, the French chef Raymond Blanc, the actor Nigel Havers and several television personalities. Needless to say, the year that Raymond Blanc joined us our caterers were a little more nervous than usual!

Upon arrival, guests were welcomed by the Earl's butler and treated to a champagne reception and canapés in the Earl's private quarters. Guests then enjoyed a gourmet luncheon in a wonderful dining room, which had a quite magical atmosphere. The fires would be lit, the candles glowing and the crystal and silverware gleaming. After lunch, Lord Lichfield would escort us to his arboretum, where each couple was invited to plant an oak sapling, personally selected by Lord Lichfield, which would be marked with a plaque bearing the guest's name as well as the variety of oak. Before departure, the guests were invited to visit the Lichfield display rooms with the Earl, to view his photographic exhibition and to hear the stories behind the pictures.

We have a wonderfully supportive vintner who provided the champagne free of charge for this event, and fabulous caterers who have been working with me for many years. Both have become friends of Acorns and have never let me down. As soon as I decided on the menu for the day, I could send it straight off to the vintner who would skilfully select the wines to match the food. The guests joining us were used to fine wines and wonderful food, so everything had to be the very best. I had to make sure that I used caterers used to working in field kitchens as, incredibly, there is no working kitchen at Shugborough (divine gourmet food was prepared on a terrace with no running water!)

Finally, each guest was presented with a special gift, and it was always a challenge for me to find something personal without spending too much money. One year, I found a company to design a presentation box (free of charge) to hold a bottle of Lichfield Gin, two specially engraved glasses, and a signed guide to the property. Another year, I managed to persuade local silversmiths to supply beautiful silver picture frames at cost, holding a limited edition print of an acorn taken by Lord Lichfield himself.

Finding a gift for the Earl, as a thank you from Acorns for opening his home to us and giving so generously of his time, was an even greater challenge. What to buy for the man who had everything? Possibly his favourite (and least expensive) gift from us was a reference book on rare trees, which were his passion. Lord Lichfield's PA kindly tipped me off that he knew the book was about to be published and was very keen to purchase a copy. He was totally amazed when he opened the gift!

Guests were invited to make a substantial (four figure) donation to Acorns, in order to experience something that money could not buy. In addition, by sharing in such an event they invariably bought in to the charity and went on to become wonderful ambassadors. Past Shugborough guests, who were at the time of joining us totally unknown to Acorns, have gone on to become major fundraisers and even trustees of our charity.

In the final year, tragically the luncheon had to be called off, due to the unexpected death of Lord Lichfield just a week before the event. It was testimony to the Earl's commitment to Acorns that his estate was still raising money for us after he died. His PA nominated us as sole beneficiary of the retiring collection at his memorial service at Lichfield Cathedral, and as joint beneficiary of the collection at the London memorial service. Furthermore, several guests who were due to have joined us at the luncheon made very generous donations to the charity in Lord Lichfield's memory, and not a single supplier penalised us for the late cancellation of the event, despite the fact that several of them must have been out of pocket.

We have so many happy memories of working with a charismatic and warm man who made everyone he spoke to feel special. Lord Lichfield is hugely missed by all of us who worked with him, and will never be forgotten. It was an honour and a privilege to have known and loved him, and he played a major part in making Acorns what it is today.

The next section looks at various other types of event which often are included in a special events manager's events plan. They do not quite come under the previous banners, although they may incorporate elements of music or culture, and provision of food and other forms of entertainment as mentioned before. Many of the key elements for organising such events are the same, but the section provides some examples of different types of event and how to make them successful.

The following types of events will be considered:

- conferences and meetings
- receptions
- family events
- festivals.

5.5 Conferences

There are many reasons why a charity may want to hold a conference – it may be to attract new donors and supporters, as a thank-you for corporate bodies or an annual supporters' conference. A conference can be used to celebrate the charity's work and say thank you to supporters, donors, volunteers and staff, and to display the growth and development of the organisation.

A conference, whether annual or, if the cost is prohibitive, every two years, is an important occasion for the charity. Key stakeholders will not only be present, but may want an input into the shape and content of the day. It is usually the special events department that is called upon to organise conferences and receptions, and it can be a huge task for the organisers, particularly given the stakeholder involvement. Therefore it is important right from the beginning to determine goals, objectives and budgets, and to be clear about who is going to be involved and who is stage managing the event. As with many other types of event, make sure you plan well enough in advance to allow for booking speakers, preparing the event and inviting delegates.

5.5.1 How to organise conferences

5.5.1.1 Planning the programme

First, you need to determine the objectives of the day and the nature of the delegates who will be attending. Next, you will need to brainstorm about a balanced variety of content that will fulfil the objectives and be interesting and attractive to delegates. Avoid having too many sessions, and make sure that you plan for enough comfort breaks and allow enough time for lunch, so that delegates can network. (The networking space is often what is praised most, even at the most highly organised conferences – so much so that there is a whole style of conference organisation based on it – called 'open space' meeting, where the agenda is set by the delegates themselves on the day. This is a specialist field of conference organising and will only work in certain circumstances; there is specialist literature which explains it in more depth – see www.wikipedia.org/wiki/Open_Space or www.co-intelligence.org.) Try to include a stimulating session after lunch, when delegates are more inclined to have a dip in energy.

5.5.1.2   Choosing speakers

Speakers should be invited after careful consideration. Again, bearing in mind the objectives of the day and the delegates, you may want to brainstorm potential speakers along with the content. Consider the following.

- Are they appropriate for the charity?
- Will they be sending out the 'right messages'?
- Will they be controversial (if that is what you want)?
- Do they come with a good track record and recommendations?
- Will they attract delegates?

Do not book a speaker that no one in your organisation has heard before in person. They may be very knowledgeable, but perhaps not so interesting when speaking. Always go on recommendation so that you are confident that they will be effective.

Once you have decided on the speakers, send them invitations. You need to make sure that speaker invitations are sent far enough in advance so that you can get your event in their diaries before they fill up, and so that you can invite back-up speakers if some of your first choices are unavailable. Depending on your relationship with the speakers, you may wish to make the initial approach face-to-face or by telephone, but make sure you follow up with paperwork (or email) explaining fully what is expected, when and where the event and their session will take place and any arrangements for accommodation and expenses that the charity will be providing. Once the speakers have confirmed, ask them for any information needed in advance – for example a short biography and outline of their session for inclusion in the conference programme. You may also want to know whether they need to use slides or other visual aids, and gain their approval for copies to be available for the delegates after the conference. It is useful to include deadlines for submitting material for the programme and when you need final notes and slides for packs you may provide on the day itself.

Top tips

These comments and tips have been collected from a number of colleagues and friends in the sector involved in speaking at conferences, about how not to treat speakers, adding some from my own experience:

- send out precise information on the venue and timing of the conference;
- brief the speaker regarding the audience's profile;
- be sure about times of presentation;
- always meet and greet speakers;
- allow speakers enough time to set up their presentation equipment;
- check that the visual aid equipment is functioning;
- remember to supply visual aid equipment, if you have agreed to supply it;
- brief staff that speakers need to be shown where they are presenting, and ensure that they are not abandoned;
- telll each presenter how long their presentation should last, and allowing presentations to overrun, thus hampering the next speaker;
- finally, at the end of the conference, show the presenters the way out, and thank them.

5.5.1.3 Stands and exhibitors' area

Depending on your venue and the object of the conference, you may wish to include an area for stands displaying aspects of your charity's work, or an opportunity for the event sponsors to have stands and displays for delegates to look at during breaks and networking time.

All departments at the charity should have a stand in reception or in the designated room (usually where coffee or tea breaks are held). (I have found that departments in a charity will welcome the chance to exhibit their work.) It will increase supporters' general knowledge of how the charity functions, and gives guests an opportunity to engage with members of staff. Staff also have the benefit of meeting supporters directly – something that they may not normally do.

You may find it helpful to provide display boards behind each table to provide a coordinated look, and encourage each team to present its work in an attractive manner. You will need to brief all staff, emphasising the impact you wish to make – tell them the key message you want to get across and the objectives of the conference. Stands should be tidy and clear of coffee cups, with display information being visual, with photographs and pictures and not too much text. People staffing the stands are there to engage with the supporters, and may need some training or briefing on how best to do that, without being either over pushy or too engaged in conversation with their colleagues to be available to supporters.

If external organisations (sponsors or other organisations that have bought space for a stand) are involved, similar considerations apply as to stallholders at external events. Make sure that everyone is aware of their particular space, what time they can arrive to set up, and what time they have to clear away at the end of the event. You will need to be clear upfront about what materials and equipment you will provide (consider whether you will be providing tables and display stands to keep a coordinated look) and what the standholders need to bring.

Consider the layout of the space, and whether there will be easy flow of people between stands. Remember that if this is the main space for people to spend breaks, there may be a lot of people converging on it at the same time and it needs to be able to cope with this.

5.5.1.4   Registration

It is usual to provide name badges for delegates, and this is an easy way to meet and greet them and keep records of who attended. If you have a delegate pack, hand it over at registration together with any goody bag which might be provided with the help of sponsors. It is a good idea also to provide name badges for staff, volunteers and standholders. Colour coding badges will help delegates to know who's who, and who they can ask for further information about the charity or the event. Make sure the pack contains a plan of the conference centre and a programme of events, and that all staff also have a copy of this, so that they can give information when required.

5.5.1.5   Venue and layout

There are many specialist conference centres and hotels which offer conference space: usually they will have experienced support teams to help you work out your room and layout needs, and provide all the facilities required when bringing a large number of people together. You may want to have a mix during the day of plenary talks and smaller breakout rooms for workshops or a choice of speakers.

Room set	Definition	Suitable for
Classroom	Rows of tables and chairs facing the front	Smaller groups. Presentations or lectures, particularly where delegates may want to make extensive notes
Theatre	Rows of chairs facing the front, usually with one or more access aisles. Often with a dais or platform at the front	Larger plenaries. Presentations, keynote speakers, panel debates or Q&A sessions
Herringbone	Rows of chairs are angled or curved, again facing towards the front	As above. Layout will depend on the shape of the room
Conference, boardroom, U-shape, T-shape	Eight-foot tables placed in different configurations, with chairs around	For smaller meetings and breakout sessions
Crescent or cabaret	Round banquet tables with chairs around half to three-quarters of each table so that all delegates can face the front	This layout can be used in a large plenary room – but will not seat as many people as theatre style. Use for presentations, speakers and plenary panels, with flexibility to undertake exercises or networking at tables
Reception	Chairs should be provided for those who wish to sit	Larger groups with the flexibility to move around and network. May be used in conjunction with a brief address by a speaker

Remember to think about not only the mix of rooms and space that you need, but how people will move between them – you do not want to lose delegates in a warren of corridors and staircases. Having a good layout plan, signage and staff or volunteers on hand to help direct people can make it easier and quicker for people to move to their next destination.

Check what the venue provides in the way of disabled access, hearing loops and any other necessary additional needs equipment. You will need to keep a record of delegates' requirements (including dietary requirements), so include a return slip when sending invitations.

You will need to have a clear contract with your venue and conference organiser or facilitator (see section 3.7). Make sure that you send your meeting or conference details in writing to the facility. Read and update all event orders, food and drink programmes before signing. Do not make assumptions about anything – if anything is unclear, ask questions and anticipate problems. Keep the venue up-to-date with any changes you may have to your programme nearer the day.

5.5.1.6   Catering

Most venues set up for conferences and events will provide catering throughout the day, and you can choose from a menu of options, usually priced per head attending. You will need to confirm a guaranteed minimum number of people attending a meal function, and will pay for either the guaranteed number or the number of people served, whichever is the greater.

Ensure there are sufficient areas for eating, or food stands available and staff to serve it, and that the room is big enough to hold the number of delegates you expect. You may have more than one food serving area to enable speedier access to food and less queuing at lunchtime. Volunteers directing delegates to relevant serving areas will help to speed up the process, as will laying out drinks beyond the food area to encourage people to move on and free up the space for those coming behind.

Food and drink guidelines

- 20 cups to a gallon
- 5 glasses of wine to a bottle
- provide 65% hot and 35% cold beverages for the morning break
- provide 35% hot and 65% cold beverages in the afternoon break
- the general rule for coffee is 70% regular, 30% decaffeinated
- have 1 server for every 15 to 20 people at a plated meal (1 server for every 10 would be even better)
- 1 bartender for every 50 people
- host bar – host pays for the drinks (consider setting a capped amount)
- cash bar – everyone pays for his or her own drinks.

5.6 Receptions

Receptions are usually smaller gatherings which afford an opportunity to network with guests, and are used often by charities as a way of developing their donor base (usually higher value donors). Receptions can also be used to invite a number of supporters who are in a position to provide a way in to a network of decision-makers. You then have the opportunity to invite the decision-makers to be part of a small group of 'champions', meeting three or four times a year to support the charity by opening doors to leading companies or individuals who will become high-level donors.

Another form of reception including your donor base is to encourage donors to increase their pledges. If your charity is embarking on this goal, then one of the best ways is to ask your existing donors to attend a reception and network for you. People will be flattered to be asked to be a part of a pioneering group which may have an impact on the charity's income generation, and they are more receptive if they are recognised for their valued support. Moreover, people are more inclined to become high-level donors when approached by another high-level donor. Remember the adage: 'People give to people, not to organisations.'

However, it is vitally important to focus on the goal of the reception, and to decide in advance what the follow-up will be. If donors or potential donors are not contacted after the event, the purpose of the reception is devalued.

5.6.1 How to organise receptions

5.6.1.1 Venue

As mentioned previously, you will need to choose your venue depending on the people you intend to invite and your budget. As you are targeting a smaller group of people, it is likely that you will be looking at a private room in a central hotel, or perhaps a company that supports the charity may be willing to offer its facilities. Consider a venue with a good view, or with something different about it such as a gallery or museum, or even a moving venue such as a boat (guests will need to arrive on time if a trip is involved). In a good location in the summer you may consider an outside element, such as a terrace or balcony with a view, but make sure that there is easy access and sufficient space inside, should you need to make a dash for it at short notice.

5.6.1.2 Content

You need to be clear about the objective of the event. You may want to focus on a particular aspect of your charity's work, or a project that needs funding. The main activity is networking between existing enthusiastic supporters of your charity and invited guests, and the chosen supporters or donors will need to be properly briefed about the objectives of the evening. A briefing meeting may be held to explain the timetable and what is required of them. Try to match existing supporters with guests of a similar age group, interests and income.

It is important to have a speaker who will welcome guests, thank them for coming and give information about the charity. This address should last no more than ten minutes. Make sure that there is relevant display material (using bullet points, not too much text, and photographs with positive images) and flyers and leaflets for guests and potential donors to take away. You may want to accompany the event with incidental music (a piano or string quartet, for example), but remember to keep an eye on the budget. Also, beware of any background music being too loud to make networking conversations difficult.

5.6.1.3 Catering

Most venues will offer catering services for receptions. You will need to provide finger food and wine plus fruit juice and water (less wine is likely to be drunk at an early evening function, particularly if a number of guests are likely to be driving). As most people will be standing, it is advisable to have a number of small tables convenient for them on which to place their glasses. Ensure that the caterers have sufficient members of staff to hand round food and refresh drinks.

5.6.1.4 Timing

These are intended to be shorter and more focused events than a conference or a dinner. The timing should be chosen to be convenient for those attending. Often the best plan, particularly when targeting professionals in a city area, is to provide a reception early after work. The reception should be two hours or even less, as people will want to get home. Therefore, it is important to keep to time on the evening – people will be more encouraged to support your charity if they gain the impression that the reception is well organised.

Here is a suggested time plan for the event.

5 pm	Staff arrive and set up a registration table and display boards
	Check with the banqueting manager and venue contact that all is in place as agreed
	Check the microphone for the speaker (have another in case of a problem)
	Check the room for small tables for drinks and glasses
5.45 pm	Existing supporters arrive and are issued with name badges
	Renew briefing details
6–6.15 pm	As guests arrive, register and receive their name badge, one member of each group greets them and introduces them to other members
	Drinks and finger food are served
6.40 pm	Speaker
6.50 pm	Continue networking
7.45 pm	Guests depart and staff clear room

5.6.1.5 Follow-up

The day after the reception, hold a debriefing session and collate any information gained about the guests' interests and desire to support the charity. Within the next week, start telephoning to make appointments with potential donors. The aim is to contact the guests of the reception within seven days to arrange a meeting. It may either be appropriate to visit the potential donor (usually a senior member of staff accompanied by the existing donor who provided the contact), or to arrange an invitation to the charity's offices. The object is to have a follow-up meeting of like-minded people in order to encourage the donor to support the charity as a major donor.

5.7 Family events

All the special events mentioned so far cater mainly for adults. However, special events programmes can be broadened to include family days. A family day out needs to provide a wide range of activities and it is a challenge for any event organiser to make sure that it gives value for money. As with all events, proper planning, including making sure that you are clear about the aims of the day and researching the audience you are trying to attract, will help to make this a success. However, family days can be enjoyable for the organiser as well as the public. If you think you will not have enough volunteers or staff, you may want to employ an organisation to run the event for you. The cost may be acceptable if it gives you the opportunity to recruit new supporters and volunteers, but do your sums carefully.

5.7.1 How to organise family events

5.7.1.1 Theme

It is best to think of a theme rather than staging a general day out – then you can franchise activities and stalls in keeping with the theme, making the event more fun and memorable, while providing more general activities. Here are some suggested themes:

- teddy bear day – I have been involved in a number of these and they have been extremely popular not only with children, but also with adults who take their teddy bears very seriously. Stalls and merchandise can be themed along the line of old-fashioned toys, rocking horses, wooden toymakers, teddy hospitals, etc.;
- vintage cars – invite people to exhibit cars built before 1960, contact car clubs within the area for their support, and advertise in the specialist press;
- steam rally – again, contact specialist clubs for exhibitors;
- country crafts – this could include anything from toys and hobbies, jewellery, lace and furniture making to paintings, willowcraft, blacksmithing and wooden sculptures.

5.7.1.2 Activities and entertainment

As well as the themed events and stalls, you may want to attract a broader range of merchandise stalls. Try to find unique manufacturers, away from the usual high street retailers. Consider having a static hot air balloon, bouncy castle and slides. Before you book a tethered hot air balloon, you will need the permission of the venue owner and to ensure there are no telephone or high power cables nearby. If you have enough space, consider a mini go-kart track, or full size table football.

Pony rides, face painters, archery and various fairground activities (games with a certain element of skill to win simple prizes, such as a coconut shy and quoits) will provide a range of activities for a range of ages, and not just the children. If you know a local farmer, city farm or animal centre, they may be able to provide a pets' corner, which could be popular with the smaller children. Make sure the animals are well enclosed, and that the owners are suitably insured.

Consider contacting local sports clubs, which may have funding for outreach programmes and would be happy to attend to encourage people to take part in 'have a go' sessions – for example five-a-side rugby. Contact local clubs or Sport England (www.sportengland.org) to find out where they are. For a local archery group with qualified coaches, contact the Grand National Archery Society (www.gnas.org).

Stiltwalkers, jugglers, clowns and acrobats can mingle with the crowd, or you can have specific displays at various times throughout the day, if you have a central theatre-style space. This would be the place to programme any competition results (best vintage car/steam engine/teddy bear), and while the crowds are gathered, to provide information about your charity and how to support it further.

Some form of live music, such as jazz bands, steel bands and brass bands are always entertaining for this type of event. The music can be heard as background throughout the site, with the bandstand forming a focus for those who want to put their feet up or have a picnic, while resting from the other entertainments on offer.

Several marquees may be needed, in case of bad weather, or as areas where people can picnic or rest if it is very hot. It is certainly advisable to have at least one central marquee as a central point of information, announcing programmes and activities, lost property, reporting lost children and to organise response to emergencies.

Make sure that there are sufficient food outlets to keep everyone happy. It is best not to underestimate the number of outlets you will require. You may want a catered refreshment tent, or to allow food franchisers to set up their stalls throughout the site, with an agreed percentage at the end of the day going to the charity. Think about the food and try to avoid the standard burger and chips, as there are plenty of caterers who provide interesting and good quality food for a family day out. Remember to include ice-cream vendors and a variety of drinks, both hot and cold, soft and alcoholic.

5.7.1.3 Funding and sponsorship

It may be difficult to find an overall sponsor for a family day event. It is recommended that you split the packages of sponsorship for activities on the day. In return for the agreed amount of sponsorship, your sponsors would get their company name and logo in the programme, and depending on the level of sponsorship, they may have a marquee or competition named after them, and perhaps be involved in any prizegiving and subsequent publicity. Local firms are most likely to be interested, as well as branches of national firms that want to raise their profile and community involvement in a particular area.

If you receive any support from companies, businesses, individuals, local groups, clubs and local authorities, remember to mention and thank them all in your programme.

5.7.1.4 Charging and fundraising

The amount you charge needs to be realistic to cover at least any costs after sponsorship and stall fees, and hopefully to make a return for your charity, so that the event provides you with added income as well as raising your charity's profile and potential supporter base. At the same time, entry costs need to reflect value for money for the public, and as a family day out you will need to ensure that it is affordable for the whole family to attend. As part of your planning you will need to compare prices of other family day outs (they are your competition), and see whether the event can meet your costs.

Consider whether you will charge per car (with parking included in the price of the ticket) or for individuals. If charging per car, you will also need to have a rate for those who come on foot. In addition to individual adult tickets, provide a family ticket and concessions for over-60s, unwaged people and children (if not included in a family price), with free entry for children under five.

Look at the HMRC guidance on entrance fees and Gift Aid, and consider whether it is worth the effort to add a further option of an enhanced price ticket which contains a sufficient donation to enable the visitor to Gift Aid the whole amount (see section 4.10.2).

Remember that this event is not just about putting on a successful family fun day; the event is supposed to raise your profile and hopefully raise funds and increase your supporter base. So consider all the opportunities to raise awareness and funds for your cause. You could hand out leaflets and/or direct debit forms along with the tickets as people enter. In addition, you should consider having at least one information point including a display board with photographs and information about the work of the charity, and more leaflets for distribution and opportunities to give out. You should have volunteers or staff running the stall who will have the opportunity to engage with people and see if they would be interested in supporting the charity in the future. Moreover, this could be an opportunity to have a stall selling charity branded merchandise. You may have an already established range of goods, but if not, some ideas would include T-shirts, baseball caps, mugs, badges, keyrings, cuddly toys, wellington boots and umbrellas. Suppliers that will provide such goods with your logo and design of choice can be found on the internet easily, or ask colleagues from other charities for recommended suppliers. Once you have managed a few events, you will soon build up a database of reliable suppliers.

Top tip

Don't include the date of the event on the merchandise, as you cannot possibly guarantee how many will attend the event and how much merchandise you will sell.

5.7.1.5   Venue

You will need to book your venue well in advance. When fixing the date, as with all events, check the events calendar in the area in order not to clash with another. As family fun days are primarily outdoor events, the best locations can be country parks – these tend to have good public access and car parking facilities, and equal access for people with disabilities.

Consider putting on the event in partnership with the venue if it is a National Trust property or stately home. Make sure that both partners are aware of the terms of the arrangement, who will be responsible for organising what, and how the benefit will be distributed. The venue needs to be of a suitable size and capacity for the numbers you are expecting. Take note of any restrictions, and make sure that the venue complies with health and safety rules. Most country house sites have the bonus of being situated away from residential areas, which will help to avoid complaints about disturbance from noise and traffic congestion. However, for a large event, particularly if it is not far from an urban area, make sure that you inform the police and local authorities of your plans, so that they can advise on traffic management.

It is also possible to put on a family fun day in a more urban environment – most cities in the UK are well endowed with parks and green spaces. You will need to approach the local authorities and parks authorities to obtain permission and discuss restrictions with them. Parking will be more of an issue in this environment, and you need to encourage people to come on public transport whenever possible.

5.7.1.6 Volunteers

You will need a number of volunteers to help throughout the day – with car parking, taking money at the gate, assisting at the information point and the charity's stall, and keeping an eye on the event as a whole and being helpful to visitors. To make volunteers easier to be identified, they should wear charity tabards or sashes (badges are too small). Car parking marshals should wear yellow safety vests.

Be sure to look after your volunteers, and avoid keeping them on one particular activity for too long, especially on car parking if the weather is very hot, very cold or wet. Organise a rota so that volunteers have breaks and do different tasks throughout the day. Whatever duties they are carrying out, make sure that you make provision for supplying them with refreshments throughout the day. Have a good supply of hot or cold drinks, whichever is appropriate to the weather. If it is hot, make sure that volunteers are informed about the importance of wearing hats and using sun protection, as well as keeping hydrated. Consider providing cover, such as a small booth or a plastic gazebo to protect them.

Volunteers need adequate training for the tasks that you ask them to do. They will need experienced help on the most efficient method to control cars. There may be a local car club with experienced marshals that may be happy to help (to secure this you can offer a free information stall promoting their club activities, or a display of their cars). In addition, you can help the job of the volunteers by ensuring that there are clear signs and information about prices and payment methods, to save them from having to repeat the information continuously. Clearly signing exits for cars will help to avoid congestion problems. Volunteers and staff also need proper briefing on their responsibilities and duties when staffing the information point, particularly if these responsibilities may involve handling lost property and looking after lost children. Everyone should be aware of the site layout and emergency procedures.

5.7.1.7 Issues to consider

You will need to consider the following.

- *Litter* – provide bins, but plan for litter collection at the end as unfortunately the general public will throw litter on the ground. Consider approaching the local scouts or a secondary school for volunteers to help in return for a donation to the group or school. Provide your litterpicking group with black bin liners, rubber gloves and a supply of soft drinks and food, and arrange for them to go round and collect litter from people or pick it up. There should be an arrangement for collection of the rubbish off site at the end of the day.

- *Toilets* – estimate realistically how many you will need, and check with the landowner regarding either access to existing toilet facilities and/or permission to put portaloos on the site.
- *Emergency services* – these need to be alerted to your plans before the event, and contact numbers of local hospitals should be on record at the central information point.
- *Information point* – This should be fairly central and easily accessible. As previously mentioned, it should contain information about programme activities and site layout and be staffed by a rota of people all the time that the event is open. Ideally, there should be access to the PA system from this point.
- *Lost property or children* – make clear that any losses should be reported to the information point, and brief all staff, volunteers and stallholders about this procedure so that they can help any visitors who may be distressed. Also, any items found should be handed in here, and lost children may need to be looked after until their parents come to collect them. Be careful when giving out information on property found – keep it simple and general, so that you can ensure that the item is correctly identified by the owner. Again, make sure that staff at the information point are properly trained on this.
- *PA system* – You may need to hire a public address system for the information stand. Often rental companies will supply a generator for an extra fee.
- *Electricity* – you may need a supply of electricity for the caterers, attractions and toilets. Most will come with their own self-operated systems, but you will need to check this and whether an alternative supply is available. If making connections yourself, make sure you only engage a qualified electrician to undertake the connection of electricity.
- *Cash float* – never underestimate how much cash float you will need at the admission booth or at any stall selling merchandise. Bear this in mind, particularly when collecting money at the gate – keep it simple, such as £5, £2.50, £1.
- *Car parking* – consider the signposting, the distance from venue and safety. If it is a grassed area, how likely is it to become a quagmire if it rains?
- *Programme* – this should contain information about the day, including a layout plan and listings for stallholders. Make sure that you provide information and offer the chance to support your charity. Mention and thank all supporters and sponsors. Either get sponsorship for the programme, or consider charging for copies to help cover your costs.

- *Thanks* – when the event is closing up, go round and personally thank all the volunteers, helpers and stallholders – try not to leave anyone out. If you follow up the next day with a letter of thanks, then you will find that, if asked again, those involved will be likely to offer their services.

5.7.1.8 Layout

Whenever stalls or stands are available to rent as a part of the event, you must provide a site layout plan. You should present this plan to the landowner for approval, and it will form the basis of discussions with the local council and the fire service concerning safety.

Mark out plots for stalls (e.g. 3 x 3 metres up to 6 x 12 metres), leaving ample room for walkways and emergency access, if required. It helps to draw up the plan to scale, marking out the stalls and other activities with pieces of card representing each one, so that you can move them around to find the best layout. You may want to group certain types of stall together, perhaps all the crafts, and create a food and drink area. It can help to colour code areas, both for the planning and the final programme guide. People will tend to gather outside a stall, so allow enough space for others to walk past freely.

Once approved by the landowner, local authorities and emergency services, your final layout plan can be used when booking stallholders, so make sure that all the plots have a number for easy reference, both when booking and setting up on the day, and that it is easily visible for stallholders when they are setting up.

5.7.1.9 Stallholders

It is a good idea to sell the plots on your layout plan to stallholders by size. Have a variety of plot sizes available, or stallholders wanting a larger site can rent two adjacent sites. Make the prices clear and payable in advance to reserve that site.

Top tip

It is not unknown for stallholders either to move their numbers or plot markers or to pitch at the wrong site, so this needs to be managed on the day. Make sure that someone is tasked with checking on progress as the stallholders arrive and set up, and that they have a masterplan so that they can make final decisions in the event of a dispute.

You must draw up a contract with clear terms and conditions (see section 3.7).

Checklist: stallholder contract

- Specify the time when access to the venue is available. Stallholders will not be allowed to set up before the official time.
- Parking information for stallholders' vehicles.
- Pitch information, confirming number, size and location of pitch(es), and the price payable in advance.
- The stalls must allow for emergency vehicle access.
- Should electricity be necessary for the stallholders, the location of access and the supply details should be specified when known.
- Stallholders should supply their own extension leads.
- Stallholders' electrical equipment must be portable appliance testing (PAT) tested (you will need a qualified electrician to arrange these outlets – check with the venue owner, who may have this organised).
- Make clear what equipment is or is not provided (for example, no tables or chairs).
- Stallholders are responsible for their own insurance requirements.
- Stallholders are responsible for leaving their pitch clean and litter-free.
- There should be a clause forbidding sub-letting of the pitch.
- There should be a clause indemnifying the organisers against loss, damage or injury (take legal advice to make sure this is worded properly) and that the organisers cannot accept any responsibility for loss or damage to stallholders' goods or equipment.
- You may wish to add a clause of conduct for stallholders – for example, not to create a disturbance with loud music or noise, not to cause an obstruction or behave in any way which the organisers deem to be unacceptable.
- It may be advisable to include a clause relating to the safe and proper use of potentially dangerous materials and appliances, such as naked lights, oil lamps or emergency electrical fittings. Make it clear if anything is forbidden outright.
- There should be a clause covering the provision of food to the public – if the stall is not a recognised food outlet, no food or drink must be sold to the general public.
- There should be a clause covering sanctions for failure to comply with the terms of the contract – for example, being denied entry or being removed if in breach of contract.
- The contract should cover stallholders' liability if they cancel. A clause can be included to cover a refund, if the cancellation is sent in writing one calendar month before the event; after this date, no refund will be issued.

Top tip

Make sure someone checks that stalls are properly erected and present no hazards such as long guy ropes or protruding objects, etc. Your main concern is for the safety of the public.

When stallholders confirm their booking, it is important to determine their needs for access and parking requirements. They may need to bring a large van or low loader, and will require suitable access. The ground may be unsuitable for heavy vehicles, especially if it has been raining. The owner of the venue will advise, since it is to their benefit that no vehicles are stuck in the mud. There are various types of tracking available to help stabilise ground which needs to be driven over, ranging from sawdust and straw to plastic and metal tracks. Make sure that you agree with the venue owner before strewing straw on their field, as you will find it difficult to pick up and remove when the event is over.

When terms and conditions have been agreed, the contracts should be signed and a copy sent to the organisers.

5.8 Festivals

Festivals usually revolve around some form of celebration, whether of an anniversary or other event to mark (such as the birthday of a key figure). However, an anniversary of your charity may not be something in itself that the general public feels strongly about, and its celebration may be best held as a theme at one of the charity's annual conferences. However, an anniversary or other occasion may be the impetus for considering a festival, while the draw to the public will be a particular theme that you attach to it. Music festivals are popular with the general public, but all festivals require substantial organisation and are certainly a challenge. Consider inviting bands and groups from youth groups and schools as a way of involving the local community. You could encourage dance and costumes as well as music by introducing an element of competition between different groups, with different categories of prizes.

5.8.1 How to organise a festival

A festival is usually an event that is celebratory in nature, and often has a community focus. Some organisations run successful festivals for a few years but then but find it extremely difficult to keep the momentum going. The trick is how to sustain the interest of the general public and attract different music, bands, speakers or entertainers consistently for a number of years. Think very hard before attempting such an event and ensure that you have a good strong committee to help you pull it together.

Case study: Rosie's walk and festival

Karen and Sean Ross, Rosie's Helping Hands

Figure 14: Rosie's walk and festival (reproduced with kind permission of Dean Staples)

What is Rosie's walk and festival?

A fun family event which began five years ago as a sponsored walk in remembrance of Rosie Ross, an Aldridge teenager who was fatally stabbed in a random and unprovoked attack while relaxing in a park on an afternoon in 2001. The sponsored walk has now grown into a walk and festival incorporating different themes. It has become a popular afternoon of entertainment and activities for all ages.

What happens to the money raised?

Rosie's Helping Hands raises money for local children and young people and local A & E departments, and funds specialised equipment and training for the Institute of Cancer Studies, University of Birmingham. The funds raised have paid for equipment and toys for toddler groups, specialised medical treatment for autistic children, sensory rooms for children with additional needs, equipment for youth clubs and staff to run children's projects. In 2005 £20,000 was raised from Rosie's walk to buy a portable ultrasound scanner for Walsall Manor Hospital A & E department. In 2006, the money raised from the walk and festival was for the Institute of Cancer Studies at the University of Birmingham.

The festival and walk

One year the festival had a country and western theme. It opened at high noon and went on until 5 pm. During the afternoon families enjoyed a beautiful four-mile walk in Walsall's hidden countryside. Every mile counts by raising money for local causes and sponsor forms were provided.

For those unable to participate on the walk there were numerous other activities, including live music provided by country and western band Indiana Rain. In addition, there was live entertainment for all the family, including dancing displays by local young people. To follow the theme there was line dancing with Par Harris, singalong with the wonderful Melody Maker, and new music performed by an all-girl band, IntroVenus. There was a line dancing display from Manic Mutts.

Special guest TV Robot Wars' double world champion Razer was on display in the 'Robo Challenge' area along with its builder and driver Ian Lewis. Other family entertainment included children's rides, circus skills, 'have a go' art and crafts plus a raffle. Bostin' Art was on hand to help make talking head puppets with natural materials collected along the walk. Aspiring cowboys could saddle up and put themselves to the test with the Rodeo Bull Ride.

One of the many responses made after the day was from a family who said:

> A lovely day enjoyed by us all. An important date on our calendar – we would not miss it for the world. We were on TV too! A real tribute to Rosie.

6 ESSENTIALS: LEGAL REQUIREMENTS AND RISK MANAGEMENT

Much law and regulation surrounds many fundraising activities, because you are taking money from the public, and because sadly there are unscrupulous people who will take advantage if the activity is not regulated. You need to be aware of the key areas of law which are likely to affect fundraising, and be satisfied that your staff know about and are able to comply with them. Similarly, events involve a lot of people, and various factors in the environment, from equipment to food to the venue itself could pose a risk to them. It is vital that you are familiar with health and safety and fire regulations so that you can minimise the risks and know what to do if the worst should happen.

This chapter highlights some of the key areas that you need to know about and consider, whatever type of event you are organising. It is not an exhaustive legal guide to your responsibilities, but hopefully it will raise your awareness of the issues and point you in the right direction for further information, should you need it.

6.1 Charity law and regulations

Charity law is a complex area, and it develops and changes over time, so this sector gives only an overview of the key areas relevant to events as at the time of publication.

The Charities Act 2006 introduced some changes and simplifications to charity law in England and Wales, but not all of it has come into force at the time of writing. For up-to-date information check the websites of the Charity Commission (www.charity-commission.gov.uk) and the Office of the Third Sector (www.cabinetoffice.gov.uk/third_sector). The 2006 Act is also primarily an updating Act rather than wholly replacing what has gone before, so some parts of previous legislation (principally the Charities Acts 1992 and 1993) are still in force, and this may remain the case unless and until a consolidating Act is made.

This chapter focuses primarily on the law in England and Wales, but identifies where there are key issues in Scotland and Northern Ireland – again, it is always worth checking the websites of the Charity Commission for Northern Ireland (www.dsdni.gov.uk/ccni.htm) and the Office of the Scottish Charity Regulator (www.oscr.org.uk) for up-to-the-minute information.

6.1.1   Charity name and registration number

In all appeals for funds, a registered charity must clearly state its status. This is a requirement of the Charities Act 1993 and includes appeals on websites or on literature advertising a charity fundraising event. There is a similar requirement to be absolutely clear about the registered charity status on bills, invoices and so forth issued in the charity's name. Most of the time this requirement is fulfilled by providing the charity's name and registration number, and these may be included as a matter of course on any headed paper for the organisation.

6.1.2   Restricted purposes

The funds raised from an event must be spent for the purposes advertised. If you hold an event to raise funds for a specific appeal, rather than the general purposes of your charity, you can use those funds only for that particular appeal. If you do not raise enough to achieve the appeal's purposes, or if you raise more than you need, you are required by law to contact donors wherever possible and offer to return the money, or gain their consent for you to use the money in other ways.

Clearly, this can be a costly process, and it is better to avoid it. Therefore, you should be very careful when producing promotional literature – make sure that it clearly identifies what the money raised will be used for, and what will happen if this is not possible. Another way to deal with this issue is to state the specific aim but clearly add that, alternatively, the money will be used for the general purposes of the charity: this is the equivalent of gaining donors' consent upfront to use their money in this way. If you find yourself in the position of having raised restricted funds from your event which cannot be used for that restricted purpose, you may need to contact the Charity Commission for advice on how to release the funds for other charitable purposes.

6.1.3   Professional fundraisers and commercial participators

There are specific legal definitions of what constitutes a 'professional fundraiser' and a 'commercial participator', contained in Part II of the Charities Act 1992. You may find that in the course of organising your event you are making contracts which fall into one of these categories, whether it is because you have a professional firm organising your event, or the nature of your sponsorship arrangements with companies constitutes 'commercial participation'. There are legal regulations (set out in the Charitable Institutions (Fundraising) Regulations 1994) about what such contracts should contain, how records should be kept and what statements should be made to the public about the relationship with the charity.

If you obtain advice from a fundraising consultant, this may not constitute a relationship with a 'professional fundraiser'. If the consultant actually raise funds for you, or your contract stipulates fundraising targets, then he or she is likely to be seen as a professional fundraiser.

Straightforward sponsorship of an event by a company may not constitute commercial participation if clearly the event is run by and for the charity, the sponsorship is a donation, and the return to the company consists of relatively low-key advertising of its brand and some tickets to the event. However, if the event involves a greater opportunity for the company to sell its services, or the arrangement goes beyond pure sponsorship to a deal where money will be given to the charity each time one of the company's products is purchased, then this is likely to qualify as commercial participation.

The requirements for professional fundraisers and commercial participators to make public statements have been updated in the Charities Act 2006, and the updated requirements came into effect on 1 April 2008. According to draft guidance produced by the Office of the Third Sector, professional fundraisers have to state that they are contracted by the charity and how much they are paid to do the fundraising. If contracted as an individual, they have to state their hourly rate and the overall amount that they expect to receive. If part of a fundraising company, they have to state the overall amount to be paid to the company, or an estimate of this, if it is not known upfront. Commercial participators have to state the nature of the relationship, and the return to themselves and to the charity. Often due to the complicated financial arrangements involved, there are many ways of doing this, and it is best to refer to *Charities and fundraising* which contains examples of different statements to cover different circumstances (see Appendix 1).

There is also a new requirement for employees of the charity who are involved in fundraising to state that they are paid by the charity, but they do not have to say how much. Volunteers do not have to make a statement at all.

6.1.4 Public collections

If as part of your event you intend to make a direct appeal for cash or direct debit sign-ups, and your event is in a public place, you may need to comply with public collections legislation. This is highly unlikely, as most of the time you will be in a private venue where all you need is the owner's permission, and you will be allowing access on a ticketed basis only: people will be electing to attend on the basis that they want to support your charity, and so your appeal will not be made to the general public.

Where you may need to have a public collections licence is collecting at an outdoor event such as a sporting challenge, where supporters and spectators have unrestricted public access. At the time of writing public collection licensing falls under the Police, Factories and Miscellaneous Act 1916, which also applies in Northern Ireland. You will need to obtain a licence from the relevant local authority, or if you are in the Greater London area you will need to apply to the Metropolitan Police. Different local authorities apply different criteria for granting the licence, so do apply in plenty of time.

The law around public collections has been updated in the Charities Act 2006 but is unlikely to come into force before 2010. The new provisions should make life easier if you carry out public collections regularly in different locations, whether at events or house to house. The Act provides for a single nationwide public collections certificate to be obtained from the Charity Commission, which essentially vouches for the charity's bona fide status. Local authorities still need to be approached for collections in public places, but the criteria for considering whether to issue a permit will be much simpler, based on whether a collection is likely to cause a public nuisance.

6.1.5 Duty of care

Underlying all charity law is the general duty of care that all trustees have under the Trustee Act 2001. This covers such issues as not proceeding to engage in contracts while knowing that the charity cannot honour them, and generally exercising reasonable prudence in administering the charity so as not to put the charity unreasonably at risk, both financially or reputationally.

You need to ensure that you are aware of any financial or reputational risks, that you exercise due caution in contracting to put on your event, and that you have procedures in place to inform or warn senior people if you become aware of major risks arising.

6.2 Data protection

In the course of planning and marketing your special event, you are likely to be using lists or databases of existing supporters or building up databases of potential supporters. You may go on to gather information at the event itself to enable follow-up with attendees. Basic data housekeeping makes sense to enable you to make the best use of the data available, but you also have a requirement to comply with the Data Protection Act 1998, which exists to protect personal data from misuse while being used for legitimate or beneficial purposes.

Although there are a few limited exemptions from the requirements of the 1998 Act, you should assume that any database used for fundraising is covered by it. This applies whether the people on your database come from your own members, people who have made enquiries or bought tickets, a list taken from a reference book or a bought-in list. It applies in most cases even if you are taking names from paper rather than computer files. Once you begin to compile your list, even before you use it for fundraising, data protection will apply.

The following sections will give you an overview of the principles of the Data Protection Act 1998, its key provisions and some practical tips on how you can ensure compliance with it. (Note that this is a guide only and not necessarily a full statement of the law or a replacement for obtaining professional advice.)

6.2.1 Data protection principles

At the heart of the Data Protection Act are eight commonsense rules known as the Data Protection Principles. These require personal information to be:

1. fairly and lawfully processed
2. collected only for specified and lawful purposes

3. adequate, relevant and not excessive
4. accurate and up to date
5. kept no longer than necessary
6. processed in accordance with the data subject's (about you hold data) rights
7. kept secure
8. not transferred to countries outside the European Economic Area without adequate protection.

6.2.2 Data controller

The data controller is the person in charge of determining how the data are to be held and processed, and it is the data controller who is responsible for complying with the Act. 'Person' means legal person, and this is likely to be the organisation itself or an individual appointed to be the data controller on behalf of the organisation.

6.2.3 Registering with the Information Commissioner's Office

All data controllers who process personal information must notify the Information Commissioner's Office (ICO) (www.ico.gov.uk) unless they are exempt. Failure to notify is a criminal offence. Notification is a simple process and can be done online, or by requesting a postal notification form. A small annual fee is charged.

The form asks for basic information such as the correct legal title of your organisation, the nature of your business, your registered office address and contact details. You will also need to identify the purposes for which you intend to use the information you process, the likely data subjects, data classes (what type of information you are holding) and recipients.

It is likely that your organisation will be registered at the ICO already for general business administration purposes, realising the objectives of a charitable organisation or voluntary body, and probably for fundraising, if you have an established fundraising function. You can check on the ICO website to see if you are already on the register, and for what purposes – make sure that fundraising is included. If you think any changes need to be made, or you need to be registered, check who is responsible for data protection in your organisation.

There is a small range of exemptions for not-for-profit and small businesses, but it is likely that if you regularly fundraise you will not qualify for one. Even if your charity is exempt from the requirement to notify, you can register on a voluntary basis. If you are in any doubt, contact the ICO for more advice (see Appendix 2). Once you have notified the ICO, your basic registration details will be available on the public register on the ICO website.

6.2.4   Responding to requests for information

The point of the Act, with its requirements for notification and registration, is to increase accountability and transparency. The Act gives individuals the right to be informed whether you hold information about them, and to be given a description of the personal information that you hold, for what purposes you hold it, and to whom you may disclose the information.

Once you have received the request in writing (a 'subject access request'), you should respond promptly (within 40 days, which is the maximum time allowed by the regulations). You are allowed to charge a fee of up to £10, and should ensure you have enough information from the requester to be reasonably sure of their identity. The 40 days run from the point at which you have all the information and fees you need to process the request. You do not have to respond to a request if by doing so you will breach the confidentiality of other individuals, or if it will take 'disproportionate effort' to provide the information. However, you should aim to provide as much information as possible, perhaps by editing references to others. There are some other specific circumstances where you do not have to provide information – these are detailed in the Act and in guidance provided by the Information Commissioner's Office.

Checklist

- Do you have permission to hold the data?
- Do you have a use for all the data you hold?
- Are your systems secure?
- Do you regularly check and clean lists?
- Are you collecting and processing personal data as part of your event?
- Is your organisation registered with the Information Commissioner's Office?
- Does your registration cover fundraising activity?
- Have the people on your list been told that their information might be used for fundraising?
- Have the people on your list been given the chance to opt out of their data being used for fundraising?

- Do you have systems in place for removing or suppressing names on lists, if people have told you not to use their details for fundraising?
- If you have bought in a database, do you have appropriate assurances that you can use it for the purposes you require?
- If you are using an agency to do telemarketing or mailing on your behalf, have you got a suitable written contract in place with the agency? Are you satisfied that the agency complies with data protection requirements?
- If you are phoning people to ask for their support, have you checked that their number is not on the Telephone Preference Service register (see www.mpsonline.org.uk)?
- Are your staff properly trained to use data correctly and to respond to requests for information?
- If you use a website, or if you share information with organisations overseas, are you complying with special rules about transferring data abroad?

6.3 Health and safety

Most special events will involve a lot of people, for whose well-being you will become responsible, at least in part, during the event. You will have a legal duty to protect staff, volunteers and members of the public from foreseeable hazards. Health and safety considerations may cover access to the site, the equipment being used, the food eaten and the ability to apply emergency procedures. Of course, you do not want anyone to be harmed at an event you have organised or for anything negative to happen and be associated with your charity, especially when you are trying to raise support.

Although it is important to have emergency procedures in place, the key thing is to plan ahead and act to minimise the risk of anyone getting hurt in the first place. The following sections will look at how to build health and safety considerations into the planning process, and give an overview of the kinds of issues that might occur in common events and how to manage them.

6.3.1 Risk assessment

Section 2.5 looked at undertaking a risk assessment for the event as a whole. The same principle and process apply to undertaking a risk assessment which focuses specifically on health and safety issues for the event. This should happen at a more detailed level than your overall event risk assessment, but will follow the same kind of structure:

- identify risks;
- prioritise risks by likelihood and impact;
- create an action plan to manage and mitigate risks.

6.3.2 Fire regulations

The Regulatory Reform (Fire Safety) Order 2005 came into effect in October 2006, replacing more than 70 pieces of fire safety law. It is applicable to charities and voluntary organisations. There is more detailed information and guidance on the Communities and Local Government website (www.communities.gov.uk). A key provision is that you must have a defined responsible person in charge of fire risk assessment, and that the responsible person must implement and maintain a fire management plan. If, having completed a fire risk assessment, you need more advice, seek professional advice from your local fire service.

Ask the venue the maximum number of people allowed to conform with fire regulations. Check that fire exits are clearly marked and are clear in case of evacuation. Discuss with venue staff and the duty manager their evacuation procedures and what staff will be on duty to assist, and ensure that all volunteers and staff are aware of their roles. Confirm all agreements in writing and ensure that each party has a signed copy.

If there is a higher than usual potential for a fire or explosion, such as holding firework displays or a bonfire, make sure that you inform the local fire brigade well in advance. It may want to be present, but even if it does not, make sure that you have taken appropriate fire prevention and safety advice, you know how to contact the fire service in case of difficulties (always 999 in an emergency), and have located the closest access to the water mains.

You must record the key findings of your fire risk assessment, clearly identifying the following:

- the key hazards;
- the preventive measures taken;
- the people at risk and those at special risk;
- the measures taken to reduce that risk (protective measures);
- your emergency plan identifying the people nominated for any particular function and the actions that people need to take;
- the information, instruction and training that people will need, and how it will be provided.

Fire safety checklist

- Who is the responsible person?
- What are the main fire hazards?
- What safety measures will minimise risk of fire or damage caused?
- Is there an evacuation plan?
- Are fire exits clearly signed and clear of rubbish and obstacles?
- Are there sufficient escape routes to enable the site to be cleared rapidly, considering the number of people attending?
- Where is the assembly point?
- What is the evacuation plan for disabled and other vulnerable people?
- What fire detection equipment is in place, and is it in working order?
- What fire fighting equipment is available – is it in working order, in the most suitable places, and are there suitably trained people to use it?
- Have key staff and volunteers been adequately informed and trained in fire safety procedures for this event?

Example: fire risk assessment

Potential fuel identified:

- dry grass
- tents
- cooking oil
- gas cylinders.

Potential sources of ignition:

- cigarettes
- lighters and matches
- electrical faults
- overheated oil
- naked flames in catering area.

People or property at risk:

- members of the public (especially children separated from parents, people with reduced mobility)
- stallholders and support staff
- vehicles parked in field
- marquees and contents.

Actions to mitigate risk:

- full plan and checks of electric cabling and connections
- rules to catering stallholders regarding temperature, supervision and proper disposal of cooking oil, and supervision at all times of cooking equipment when in use

- 'no smoking' and 'fire risk' warning signs in car park and throughout the site
- sand buckets and appropriate extinguishers (especially non-water extinguishers in catering areas) to be placed at well signposted fire points throughout the site
- brief all stallholders and volunteers on procedures for raising the alarm and evacuation procedure
- ensure the alarm can be raised via PA system
- ensure adequate supervision of car parking area.

6.3.3 Emergency plan

In the event of an emergency, you need to make sure that speedy and effective decisions are made and carried out – it is vital to designate one person to be in charge, and to make sure that everyone knows who this is and how to contact them.

You need to have a plan in place to deal with all the types of emergency you can imagine, from fire to flood, high winds, accidents and crashes. It is not that you expect these things to happen (hopefully your planning will have minimised the risk), but that everybody needs to know what to do, should the worst occur. What would happen if somebody collapsed at your event? Would people likely to be nearby know what to do?

Identify clearly the actions to be taken in different circumstances, and who is responsible for what. Record this on a side or two of A4, together with emergency numbers to call, and include a site plan which identifies escape routes, fire extinguishers and first aid points. Make sure that all stewards and responsible staff have been well briefed on the emergency plan, and that each has a copy of it.

6.3.4 Crowd control

For ticketed events, you should have a good idea of how many people you are expecting, and roughly when they will arrive and leave. If large numbers are involved, you will need to consider how to minimise bottlenecks on arrival or departure, and how to minimise the impact that such large numbers of people and, potentially, vehicles will have on the neighbourhood and passers-by.

Talk to the local police well in advance, telling them the nature of your event and numbers expected. They will be experienced in traffic management and crowd control, and will be able to advise you or decide that their presence may be needed to help manage the situation. Try to keep main traffic routes for cars and people separate wherever possible. Consider any special arrangements that may be necessary to enable access for any disabled guests or those with other additional needs.

6.3.5   First aid

You need to be prepared for someone falling ill, hurting themselves or suffering the effects of the weather. You should have an adequate number of trained first aiders on site for the number of people attending. The first aid post should be easily identifiable, as should the first aiders themselves. If at an indoor venue, check to see if they have first aid trained staff who will be on duty during your event, and how best to contact them. For large outdoor events, contact St John Ambulance well in advance to request their attendance at your event.

6.3.6   Food

As previously mentioned, make sure that any contracted caterers have the necessary food safety certificates, and that you are satisfied that they are competent to handle, cook and deliver food in a hygienic and safe manner. Do not allow volunteers or non-licensed people to cater for an event. You have far less control over safety standards, and they are not likely to be insured or able to cover liabilities should food poisoning arise – in all likelihood it will be your liability for allowing non-professional catering at the event.

6.3.7   Overseas events

As previously mentioned in Chapter 5, you should check the references, competence and insurance cover of contracted agencies, and ensure that participants know the level of fitness required – consider fitness screening.

6.3.8   Be prepared

If there is an incident, you need to be prepared to deal with it, to bring in help if necessary, and to make an accurate record of what has happened and how, in case of future investigation. Always make sure you have the following:

- the emergency plan;
- a site plan;
- key numbers – first aiders, fire brigade, police;

- a charged mobile phone (check that there is reception);
- a camera – if there is an accident, take pictures from as many angles as possible and include the whole scene;
- notepad and pen or dictaphone – take full details of the following in the event of an incident:
  - time, location and weather conditions;
  - the services attending – ambulance, police, etc.;
  - the details of people involved;
  - were the injured people behaving responsibly – note any suspicions of drink or other substances being involved;
  - were safety signs clearly displayed? (take photographs);
  - take witness statements – remember to include names, addresses and contact numbers.

6.4 Insurance

While you should do everything that you can to assess risks and take action to minimise them, you still have to expect the unexpected, and you cannot ever have a fully safe event. The potential liabilities which could arise from a special event could cripple a small to medium-sized charity, and seriously affect a larger one. Any fines, financial payments and court costs are not money spent on the charity's beneficiaries, so it is vitally important to make sure that your event is appropriately insured.

The following sections will provide a brief guide to the types of insurance you may need to consider. Of course, for a complex event this does not replace the need to take professional advice on your specific circumstances.

6.4.1 Public liability insurance

Public liability insurance indemnifies a charity, its trustees, staff and volunteers against any claims from members of the public for loss, injury or damage inflicted during the course of an event. You should check that the charity has current public liability insurance, and confirm that the insurance policy provides cover for the event that you are staging. Also check that you are satisfied that the maximum amount payable under the policy (the 'limit of indemnity') is sufficient for the type of activity or event, and the level of risk, which you should have identified already, is covered.

6.4.2   Third-party insurance

Every effort must be taken to avoid taking responsibility for insuring public liability risks for events when an event is arranged for the benefit of your charity, but not organised by you. If someone else is organising the event on your behalf, you need to ensure that they are both competent and adequately insured themselves: confirm this in writing and take advice on whether it is appropriate to issue a disclaimer making clear who is responsible for the event. However, be aware that a disclaimer (such as those often found in car parks or cloakrooms) in itself will not avoid liability for loss or damage if it is caused by negligence.

6.4.3   Equipment insurance

If you are borrowing or hiring equipment for the event, make sure that the owner has insured the equipment adequately, and that their insurance covers your use of it. You should avoid insuring any equipment which does not actually belong to the charity – many policies will not cover equipment that is not your own property.

6.4.4   Contractors' insurance

Check that all contractors have appropriate insurance, and make sure that responsibilities for defaulting, cancellation or harm caused by them are covered in contractual terms. In the case of outside activities involving any degree of risk to the person, such as hot air ballooning or Ministry of Defence assault courses, you must satisfy yourself that suitable insurance cover is in place before proceeding with the event.

6.4.5   Venue's responsibility for insurance

Whether indoors or out, you should seek assurance from the owner of loaned or hired property that they have complied with the following:

• they already have insurance cover;
• their insurance covers the event;
• their insurance covers a sufficient amount;
• there is a waiver of subrogation rights.

'Waiver of subrogation' means that the insurance company cannot turn to the charity to recover any payments that the insurer may have made. In most cases, it will not cost the insurer any extra in premium.

6.4.6 Bad weather insurance

If your event is being held outside, and especially if it depends on good weather, you may want to investigate the cost of taking out cover against losses arising from cancellation of the event due to bad weather. This is commonly referred to as 'pluvius insurance' ('pluvius' meaning 'rain'). It is likely to be expensive but worth considering if you have a high risk of losing all your set-up costs in the event of cancellation. Check the terms and conditions of this type of insurance carefully, and take professional advice as to whether it is appropriate for your event.

6.4.7 Cash

There are policies available which provide cover for the loss of cash collected at an event, when being carried or kept overnight at the private dwelling of a nominated individual of the charity. However, do check the conditions very carefully and make sure that you abide by them. You will have to take certain security measures, are likely to have to ensure that only named individuals are responsible for holding the cash, carrying and keeping it in a secure manner, and that the cash is banked as soon as reasonably possible.

6.5 VAT

Special events often involve the buying in of goods and services (from printers, marquees, caterers, etc.) which may include a VAT charge, and the selling of goods and services (tickets, food, other products), which may need to have VAT charged on them. Sometimes the event will be run entirely within the charity, but its complexity and risk means that it may be run through a trading subsidiary. The tax implications in terms of how profits are to be treated, or VAT charged and/or reclaimed, can be complex, and it is important to address tax issues directly. There are two reasons for this: first, because you have a duty to maximise the return to the charity from the event, so you do not wish to incur any more tax liability than is absolutely necessary; second, because if you get it wrong, the implications and the costs for the charity as a whole can be very significant.

The following sections provide a brief overview of the key issues relating to VAT. It is advisable to obtain more detailed professional advice for any large-scale fundraising event programme.

6.5.1　Exemptions

For most of their activities, charities are not exempt from VAT. This means that they have to pay VAT on the goods and services they buy in, and, if VAT-registered, can charge VAT on goods and services they provide. They can also offset VAT paid against VAT charged.

However, there is a fundraising events exemption from VAT for events which are primarily for the purpose of raising funds for a charity, and where the profits are transferred to the charity. There is a restriction to the exemption of 15 events per year of any one kind at any one location. Although you are unlikely to have more special events than this in any one year, it is worth knowing that you can have more than 15 as long as they are not at the same location. However, if you go over the 15 at one location, all the events at that location will be liable for VAT, not just the excess. Therefore, it is worth communicating with other event organisers within your organisation to check that you do not go over the limit. The exemption does not apply to any event where accommodation is provided for more than two nights, so some challenge events may be excluded. This exemption also applies to direct tax on profits – but different considerations may apply if the event is run by a trading subsidiary.

You need to balance carefully the benefits of taking advantage of the exemption with any potential costs (such as not being able to offset VAT on goods and services bought in) and risks (such as not running an event through a trading company), and it is usually advisable to obtain professional advice on the correct route to take.

Certainly, you should discuss the VAT and tax position with your finance division, as a particular VAT treatment for your special events could have a significant impact on the tax treatment of the rest of the charity.

6.5.2　VAT and sponsorship

The VAT liability arising from income from sponsored events (marathon, overseas challenges etc.) depends on a balance of benefits to participants, whether there is a fee for them to participate (or a minimum level of sponsorship), and ultimately on careful wording to minimise VAT liability.

Supplying a runner with a T-shirt is unlikely to be seen as a benefit by HMRC, so won't incur VAT liability. However, requiring a runner to raise a minimum amount in order to earn their place at the event will be classed as a registration fee, and VAT will be due on the minimum amount raised. Any donations over and above the minimum amount will be tax free. If a participant is asked to pledge or commit to raising a certain amount, and this amount is not insisted upon as a pre-requisite to taking part in the event, then the whole of the sponsorship money would be classed as a donation, and no VAT would be charged.

6.5.3   Tax and Gift Aid

Section 4.10 gives more information on making the most of the Gift Aid possibilities to maximise the income to your charity from the event.

Dos and don'ts

Do consider the tax implications and take appropriate advice to make sure you make the most of your event.

6.6   Licences

6.6.1   Premises licences

The Licensing Act 2003 brings together different licensing regimes for the provision of alcohol, regulated entertainment and late-night refreshment. Most of the venues you are likely to use for your special event should have applied for and hold a premises licence from their local authority already. It is worth checking whether their licence covers the activities that you are planning. Licences can cover the provision of alcohol, performance of music (whether live or recorded), dance and dancing, the exhibition of a film or performance of a play, the provision of hot refreshments after 11 pm, and any combination.

If any of your proposed activities constitute a regulated entertainment that is not covered by the premises licence, you may need to provide a temporary event notice (TEN) to the licensing authority and to the police at least ten days before the event itself. A TEN can be used to authorise relatively small-scale events involving no more than 499 people at any one time. However, there are other limits to using a TEN, involving how often one has been used concerning the particular premises in any one calendar year, or allowing at least 24 hours between events notified by the premises user or at that premises.

A premises licence is required if the regulated entertainment is to take place outdoors. Again, if the venue is used regularly for outdoor events, the owner is likely to have a licence already. If not, it may need to apply for one, or a TEN may be appropriate.

6.6.2 Music licences

As mentioned previously in Chapter 5, if live or recorded music is to be played, you should contact PRS for Music (www.prs-alliance.co.uk) and/or Phonographic Performance Ltd (PPL, www.ppluk.com). This is in addition to any premises licence covering public entertainment as discussed above, and ensures that copyright is upheld and appropriate royalties distributed to the copyright holders.

PPL is a music service company working on behalf of performers and record company members. It licenses sound recordings and music videos for use in broadcast, public performance and new media. PRS for Music brings together two royalty collection societies: MCPS and PRS. It collects and pays royalties to members when their music is distributed to the public, performed or played in public, broadcast or made publicly available online.

6.7 Best practice

Most of this chapter has dealt with the legal basics that you should be aware of, in order to ensure that your event complies with legislation and does not get you or your charity into trouble. However, most charities aspire to go beyond the legal minimum and apply higher standards to their fundraising, conscious of the fact that fundraising is a major form of communication with the public about the charity, which can have a huge impact on its reputation.

The collective experience of the sector has led to best practice standards being developed by the Institute of Fundraising to cover various forms of fundraising. This section provides an overview of some of the key elements of best practice as they relate to special events.

6.7.1 Fundraising Standards Board

The Fundraising Standards Board (FRSB) is a body established in 2007 to administer a self-regulation scheme for best practice in fundraising. By joining the FRSB, charities demonstrate their commitment to best practice by signing up to the 'Fundraising Promise', a public declaration of the following key principles of behaviour:

- committed to high standards
- honest and open
- clear
- respectful
- fair and reasonable
- accountable.

By joining the scheme, charities also commit to abide by the Institute of Fundraising's Codes of Best Practice in Fundraising (see section 6.7.2), and to establish a transparent complaints system, informing members of the public that if their complaints cannot be resolved internally, they can have recourse to the FRSB to adjudicate. Member charities can display the best practice logo of the fundraising tick (see below), and in turn help to drive up standards and public confidence.

This form of self-regulation was recommended in the government review of charity legislation, 'Private Action, Public Benefit' (Cabinet Office, 2002), as a preferred method of raising fundraising standards instead of creating more statutory legislation. However, the Charities Act 2006 includes a back-up clause allowing the secretary of state to impose statutory regulations regarding fundraising practice if self-regulation does not work. It is up to the charity sector to make self-regulation work, or face the consequences of increased legislation in this area in the future.

Hopefully you will know if your organisation is a member of the FRSB; if not, check internally or on the FRSB website (www.frsb.org.uk), which contains a register of members. If you are not yet a member but think you could (or should) be, talk to your fundraising director and consider putting a case together. Membership can raise the profile of fundraising at board level and add to your external fundraising PR and marketing by enabling you to display the FRSB quality mark tick.

6.7.2   Institute of Fundraising Codes of Best Practice

The Codes of Best Practice cover many areas of fundraising, and are a peer-reviewed, technical guide to minimum legal standards and expectations of what is best practice. Some codes cover more generic fundraising topics such as payment of commission to professional fundraisers and managing volunteers; others are more specific to event fundraising, such as the following:

- charity challenge events
- event fundraising
- outdoor fundraising in the UK
- best practice for fundraising contracts
- charities working with business
- data protection.

7 IF THINGS GO WRONG

Planning, risk assessment, using recommendations and entering into robust contracts – many of the aspects covered in this book are designed to minimise the risk of avoidable disasters occurring. However, experience tells us that no matter how much well the event is planned and organised and how experienced the event organiser is, there will in all probability be a crisis during the planning stage or at the event itself.

7.1 Crisis? What crisis?

Even with the best laid plans, things can and do go wrong. Your job as event organiser is to keep calm, assess the degree of the problem and be flexible and in control in dealing with it, in order to minimise the impact and salvage the event for your charity where possible. Firefighters are trained to put out fires; if you do not identify and plan for possible problems you will become a firefighter by default without the necessary tools. You need to develop an ability to anticipate possible problems. In making decisions and problem-solving it is vital to be aware of factors that could lead to a crisis. You also need to be able to judge when to take immediate action and deal with the situation and ask questions later.

Remember, risks are not problems: you need to be aware of risks in order to manage them. They have to be solved quickly or they will develop into a crisis. Keep a notebook with you and jot down possible problems that could occur and manage them at the risk stage.

Without being gloomy or overly pessimistic, the following sections aim to highlight some of the key areas where things can go wrong, how to minimise the risk of them happening, and how to recover or deal with these situations.

7.2 Project planning schedule takes longer

At the beginning of this book, it was stated that no matter how early you begin the planning stage, invariably you will run out of time. Most failures in event management project planning are a result of being unrealistic about how long and how many hours you will have to spend putting an event together. You can minimise this by being realistic in the first place, and allowing enough slack in the schedule, so that you do not play 'catch-up' all the time.

If you begin to run out of time, one solution is to bring in extra help. This will cost money and play havoc with the budget, but if you do not complete the project, you will lose more than money. If your schedule is seriously slipping, do not ignore it; step back and review the situation, identify your really critical points and timescales, and focus your efforts on these. You may need to cut back on some extras that are not crucial to the event.

7.3 Inaccurate estimates

Do not underestimate the time that people take to deliver estimates and complete a task. You could be facing a very difficult situation if you are a long way into an event plan before you discover that suppliers are unable to meet schedules or estimated costs. You need them to deliver in order for the event to go ahead, but paying extra could seriously undermine your budget and the value of the event.

You can minimise this by getting all costs in writing and confirming delivery dates. Wherever possible, avoid paying the full cost upfront – keep some in reserve for payment on delivery, as this will put you in a stronger position should attempts be made to charge extra. If you have hardcopies of all agreements, there should be no dispute about costs, and you should make sure that contracts are clear. Keep to your side of the bargain, and do not change your brief mid-delivery without negotiating and confirming in writing the cost of doing so.

You may need to draft in additional support to ensure delivery to time, or pay the extra requested – either way, this will cost the charity and may undermine the effectiveness of the event. You could call the supplier's bluff – it is a risky situation but most suppliers will want repeat business, so if they agree to complete on this occasion you can agree to sit down and work with them to develop more realistic contracts in future.

7.4   Technical difficulties

From concerts to after dinner speeches, we barely notice the technology until it fails – microphones that do not work, or that painful screech of feedback. A lot of work goes on in the background to ensure that the event goes smoothly for those attending, and it can be very noticeable if what we take for granted stops working.

Make sure that everyone concerned with the technical set-up meets with you at the venue a month or two before the event to determine what is required. They must arrive at the venue well ahead of time – the day before, if the event starts in the morning, and in the morning for an evening event. Build tests and rehearsals into your timings.

Check the simple solutions first – is everything wired up and turned on? If there is equipment failure, use the back-ups you have brought with you. Good sound engineers always have extra of everything in case something fails, so check when booking them. If there is a minor problem, try to fix it as unobtrusively as possible so as not to distract the audience. If it is more major and that particular part of the event cannot continue until it is fixed, try to keep the audience or attendees informed, and consider buying your technical support some time by rescheduling the programme if possible.

7.5   Unforeseen absence of resources

Failure to deliver on promises, whether contractual or otherwise, is a nightmare. This can be key raffle prizes, or chairs or glasses not arriving at the site.

You can minimise this by making sure that contractual agreements are clear, and that voluntary offerings are confirmed in writing. At least one week before the event, confirm resources requests, with a further reminder and confirmation the day before to be on the safe side. If necessary, give this task to a team member to chase during the run up to the event.

Consider where else you might be able to obtain the necessary resources at the last minute – would the local church or school be able to help with chairs? They may not be as smart as the ones you had ordered, but people will be able to sit on them. Can you make an appeal to a local supermarket or off-licence to borrow glasses? Think imaginatively and talk through the problem with someone else on the team.

Case example

I was managing a large event and a trustee had offered to supply the champagne for the reception for 350 VIP guests. I confirmed this generous gift in writing, rang the trustee up the week before to ensure that there were no problems, and was given confirmation that the order been placed and delivery would be at 1 pm on the day. When 2 pm came I rang again, got the answerphone and left a message. Fortunately I knew the name of the wine supplier, which was not too far away from the venue. I rang them and was told that they had no record of this order. They suggested that I should come and speak to the manager personally, which I did, and true enough, the trustee had forgotten. Fortunately, the manager was very sympathetic. I did emphasise that I was not blaming him and asked how I could resolve this. They managed to get enough champagne from their depot (miles away) to the venue by 5 pm – the reception was at 6.30 pm. We managed to get it sufficiently chilled just in time – and the bill went on the trustee's account.

7.6 Venue lets you down

While hopefully this will not happen often, being let down by a venue at short notice is most likely to create a major headache and lead to the cancellation of an event. The booking may have been made in the wrong diary or not at all, the company may have gone into receivership, or – as has been the case recently – strike action may lead to buildings remaining shut to the event or field catering staff.

You can minimise this by having a robust and clear contract with the venue containing penalty clauses for failure to meet contract terms. Confirm the booking both one month and one week before the event to make sure that it is in the diary, as well as confirming numbers. Use recommended and reputable venues. Look into the viability of event cancellation insurance – usually, this is only practical if it is a very major event.

It may seem like a nightmare, but keep calm and use your records of other venues in the area to see if any are available at short notice. Your priority will be to see if you can continue with the event successfully – if costs are prohibitive, you may be best advised to cancel. However, remember that other venues may offer good deals, as it is a benefit to them to get a last-minute booking of space which otherwise would be empty and not paid for at all. You will need to notify all attendees of the change of venue, or if this is not possible, the cancellation. Write, email or text all ticketholders, put notices out via local radio and papers if necessary for an open event, and make sure that there are clear notices and people at the original venue on the day to redirect anyone who forgets or arrives anyway. Whether or not you have managed to rescue the event, look at whether you can recoup costs from the original venue – if it has gone into receivership, make sure to register as a creditor of the company, as you may be able to retrieve your deposit and compensation from the administrators.

7.7 Entertainer or celebrity lets you down

If your event has been advertised by promoting the attendance of a particular speaker, act or celebrity, what will you do if you get a call the day before or on the morning of the event – or even after it has started? Unavoidable mishaps do occur – singers and speakers get laryngitis, people become ill or stuck somewhere on the way.

You can minimise this by forging a genuine relationship with the celebrity or headline act – if the cause is close to their heart, they will be more likely to pull out all the stops to meet their commitment to you. This should be underpinned with a clear and strong written agreement or contract to attend, in most cases made through their agent. As with the venue and other resources, follow up on the original booking to confirm attendance. Arrange for the guest to arrive in plenty of time, and offer to put them up the night before if necessary or if they have a long way to travel.

If there is a genuinely unavoidable reason for the no-show, attendees are likely to be sympathetic, if disappointed. If you have other high-profile guests or acts, they may be willing and able to step in at short notice, or you will have sufficient variety of quality entertainment such that the event will be able to continue, albeit sadly without the missing celebrity. However, if the act is the main draw to the event, you may have to consider your options for cancelling or postponing.

7.8 Not enough tickets sold or people attending

You budgeted for a certain number of people to buy tickets or turn up to your open event, but the tickets simply are not selling in the numbers you need. The atmosphere will be poor with a sparse population of people, but, more importantly, it will damage the bottom line for the charity.

You can minimise this by proper planning. Did you identify the right audience for the event? Have you set the costs of the tickets at the right level – not just to cover the cost of the event, but to make them affordable for the target audience? Have you done enough of the right sort of marketing? Does your event clash with something else with a greater draw?

If you spot the low numbers soon enough, consider whether an extra push on marketing and PR will be enough to turn things around. You will need to assess realistically whether the event itself is desirable to the target audience – if it is not, then spending more on marketing will not fix things. If it is an open event such as a family fun day, where you are already set up, consider sending a team of volunteers to try to drum up awareness and attendance from the local high street. If it is bad weather which has kept people away, this will not be a useful option. Work out the cancellation costs and whether it is better to go ahead at a small loss, or cancel. Remember to consider the effect on your reputation of either cancelling or going ahead with a poorly attended event.

7.9 Too many people attending

This is a rare problem where the event is ticketed, but it can occur at an open event or where a group has been invited on the assumption that only a percentage will accept the invite.

For ticketed events you can minimise this by ensuring that you set a maximum number of tickets for the size of the venue. You must have systems in place to account for any complimentary tickets and ensure that you do not oversell. Your event must comply with fire regulations relating to the maximum number of people to evacuate the venue safely – putting attendees in danger or invalidating your insurance is not an option. For open events, do your research well and judge the numbers by the success of previous events in the area if possible. Always allow for an overspill car park when planning parking, and make sure that traffic stewards are aware of capacity and when to direct to any overspill.

If possible, keep a record of excess demand. Get the contact details of disappointed people you have had to turn away – this could be useful information when planning the scale of your next event, and you could offer priority booking to those disappointed this time. For open events, when you have to deal with additional demand on the day, consider whether you can stagger the event or issue timed tickets to relieve the rush. You may need to maintain careful coordination with local police if they are involved in crowd control and traffic management, and will have to take and communicate their advice to any volunteer stewards. Your major problem is likely to be catering and facilities. Speak to the caterers on-site, who may be able to provide last-minute back-up, or contact other local firms on your reserve list, as they may be happy to absorb the extra business if they can.

7.10 Adverse weather

The one thing you absolutely cannot control is the great British weather! Clearly, this will affect outdoor events the most, but severe flooding or snowfall can affect transport and access to any event. Remember that hot weather can cause problems for exhibitors and visitors alike.

Check the weather forecasts in the immediate run-up to the event – they will give you some notice as to whether alternative plans may need to be put into action. If very hot weather is expected, make sure that adequate water and shade is available, and consider whether dust may need to be damped down during the day. If the weather really is too awful to continue, you will have to cancel – as mentioned in section 6.4.6, it is possible to insure against such an event, so consider whether it is worth doing so.

Rosie's walk and festival

Karen and Sean Ross, Rosie's Helping Hands

One year we had to postpone to another date because the weather was so bad. We contacted as many people as we could, including announcements on local radio, however we both went to the site on the designated day, just in case anyone turned up.

7.11 Transport breakdown

This is most likely to affect London-based events, where the majority are expected to arrive via the Underground. However, if there are major issues on a mainline rail service that you were relying on to get people to your event, or major delays on a key road route, this will apply to you.

You can minimise this by being aware before the event if there are major problems with any of the Underground lines or main routes of access. You cannot control transport issues and for most of us, most of the time, they are no problem at all.

For a London event where a lot of attendees are affected, get information on the situation (is the problem causing delays or complete shutdown?) and consider delaying the start of the event to allow time for people to arrive. However, this needs to be set against the interests of those already at the event and waiting – there is a limit to how far you can disrupt your schedule.

Acorns Hospice: Marquee Week

Geraldine Mannion, corporate functions manager, Acorns Hospice

As with any major event, there is always the potential for something major to go wrong, but by trying to predict any problems we have so far managed to cope whenever disaster strikes. One year, all the electrics short-circuited minutes before the start of the AGM, but fortunately an electrician was on stand-by to restore us to full power quickly. Another year, a mini-tornado hit Selly Oak and the marquee was badly flooded. At very short notice we managed to find special heaters which we ran in the marquee all night to dry out the floor adequately before the next day's event. We also lost our key speaker one year when she broke down on the motorway with no chance of getting to us on time. The late Earl of Lichfield, founder patron of the charity who was with us on the day, allowed us to persuade him to step in, which he did splendidly, with hilarious anecdotes about photographing the royal family.

7.12 Illness or injury at the event

You will be dealing with and responsible for a wide range of people at these different events, and while the majority will have a good time and return home safely, some may not. You may have to deal with heart attacks, choking, food allergies, food poisoning, falls or more serious injuries, and particularly during challenge events, hypothermia, broken limbs or, in the worst case scenario, fatalities.

Keep calm, and remember that the priority is to deal with the injury or illness and do your best for the person involved. Use your emergency plan, and your first aiders and contact numbers. Consider whether there are any safety implications for others at the event, and take any necessary action to make sure that no one else is hurt (see sections 6.3.8 and 6.4.1)

7.13 Failure or breakdown in communication

This can be with the team, other departments, volunteers, suppliers and, worst of all, the guests. It can affect the smooth running of the day if people do not know what they are supposed to do, or do not deliver on promises you were taking for granted. If guests do not know what is going on they can become fractious, or they may have expectations of something other than what they are getting. As with so many other areas of life and management, communication really is key.

You can minimise this by following the guidance provided in Chapter 2 on planning and strategy. People will forget, people will make promises and fail to keep them, and people make assumptions. As a manager you will, with experience, learn how to work best with your team. Make sure that the publicity for your event is accurate and not misleading, and that you can deliver on what you promise.

You can manage this by ensuring that if people (guests in particular) feel the need to do so, they can find the right person to raise an issue with easily, and that it is dealt with politely, sympathetically and effectively (ideally, there will be nothing to complain about). You may need to brief or even train volunteers on how to deal with members of the public, particularly if they are going to be stewards and therefore visible and likely to be the first point of approach.

Dealing with an irate sponsor, guest, celebrity or volunteer is another matter. When people get angry they have an adrenalin rush, a situation occurs and this provokes a 'fight or flight' reaction. You may feel their complaint or the way in which they put it to you is unjustified, but in their eyes you will be the one to blame. It is difficult to keep calm in a pressurised situation, but by meeting aggression with aggression, the situation will only escalate and achieve little apart from raised blood pressure and bad feeling. Avoid adding fuel to the fire by expressing your personal opinion, even if you know that you are right.

Whatever issue they raise, do not panic. If you have time, sit down and think through the problem:
1. gather all the necessary information
2. identify the options
3. select the best option
4. prepare an action plan.

If you do not have time and the situation requires your immediate reaction, take a deep breath: if it is life-threatening, you will have your emergency plan and know what steps you have to take regarding the emergency services and so forth. If it is not life-threatening, you should take a step back and review – do not allow people to badger you for a quick decision. People will panic, shout and rage if they feel they have been let down, compromised or made to look inferior in front of friends, family and colleagues. In this instance listen, sympathise, and do not justify. Listen to their problem, reply in a composed voice. Try to match their breathing and bring it back to a slower pace. Gradually lower the pitch of your voice and decrease the volume. If possible, get them to move away from the centre of things and speak with you in a private area. Give reassuring answers such as:

> *This is very serious – I understand how you feel, but I will need time to make proper enquiries and come back to you.*

> *There are several people involved – I am going to ask you to give me some time to sort it out and come back to you.*

Top tip

There are some excellent training programmes on dealing with difficult people and situations. It is suggested that all fundraisers take advantage of these courses. You will learn to 'pace' the person you are dealing with and calm situations down (see Appendix 2).

7.14 Cancelling an event

No one wants to have to do this, and it is rarely the easy option as there will often be a lot involved (including cost) with little to show for it. Most of this chapter has been about coping with or avoiding problems. However, if you do have to cancel, you should do the following.

- Check cancellation clauses in contracts with venues, caterers, stallholders, etc.
- When it becomes clear that it is necessary to cancel, talk to people as soon as you can. The more notice they have, the more sympathetic they are likely to be.
- Explain the situation and the reasons for cancelling.
- Offer to pay contractual cancellation fees. Those sympathetic to your cause may offer to waive them, but you should be prepared to pay.

- Try to understand the position of suppliers, entertainers, guest speakers and volunteers, and keep things as polite and professional as possible. You may want to engage them for a future event, so you need to keep their confidence in you.
- You will need to contact ticketholders and potential attendees to inform them that the event is off or postponed. Again, give as much notice and explanation as possible, with an apologetic rather than a defensive tone, as this will help the bad news to be received more sympathetically.
- Offer no-quibble refunds of ticket fees. Depending on the situation (level of the ticket price, nature of the event, nature of the supporters who bought them) you may consider giving people the option to convert their fee into a donation, but this has to be entirely optional.
- Offer priority notice and booking for the next event.

POSTSCRIPT

By embarking on a career in fundraising and special events management you will be involved in one of the most rewarding jobs that you can do, but it is demanding and requires certain qualities. Therefore, in conclusion I would like to offer the following advice.

I have made mistakes. You will make mistakes too, so accept and learn from them. Remember, you cannot do it alone, there are only 24 hours in a day and you will have to learn to trust and delegate. Remember to praise frequently, communicate constantly and be very clear about your objectives.

Learn to be able to assess your own performance, and to accept criticism and advice, trust, be fair and knowledgeable. Set meaningful goals and track your progress. Avoid relying on your organisation to help you to develop your skills. Take responsibility for self-advancement and remember that you will have to manage yourself as well as others, so stay focused.

Do not lose your sense of humour. Try to find a way to relax – it is important to unwind – something that involves physical activity is often best. What is vitally important for your sanity is to retain a sense of perspective.

APPENDIX 1: BIBLIOGRAPHY

The following is a list of publications which I hope will be useful in planning and resourcing your special events. (Many of the fundraising and voluntary sector books listed are available through Directory of Social Change: www.dsc.org.uk.)

Chapter 2: Strategy and planning

The Complete Guide to Business and Strategic Planning (3rd edn), Alan Lawrie, Directory of Social Change, 2007

Create!, Mark Butcher, Directory of Social Change, 2005

Managing Without Profit: Leadership, Management and Governance of Third Sector Organisations (3rd edn), Mike Hudson, Directory of Social Change, 2009

The Mind Map Book, Tony Buzan, BBC Active, 2006

Mind Mapping: Kickstart Your Creativity and Transform Your Life, Tony Buzan, BBC Active, 2006

Use Your Head, Tony Buzan, BBC Active, 2006

Chapter 3: Making it happen

CC30 Finding New Trustees – What Charities Need to Know, Charity Commission, 2007

Cause Related Marketing: Corporate Survey 111, Katy Neep, Business in the Community, 2001

The Complete Fundraising Handbook (5th edn), Michael Norton and Nina Botting-Herbst, Directory of Social Change, 2007

The Complete Guide to Surviving Contracts, Alan Lawrie, Directory of Social Change, 2008

Friends for Life: Relationship Fundraising in Practice, Ken Burnett, White Lion Press, 1996

Handbook of Key Customer Relationship Management, Ken Burnett, Financial Times/Prentice-Hall, 2000

How to Win Customers and Keep Them for Life, Michael LeBoeuf, Penguin, 2000

In Search of Excellence: Lessons from America's Best Run Companies, Robert H Waterman, Jr, Thomas J Peters, Tom Peters and Robert Waterman, Warner Books, 1988 (out of print, available through Amazon resellers)

Recruiting Volunteers, Fraser Dyer and Ursula Jost, Directory of Social Change, 2006

Relationship Fundraising, Ken Burnett, Jossey-Bass, 2002

The Russell-Cooke Voluntary Sector Legal Handbook (3rd edn), James Sinclair Taylor and the Charity Team at Russell-Cooke Solicitors, Directory of Social Change, 2009

The Zen of Fundraising, Ken Burnett, Jossey-Bass, 2006

Chapter 4: Making the most of it

Charity Marketing, Ian Bruce, Institute of Chartered Secretaries and Administrators (ICSA), 2005

Essential Volunteer Management (2nd edn), Steve McCurley and Rick Lynch, Directory of Social Change, 2007

Keeping Volunteers, Steve McCurley and Rick Lynch, Directory of Social Change, 2007

Marketing Strategy, Peter Maple, Directory of Social Change, 2003

Strategic Marketing: Creating Competitive Advantage, Douglas West, John Ford and Essam Ibrahim, Oxford University Press, 2006

Chapter 6: Essentials: legal requirements and risk management

CC3 The Essential Trustee – What You Need to Know, Charity Commission, 2008

CC20 Charities and Fundraising, Charity Commission, 2008

CC49 Charities and Insurance, Charity Commission, 2007

Charity and Voluntary Workers: A Guide to Health and Safety at Work, Health and Safety Executive (HSE), 1999

Data Protection for Voluntary Organisations (3rd edn), Paul Ticher, Directory of Social Change, 2009

Health and Safety Handbook (2nd edn), Al Hinde and Charlie Kavanagh, Directory of Social Change/Health at Work, 2006

OG 58 A1: Data Protection Act 1998, Introduction – Data Protection, Freedom of Information and Human Rights, Charity Commission, 2005

Private Action, Public Benefit: The Journey Towards a New Charities Bill, Cabinet Office, 2002

Voluntary but Not Amateur (8th edn), Ruth Hayes and Jacki Reason, Directory of Social Change, 2009

Chapter 7: If things go wrong

Dealing with Difficult People, Karen Mannering, Chartered Management Institute, 2009

Managing Conflict, Gill Taylor, Directory of Social Change, 1999

APPENDIX 2: LIST OF WEBSITES

This is a list of websites for organisations which have been featured in the book or will be of general use to special events fundraisers.

Case studies

Acorns Children's Hospice: www.acorns.org.uk

Charity Challenge: www.charitychallenge.com

Montpellier Creative: www.montpelliercreative.com

Peckleton Arts: www.peckletonarts.co.uk

Queens' College, Cambridge: www.queens.cam.ac.uk

Rosie's Helping Hands: www.rosieshelpinghands.org

The Brainwave Centre: www.brainwave.org.uk

Water Aid: www.wateraid.org/uk

Challenge event organisers

Across the Divide: www.acrossthedivide.com

Team Challenge: www.teamchallenge-company.co.uk

Greenrock: www.greenrock.co.uk

Charities, professional regulation and best practice

Charity Commission: www.charity-commission.gov.uk

Charity Commission for Northern Ireland: www.dsdni.gov.uk/ccni.htm

Directory of Social Change: www.dsc.org.uk

Fundraising Standards Board: www.frsb.org.uk

Institute of Fundraising Codes of Practice: www.institute-of-fundraising. org.uk/bestpractice/thecodes/

National Council for Voluntary Organisations: www.ncvo-vol.org.uk

National Association for Voluntary and Community Action (covers England): www.navca.org.uk

Northern Ireland Council for Voluntary Action: www.nicva.org

Office of the Scottish Charity Regulator: www.oscr.org.uk

Scottish Council for Voluntary Organisations: www.scvo.org.uk

Donations and tax-effective giving

HM Revenue & Customs' advice on Gift Aid: www.hmrc.gov.uk/charities/gift-aid.htm

Institute of Fundraising tax-effective giving: www.tax-effective-giving.org.uk

JustGiving: www.justgiving.com

Event resources and entertainers

Agents' Association: www.agents-uk.com/index.html

Bob Lamoon: www.boblamoon.com

British Institute of Professional Photography: www.bipp.com

Canford (sound equipment):www.canford.co.uk

Entertainers: www.entertainers.co.uk

Equity (performers' union): www.equity.org.uk

Guild of Professional Toastmasters: www.guild-of-toastmasters.co.uk

Institute of Auctioneers & Appraisers in Scotland: www.auctioneersscotland.co.uk

Institute of Professional Auctioneers and Valuers: www.ipav.ie

National Association of Toastmasters: www.natuk.com

National Association of Valuers and Auctioneers: www.nava.org.uk

NMP Live (after-dinner speakers): www.afterdinnerspeakers.co.uk

Phonographic Performance Ltd (PPL): www.ppluk.com

Pro audio: www.proaudiosystems.co.uk

PRS for Music: www.prsformusic.com

Spotlight (actors and casting directory): www.spotlight.com

Stagehire: www.HPSS.Stagehire.co.uk

Tega hire (staging): www.tega.co.uk

Toastmasters General Council: www.toastmastersgeneralcouncil.org

UK Entertainer Directory: www.entertainerdirectory.co.uk

Health and safety

British Insurance Brokers' Association: www.biba.org.uk

Charities Safety Group: www.csg.org.uk

Communities and Local Government guidance on fire safety law:
www.communities.gov.uk/fire/firesafety/firesafetylaw

Legislation, government departments and guidance

The Charities Act 2006: www.opsi.gov.uk/acts/acts2006/
ukpga_20060050_en_1

The Children Act 1989: www.opsi.gov.uk/Acts/acts1989/
Ukpga_19890041_en_1.htm

The Children Act 2004: www.opsi.gov.uk/Acts/acts2004/
ukpga_20040031_en_1

Communities and Local Government: www.communities.gov.uk/
corporate

Data Protection Act 1998: www.opsi.gov.uk/Acts/Acts1998/
ukpga_19980029_en_1

Department for Children, Schools and Families: www.dcsf.gov.uk

Department for Culture, Media and Sport: www.culture.gov.uk

HM Revenue & Customs, guidance on VAT and fundraising events:
www.hmrc.gov.uk/charities/vat/fundraising.htm

HM Revenue & Customs, tax guidance for charities: www.hmrc.gov.uk/
charities

HM Revenue & Customs, 'Fundraising Events: Exemption for Charities
and Other Qualifying Bodies': www.hmrc.gov.uk/charities/fund-raising-
events.htm

HM Revenue & Customs, 'VAT for Charities and Not-for-profit Organisations' www.hmrc.gov.uk/charities/vat/intro.htm

Information Commissioner's Office: www.ico.gov.uk

Information Commissioners Office: Data Protection Act 1998 guidance: www.ico.gov.uk/what_we_cover/data_protection.aspx

Office of the Third Sector – charity law: www.cabinetoffice.gov.uk/third_sector/law_and_regulation.aspx

Protection of Children Act 1999: www.opsi.gov.uk/ACTS/acts1999/ukpga_19990014_en_1

Protection of Vulnerable Adults: www.dh.gov.uk/en/SocialCare/Deliveringadultsocialcare/Vulnerableadults/index.htm

Sale of Goods Act 1979 www.opsi.gov.uk/RevisedStatutes/Acts/ukpga/1979/cukpga_19790054_en_1

Marketing and business strategy

Business in the Community, Cause Related Marketing: www.bitc.org.uk/resources/publications/brand_benefits.html

Businesslink (search strategic planning): www.businesslink.gov.uk

Tony Buzan: http://buzanworld.com

The Chartered Institute of Marketing: www.cim.co.uk

The Management Centre: www.themanagementcentre.com

Working for a Charity: www.wfac.org.uk

Training

For event fundraising courses or for training on other areas touched on in this publication such as business and strategic planning, charity law, data protection, health and safety and managing people, go to: www.dsc.org.uk.

Volunteering

Do It!: www.do-it.org.uk

Reach: http://reach.londonmet.ac.uk/home.aspx

Volunteering England: www.volunteering.org.uk

INDEX

adding value to your event 33,
134–8, 151
advertising 109, 113
  see also marketing
aims and objectives
  identifying 12–16
  reviewing against 39
art or photographic exhibitions 28
  see also musical and cultural
  events
auctions
  generally 134–8
  and cash handling 105
  and Gift Aid 141–2

bad weather insurance 226
balls and dinners
  organising 144–59
  adding value to your event 33,
  134–8
  case study 155–9
  example flow chart 64
  example list of tasks 62
  preparation time 28
blogs, for marketing 111
bookings
  generally 88–91
  final bookings–venue 89
  timescales 27, 90
  see also contracts
Boston Matrix analysis tool 10–12
branding
  see logos and trademarks;
  marketing
budgeting
  generally 29–37
  after the event activities 105–6
  for marketing 109
  price negotiation 91–2

buffer times 65–7

cancellation
  cancelling your event 241–2
  advance preparation 69
  case study 191, 238
  clauses in suppliers' contracts
  94
  event cancellation insurance
  235
  weather-related cancellation
  226, 238
car parking issues
  to consider when choosing
  venues 89, 204, 206
  marshalling duties 101, 183,
  205
  overspill parking 237
  stallholders' 209
case studies
  Acorn Children's Hospice:
  Marquee Week 14, 239
  Acorn Children's Hospice:
  Shugborough Luncheons
  189–91
  The Brainwave Centre's royal
  event 162–4
  Charity Challenge 173–7
  Macmillan Celebrity Christmas
  Stocking Auction 136–7
  Montpellier Creative 124–7
  Peckleton Arts: Mozart on the
  Move 186–8
  Queens' College members'
  anniversary dinner 155–9
  Rosie's walk and festival
  210–11, 238
  Water Aid: job description for
  events organiser 47–50

case studies—*continued*
    Water Aid: Sydney Regatta
        177–80
cash handling 105, 226
casino nights 150
catering
    finding and booking suppliers
        90–1
    contracts 96
    general quantity guidelines
        197
    food safety 223
    in situations where more
        people than expected turn up
        238
    for balls and dinners 146
    for conferences 197
    for family events 202
    for receptions 199
cause related marketing (CRM)
    76–7
celebrities 132–4, 236
    see also VIP guests
challenge events
    generally 165–81
    preparation time 28
    sponsorship money 105,
        140–1, 171, 172, 227–8
charity law 212–16
checklists
    planning events 42–3, 181
    expenditure items 31–2, 36–7
    company sponsorship 73–4
    proposals for company
        sponsorship 79–80
    finding a venue 89
    pre-event generally 97–101
    contracts with suppliers 94–5,
        208
    working with printers/
        designers 115
    fire safety 221
    data protection 218–19

checklists—*continued*
    on the day activities 101–3
    after the event 103–6
clearing up
    allowing time for 28, 95
    practicalities of 103–4, 205
commercial participators 94, 151,
    214–15
committees 50–3
communication breakdown, how
    to remedy 240–1
concerts
    see musical and cultural
        events
conferences 192–7
contingency plans
    budgeting 32
    project management 69–70
contracting out
    see professional services
contracts
    generally 92–7
    contractors' insurance 225
    with caterers 96
    with celebrities 133–4
    with entertainment 96
    with professional PR
        consultancies 125–6
    with stallholders 95, 208
    with venues 93, 95, 197, 235
corporate culture (of your charity)
    86–7
corporate sponsorship
    generally 71–87
    and commercial participation
        214–15
    for family events 202–3
    post-event feedback 104–5
costs of events
    see budgeting
criminal record checks 57–9
critical path analysis 66–8
crowd control 222–3

cultural events 28, 181–91
   see also festivals
customer satisfaction survey 85–6

data protection 112, 216–19
debriefing 38, 104–5, 200
decorations
   pre-event activities 98–9
   for balls and dinners 146–7
deposits 89
design and print work 31, 97–9,
   114–16
detail, attention to 130–1
dinners
   see balls and dinners
direct mailing 110, 113
donors
   see supporters
dress codes 150, 161
duty of care 215–16

email, for marketing 112
emergency plans 222, 223–4
employment, avoiding *de facto*
   employment of volunteers 56
entertainment
   finding and booking 90–1
   contracts 96
   for balls and dinners 151–2
   for family events 202
   when entertainment fails to
      attend 236
equipment
   pre-event activities 98
   contracts with suppliers 95
   failure to arrive 234–5
   insurance for 225
   for musical events 185
   technical difficulties 234
estimates, inaccurate 233
event organisers
   see special events organiser

expenditure items checklist 31–2,
   36–7

family events 200–9
feedback, collecting 38, 102,
   104–5, 240–1
festivals 209–11
fire regulations 99, 145, 147, 152,
   207, 220–1, 237
fireworks 154, 184, 220
first aid 99, 172, 223, 239
fixed costs 29
flow charts 64
follow-up activities 38–43, 106,
   134, 158–9, 200
   see also debriefing; feedback
food
   see catering
forecasting (budget) 31
fun runs
   see challenge events
Fundraising Standards Board best
   practice guidelines 229–30
funds, obtaining 70–87

Gift Aid 138–43, 177
goody bags/gifts for guests 148,
   172, 190

'Heads and Tails' game 152
health and safety 99–100, 219–24
   see also fire regulations; first
      aid
hidden costs 30
hosts, role of 154

ideas, generating 17–19
illness or injury at event 239
   see also first aid; risks
income, estimating 32–3
indirect costs 30
induction
   for committee 51
   for volunteers 55

Institute of Fundraising Codes of
   Best Practice 231
insurance 26, 224–6, 235
internal promotion of events 131
internet as marketing tool 110–13
interviews, giving (publicity)
   120–7
investment return ratios 34

job description (special events
   organiser) 47–50

lead-times 27
leadership 46
legal requirements 212–31
licences
   for music 147, 229
   premises licences 228–9
   public collections 215
literary lunches 188
logos and trademarks 94, 95, 115,
   203–4

management
   of contracts 96–7
   project management 60–70
   of volunteers 55
   when things go wrong 232–42
market research 19–21
marketing 45, 107–20, 187–8
master of ceremonies 152–3
masterclasses (musical) 184–5
media
   advertising your event 109,
      113
   working with the media to get
      publicity 116–30
meetings, effective committee 51
merchandise, charity branded
   203–4
mind maps 13, 63

music
   musical and cultural events
      28, 181–91
      see also festivals
   music licences 229
   for balls and dinners 147, 150
   for family events 202
   for receptions 199

negotiating prices 91–2
network diagrams 64–7
networking
   as key fundraising skill 18, 46
   to build relationships with
      companies 75, 77–8
   to build successful committees
      51
   at conference events 192
   at reception events 199
newspapers and print media
   interviews for 121–2
   marketing your event in 113
   press releases 116–20

'open space' meetings 192
organiser, special events
   advice for 102, 243
   recruitment of (in-house)
      45–50
   role on the day 101
   sample job description 47–50
   using professional event
      organisers 57
outdoor events
   catering 91
   family events 200–9
   licences 229
   picnic in the park 28, 183–4
   see also weather
overcrowding (too many people
   attending) 237–8
overseas events 171, 223

partnerships (to raise funds) 71–87

permissions, for use of photographs 129, 130

PEST analysis tool 9–10

photographs
  publicity of your event 127–30
  photographers selling to guests at balls/ dinners 151

picnic in the park events 28, 183–4

'piggybacking'
  events 9
  surveys 21

planning events
  generally 5–43
  budgeting 29–37
  planning marketing 108–10
  remedying over-running schedules 233

pledged donations 105–6

pluvius insurance 226

police liaison 99, 204, 222–3, 237

PR consultancy, using 124–7

preparation times 27–8

presentations
  for obtaining corporate fundraising 81–4
  and working with a PR consultancy 125–6

press packs 120

press photographers 128

press releases 116–20

preview nights 182

price negotiation 91–2

print requirements
  press packs 120
  programmes 153–4, 206
  tickets, invitations and programmes 97–8

printers (as suppliers) 114–16

product life-cycle 10, 34, 40–1

professional services, contracting
  professional auctioneers 135
  professional challenge companies 174
  professional event organisers 57
  professional fundraisers 57, 166, 176, 214–15
  professional photographers 127–8
  professional PR/ marketing companies 107, 124–7
  professional pyrotechnicians (fireworks) 154
  professional toastmasters 152–3

project management 60–70

proposals, written (for corporate fundraising) 78–85

public collections 215

public liability insurance 224–5

public relations (PR) 107–20

publicity 107–30

quotes from suppliers 91–2

radio
  advertising on 113
  giving interviews for 122–4

raffles
  generally 151
  failure of key prizes to materialise 234

receptions 198–200

recruitment
  of special event organisers 45–50
  of volunteers 54–5

references, for volunteers 59

research
  committee members 51
  companies for sponsorship 74–5

research—*continued*
    identifying target markets
        108–9
    market research 19–21
    supporter research 19–21,
        108–9
reserves 71
restricted purposes fundraising
    213
return on investment ratios 34
reviewing your event 38–43
risks
    risk management generally
        22–6
    awareness of risks 4, 232
    challenge events 175–6
    emergency plans 222
    fire risk assessments 220–1
    health and safety risk
        assessments 219–20
royal events 159–64
runners, duties of 102
running orders 100, 102

safety
    see health and safety
security 95, 99–100, 111, 160
    see also cash handling
senior staff 50, 53–4
setting up 95, 100
signage 98–9, 101
singalongs 182–3
skills audits of volunteers 55–6
SMART objectives tool 15
social networking websites, for
    marketing 112–13
speakers
    for balls and dinners 154
    for conferences 193
    for receptions 199
special events, definition of 3–4
special events organiser
    advice for 102, 243

special events organiser—
continued
    recruitment of (in-house)
        45–50
    role on the day 101
    sample job description 47–50
    using professional event
        organisers 57
sponsored events
    see challenge events
sponsorhip, corporate 71–87
sporting events
    see challenge events
staff teams for events 53
stalls and stands at events 95,
    194–5, 201–2, 207–9
strategies
    events strategies 5–43
    organisational strategies 5–6
suppliers
    finding and booking 88–91
    contracts 92–7
    dealing with 234
supporters
    looking after 131, 188
    supporter research 19–21,
        108–9
    supporters as volunteers 54
surveys, of supporters 20–1
SWOT analysis tool 8–9

table plans 148
target markets, identifying 108–9
target setting 13–14
task lists, example 62
teams, putting together 44–59
technical difficulties 234
television interviews 122–4
templates
    event aims and objectives 16
    budgeting 35–7

templates—*continued*
  job description and person
    spec (special events
    organiser) 47–50
  volunteer skills audit 56
  example list of tasks 62
  project definition form 70
  press releases 118
  Gift Aid form 143
  see also checklists
temporary event notices (TEN)
  228–9
thank yous
  events aimed at thanking
    supporters 14, 192
  thanking participants 55, 104,
    106, 134, 158, 190–1, 203,
    206–7
themes 98–9, 146–51, 201
third-party insurance 225
ticket sales
  and Gift Aid 139–40
  not selling enough 236–7
timescales
  planning events 27–9
  pre-event activities 97–101
  in project management 65–6
toastmasters 152–3
tools
  Boston Matrix analysis tool
    10–12
  critical path analysis 66–8
  the five 'Ps' of marketing 108
  flow charts 64
  mind maps 13, 63
  network diagrams 64–7
  PEST analysis tool 9–10
  risk assessment 22–6
  SMART objectives tool 15
  strategic analysis 7–12
  SWOT analysis tool 8–9
trademarks and logos 94, 95, 115,
  203–4

transport breakdown affecting
  your attendees 238–9
trustees 50, 53–4

variable costs 30
VAT 32, 226–8
venues
  finding and booking 88–90
  contracts 93, 95, 197, 235
  insurance 225
  letting you down 235–6
  using their 'What's On' guides
    to advertise 114
  for balls and dinners 144–5
  for conferences 195–7
  for family events 204
  for musical events 185, 186
  for receptions 198
VIP guests 101–2, 134, 189–91
volunteers
  generally 54–6
  avoiding *de facto* employment
    of volunteers 56
  checking and vetting 57–9
  events committees 50–3
  recruitment 54–5, 111
  supporters as volunteers 54
  training 55, 205
  volunteer roles at events 154,
    205

walk-through on the day 100–1
weather
  affecting your event 26, 28,
    182–3, 238
  bad weather insurance 226
websites
  JustGiving 172
  for marketing your event
    110–11
'with great pleasure' events 188
'wow' factor 153–4, 184